Sorin deeply explores the intersection of science and creativity within marketing, demonstrating how a data-driven approach can enhance business impact. By complementing this evidence-based approach with diverse perspectives from industry leaders, this book unpacks the nuances of marketing effectiveness, from strategy formulation to execution across various channels.

Jane Wakely, EVP PepsiCo, Chief Consumer and Marketing Officer, and Chief Growth Officer for PepsiCo's International Foods

With a refreshing blend of practical frameworks and cutting-edge analytics, Sorin demystifies marketing effectiveness from a brand practitioner's perspective. A must-read for any marketer aiming to spark sustainable brand growth in data driven marketing.

Andreas Cohen, Chairman, I-COM Global

Sorin is a longtime thought leader at the intersection of applying hard marketing science to the "squishy" world of brand, sharing his playbook with both entrepreneurs and established companies. As an unusual combination of tech-forward data geek and big-brand marketer, Sorin is a passionate devotee of data and brings together insights from major brands and innovative startups, alike.

Sim Blaustein, Partner, BDMI

Sorin shows with grace how to master the AI transformation in marketing effectiveness. His unparallelled first-hand experience with scaled human data at makes it a refreshingly useful read.

Mihkel Jaatma, CEO, Realeyes

Sorin has impressed me as a thoughtful marketer, merging practicality with scientific measurement. Let him impress you in this book, bridging the gap between academic data science and actionable business strategies.

Koen Pauwels, Associate Dean of Research and Distinguished Professor of Marketing, D'Amore-McKim School of Business at Northeastern University

Marketing is an endless experiment, and this book proves it in a refreshing way. A bold, thought-provoking guide that challenges marketers to think critically, adapt strategically, and thrive in an era of relentless disruption.
David Klingbeil, CEO of Submarine.ai and Adjunct Professor of Marketing and Strategy at NYU

In his indomitable direct style, Sorin reminds us that effectiveness is not just about measuring ROI. The lens of effectiveness must be applied to all the elements of the marketing mix: strategy to pricing and product to media and advertising. The time spent on this fun, intelligent and refreshingly straight up book will be well spent.
Rupen Desai, CMO and Venture Partner, Una Terra and Co-founder, The Shed 28

Constantly pushing the boundaries of what's possible, this book is a reflection of Sorin's relentless pursuit of marketing excellence. It's a guide for those who believe marketing can always do better. It provides invaluable tools and insights that will drive real results, whether you're a seasoned professional or just starting out. A must read for evidence-based industry leaders!
Anja Spielmann, VP Global Brand Experience, Mars

Sorin is my go-to guru for marketing effectiveness. This book is a mind-blowing mashup of marketing science and strategy, with immediate applications that can make your marketing more effective.
Michael Platt, Professor of Marketing, Neuroscience, and Psychology, University of Pennsylvania and Director of the Wharton Neuroscience Initiative

Delivering and demonstrating meaningful effectiveness is essential for marketers. Key to greater impact and influence. How to do it as elusive as ever. Calling on practical experience of assessing marketing effectiveness in the round and a deep understanding of what good looks like, this is a useful and thought-provoking guide to driving brand growth.
Russell Parsons, Editor-in-Chief, Marketing Week and Festival of Marketing

Blending together insights from the brightest minds in marketing, Sorin's book is a catalyst for industry-wide effectiveness. A tour-de-force for marketers seeking better outcomes.
Stephan Loerke, CEO, World Federation of Advertisers (WFA)

Sorin has set the agenda for marketing effectiveness, not simply in arguing that marketing should be measured effectively and thus proven, but in defining how we should do it. Any fellow agency professional who shares an ambition to deliver actionable outcomes for their clients should read this book.
Simon Sadie, Global Client President, WPP

Taking scientific test-and-learn to the next level, this book offers practical frameworks for brand leaders to fuel digital growth. Sorin's insights might inspire your next big idea in marketing.
Erika Hagberg, Director, Global Client Lead, Google

Innovative, clear, and practical, this book is a must-read for retail leaders navigating a dynamic market. Sorin's insights illuminate the path to marketing strategies that drive measurable growth.
Marissa Jarrat, EVP, Chief Marketing and Sustainability Officer, 7-Eleven, Inc.

Sorin's vision of creative excellence integrates his broad and deep understanding of the best tools in the marketplace with a refreshingly business-forward pragmatism that all marketers will value. His voice is an important one for anyone who wants to understand the dominant drivers of ROI in this creatively led world.
Ben Jones, Founder, Sundogs, former Global Creative Director, Google

Sorin's book gets what too many books miss: marketing effectiveness isn't a solo act. This is a real-world guide to getting media, creative, and all other marketing levers pulling in the same direction with less jargon for more results.
Gerry D'Angelo, Senior Adviser, McKinsey and Company

Marketing Effectiveness

Applying marketing science for brand growth

Sorin Patilinet

KoganPage

First published in Great Britain and the United States in 2025

Kogan Page

Kogan Page Ltd, 2nd Floor, 45 Gee Street, London EC1V 3RS, United Kingdom
Kogan Page Inc, 8 W 38th Street, Suite 902, New York, NY 10018, USA
www.koganpage.com

EU Representative (GPSR)

Authorised Rep Compliance Ltd, Ground Floor, 71 Baggot Street Lower, Dublin D02 P593, Ireland
www.arccompliance.com

Kogan Page books are printed on paper from sustainable forests.

© Sorin Patilinet 2025

The moral rights of the author have been asserted in accordance with the Copyright, Designs and Patents Act 1988.

ISBNs

Hardback   978 1 3986 2106 0
Paperback   978 1 3986 2105 3
Ebook   978 1 3986 2107 7

British Library Cataloguing-in-Publication Data

A CIP record for this book is available from the British Library.

Library of Congress Control Number

2025940726

Typeset by Integra Software Services, Pondicherry
Print production managed by Jellyfish
Printed and bound by CPI Group (UK) Ltd, Croydon CR0 4YY

Marketing is about understanding people, but no lesson on connection or love could ever compare to what I've learned from my family.

Felicia, your steady support has been my foundation, anchor and quiet strength through every challenge.

Emma and Sebastian, your laughter, curiosity and boundless imagination remind me daily why I do what I do.

You are my greatest inspiration, my proudest legacy and the true measure of my success.

This book exists because of you and for you.

Thank you.

CONTENTS

LIST OF FIGURES AND TABLES

ABOUT THE AUTHOR

Sorin Patilinet is a global marketing executive with over two decades of experience across multiple consumer product categories, companies and geographies. Throughout his career, he has excelled at the intersection of marketing strategy, data sciences and deciphering customer behaviour, helping numerous brands unlock the power of marketing.

A recognized industry expert in marketing effectiveness, Sorin has dedicated much of his research to understanding what drives humans to act the way they do. His expertise has made him a sought-after adviser for companies aiming to optimize their marketing performance and measurement strategies.

Sorin is a passionate speaker at marketing events and an academic lecturer on marketing and creativity, sharing insights on the evolving role of data, storytelling and brand effectiveness. His work has been featured in numerous industry publications, learning programmes and executive education curriculums, shaping the thinking of marketing leaders and students alike.

Sorin lives in Brussels with his wife, Felicia, and their two children, Emma and Sebastian. When he's not decoding the science of marketing, he enjoys listening to indie rock music, watching his favourite team, Liverpool FC, win, and reading non-fiction books.

Thriving through marketing effectiveness

In the marketing industry, the tools and technology we can employ today have propelled us significantly forward from John Wanamaker's famous provocation that 'Half the money I spend on advertising is wasted; the trouble is I don't know which half.' However, even the most successful marketers continuously challenge themselves to maximize effectiveness for their brand and category, seeking to deliver value both today and for the long term.

This leads me to marketing effectiveness, the core of measuring success against desired outcomes like increased sales, brand growth, and consumer behaviour change. Marketing effectiveness and measurable impacts are increasingly critical in a highly fragmented and uncertain business context. The distinction between companies that merely survive and those that thrive lies in marketing and communications strategies that drive sustainable growth – unlocking consumer behaviour shifts – not just attitude.

If you're reading this, you recognize that effective marketing and communications are crucial for business success. Wouldn't it be great if there were a formula for marketing effectiveness? Although I can't promise one, Sorin's book unpacks guiding principles that have benefited many renowned brands.

For over a decade as a Chief Marketing Officer at Mars, I had the pleasure of collaborating closely with Sorin to foster an internal culture of effectiveness. Together with many talented individuals in the team our shared commitment to rigorous, science-based marketing strategies consistently delivered solid brand growth and industry recognition.

I am still passionate about delivering end-to-end growth strategies and quality campaigns that build brand meaning and distinctiveness with people whilst achieving strong tangible growth and business results. This is a challenging endeavour. Marketers confront this challenge daily, driven by an insatiable desire to push boundaries and create work that engages consumers while innovating to drive brand growth.

In the current economic climate, companies face multi-faceted issues, all while having access to similar information and technologies. To stand out and transform your business, place creativity at the forefront. While creativity without effectiveness is futile, effectiveness without creativity is unattainable. This tension is central to our industry – marketing effectiveness is key.

Sorin deeply explores the intersection of science and creativity within marketing, demonstrating how a data-driven approach can enhance business impact. By complementing this evidence-based approach with diverse perspectives from industry leaders, this book aims to unpack the nuances of marketing effectiveness, from strategy formulation to execution.

The practical sections are designed to empower marketers at all levels, illustrating how to embed effectiveness into every aspect of a marketing plan. By emphasizing the importance of data, you will learn to develop end to end strategies that resonate with consumers while addressing complexities in product positioning, pricing, and media effectiveness.

Additionally, discussions on creativity and advertising reveal the art and science behind impactful brand communication, debunking persistent industry myths. Looking ahead, Sorin addresses the transformative role of AI in marketing, preparing readers for upcoming challenges and opportunities.

At PepsiCo, we continue to evolve our consumer functions to be human-centric, agile, and innovative – equipped to thrive in a technology-driven world. This evolution aims to inspire a new generation of marketers who embrace both analytical rigor and creative ingenuity. We believe in the synergy of 'art' and 'science'. The art of brand building harnesses our brands' power to create cultural impact, while the science of growth applies a rigorous approach to drive sustainable, profitable brand growth. Central to this is our beating heart: human-centricity. By placing people at the centre of our worldview, we enhance our role in their lives. Applying marketing. Science and behavioural economics to improve effectiveness is crucial for achieving long-term growth, particularly when paired with high-quality creative.

As you read this book I encourage you to embrace the mindset shift of effectiveness – embracing the tools and the rigor to identify the key drivers of growth for your brand and category. I hope like me you find something in Sorin's examples to inspire and aid your own personal learning and development to further refine your own mastery of marketing effectiveness.

Jane Wakely, PepsiCo Executive Vice President, Chief Consumer and Marketing Officer and Chief Growth Officer for PepsiCo's International Foods business

PREFACE

The art of engineering marketing

Why I wrote this book

A renowned marketing professor turned entrepreneur, Scott Galloway, famously stated that the quality of your decisions determines the quality of your life. Your top three life decisions are who you marry, where you live and your chosen career path. All of these predict your happiness.

Many twenty-somethings delegate these life-changing decisions to others: family, friends or teachers, or, worse, fail to spend enough time reflecting on their true desires. I admit I have been guilty of this at times as well. We all need advice and self-reflection to make better decisions at different ages.

Precisely the same, in our professional lives, in marketing, we frequently get caught up in minutiae, sweating over small stuff and procrastinating on the most critical top decisions.

Why do we do this? Because big decision-making is inherently challenging and perceived as risky, mastering decision-making is one of the most crucial skills a person can develop.

Having navigated hundreds of decisions daily over a marketing career spanning 20-plus years, I want to help you improve your chances of success in marketing decision-making. This book was born from a personal conviction that marketing can be approached with scientific precision and analytical rigour.

The stereotype of marketers as mere extroverts or showmen is a misconception. Data should lead; gut feelings or experience, while important, should follow. That's the only way your top decisions will ultimately contribute to your happiness.

Who am I?

My life journey began in a challenging setting. I was born in communist Romania in the 1980s. When you have close to nothing, anything is possible. Like most of Eastern Europe then, Romania was a closed economy, a place of scarcity and permanent out-of-stocks, of rationing for essential goods like bread, oil or fuel. On top of this, any foreign travel and even contact with the Western world was illegal. Food shops (*alimentara* in Romanian) were famous for their empty shelves, but when any product became available, everybody rushed to get it, sometimes without knowing what product had arrived. It was all about product availability, not branding.

Advertising, as the Western world knew it, was non-existent. It's possible that the stark scarcity of those times fuelled my nation's fascination with the 'outside' world and its myriad brands, fresh ideas and famous sights. This curiosity exploded with the fall of communism in 1989. Suddenly, the floodgates opened, we started to travel and Romania was inundated with Western products.

My first comprehensive exposure to this new world was during 'The Night of Ad-Eaters', an event that gathered people in a cinema theatre to watch international advertisements from dusk till dawn. Just imagine spending ten hours in a cinema to watch ads. I loved it.

But despite my growing passion for advertising, I knew I was not creative. I loved mathematics and solving puzzles, not drawing or crafting narratives. A future career in an advertising agency didn't seem like a fit for an analytical introvert. I chose the best choice for geeks, studying engineering at POLITEHNICA University of Bucharest. Over five years, I prepared for a career in building telecommunications networks, programming robots and creating innovative billing architectures for mobile 3G systems.

Twenty years later, I've counted zero days employed as an engineer. Instead, I apply my engineering mindset every day in my international marketing career. I am a living example that engineering and science principles can powerfully enhance marketing strategies.

This book is my effort to share these insights, hoping they will guide you as you make your own decisions in the complex world of brands.

Wait ... but what is new here?

I firmly believe that marketing can be engineered. I strongly believe that existing stereotypes of marketers as extroverts, showmen or even magicians are inaccurate. I am a supporter of engineers in marketing. But if you are not trained as an engineer, don't despair. This book gives you the key concepts that will make you a Marketing Engineer, too.

This book offers you the practitioner's point of view on marketing sciences.

Outstanding individuals like Byron Sharp, Mark Ritson, Philip Kotler, Peter Field, Les Binet, Karen Nelson-Field, Scott Galloway and Seth Godin, to name just a few, are the giants on whose shoulders I stand today. They have each made tremendous contributions to the marketing body of knowledge and to my own ideas. Without their publications, we would still be in Marketing 1.0.

Yet, I feel that the voice of the practitioner, the voice of a brand leader, is rarely present in the marketing industry discourse. That's my unique selling proposition. I complement what academics and agency experts have offered you already, with a personal take on the art of marketing effectiveness.

Who is this book for?

- Marketing professionals will access proven practical insights and simple tools to make better day-to-day decisions in their role.
- Advertising and media agency professionals who create and execute marketing campaigns will get the insights to be more effective. Why not shine in front of their clients?
- Entrepreneurs and business owners who try to accelerate the growth of their brands will benefit from proven best practices and the application of engineering principles in larger organizations.
- Students of marketing and engineering can use this book as a valuable resource to complement their academic curriculum and find inspiration for their future careers.
- Academics teaching marketing courses can also incorporate the book into their curriculums to provide real-life examples to their teaching.
- C-Suite executives and board members responsible for steering their companies towards growth will appreciate the book's insights on using marketing more scientifically to drive results and secure a competitive advantage.
- Consultants advising on marketing will benefit from staying current with the latest trends and best practices while deepening their understanding of key subjects like consumer behaviour, growth models and advertising effectiveness.
- You: the person brave enough to open this book and desiring to become a better version of yourself. This book is you, for the marketer in you or the entrepreneur starting to build their brand today.

ONE MORE THING...

Want to stay effective and ahead of the curve? Scan this QR code to access extra book content and updates online.

LIST OF CONTRIBUTORS

This book would not have been possible without the insights, guidance and contributions of the following friends, each of whom has played an essential role in shaping this book.

Jane Wakely – a visionary leader whose strategic thinking continues to shape the future of marketing at peak levels.

Karen Nelson-Field – a pioneer in marketing sciences whose research transformed how we think about attention.

Fergus O'Carroll – an advertising industry expert in strategy and a widely recognized podcast voice in marketing.

Joe Zawadzki – a serial entrepreneur and investor whose understanding of the marketing ecosystem is unmatched.

Danilo Tauro – a forward-thinking influencer in MarTech with deep expertise across multiple business models.

Paolo Provinciali – a marketing effectiveness leader dedicated to excellence in data, media and creativity.

Anastasia Leng – a brilliant entrepreneur pushing the boundaries of creativity and data analytics daily.

Jon Lombardo – an evidence-based B2B marketer and innovative entrepreneur, building the future of marketing research.

Thomas Kinley – the best insight translator between academia and business.

Stefano Puntoni – a distinguished academic whose research in decision-driven analytics and AI interactions is all-star.

At the end of each chapter you will find their insightful contributions to this book, complementing my ideas. I am profoundly thankful for their friendship and contributions.

01

Marketing science: buzzword or academic reality?

Introduction to marketing science

Marketing is the imaginative application of insight. The best marketing fuses creativity with data-driven truth. Science pursues truth through evidence, and in marketing, science helps uncover customer realities. Welcome to the world of marketing science.

This first chapter introduces three primary concepts and the interplay between them. These concepts and their interactions are what we will explore in depth throughout this book: science, engineering and marketing.

We'll examine how the analytical mindset has fuelled global progress recently and why engineering has emerged as the leading field of study for many successful business leaders. I was shocked to discover that almost all CEOs of leading companies are engineers.

DID YOU KNOW?

9/10 of all CEOs leading the world's top companies are engineers

At the time of writing, in an era where technology and data-driven decisions shape industries and influence stock markets, it's no surprise that engineers are at the top of the world's most valuable corporations:

- Satya Nadella (Microsoft) studied electrical engineering before pursuing an MBA, while Sundar Pichai (Alphabet) has a background in metallurgical engineering and material sciences. Jensen Huang (Nvidia) holds a degree in electrical engineering, and Hock Tan (Broadcom) is trained in mechanical engineering.

- C.C. Wei (TSMC) earned a PhD in electrical engineering. Elon Musk (Tesla) majored in physics and economics, combining science and business. Even

Tim Cook (Apple), who was known as a supply chain expert, studied industrial engineering. Amin H Nasser (Saudi Aramco) specializes in petroleum engineering. Mark Zuckerberg (Meta) studied computer science but didn't complete his degree.

- The exception is Andy Jassy (Amazon), who has a background in business.

This overwhelming correlation highlights the success of analytical, problem-solving and engineering thinking in guiding the world's largest businesses. Engineering is no longer merely about building bridges and factories; it's about influencing the future of global markets and society.

While this book can't replace an engineering degree, this chapter will unpack the basic concepts of marketing science and marketing engineering, exploring the application of engineering and scientific thinking to the art of growing brands.

My personal highlight is the last part of the chapter. I'll introduce the Engineering Marketing Framework – my contribution to elevating the quality of your future marketing decisions. The framework offers a set of practical tools for growing brands through science.

Marketing science: a clear vision for brand success

During a recruitment interview for my first marketing research role, I was asked an open question that influenced my career path. A hiring director put me on the spot by asking me to explain what I understand about marketing science.

'What is marketing science, Sorin?'

I immediately sensed that a Kotlerian textbook[1] answer wasn't enough; I knew marketers are storytellers. So, I took my chances and compared marketing science to an eye test at the optometrist. The recruiters were intrigued, but I continued. I explained that marketing plans often need different tactics and execution paths.

Like an optometrist switching lenses, marketers need to test various approaches. Each adjustment brings the effectiveness goal into better focus. Eventually, the right lens clicks and everything becomes sharp.

Marketing science is an approach that uses robust measurement to achieve effectiveness.

The director liked my explanation, which probably got me the job. Scientific-style testing then became my go-to way of thinking about marketing in general.

Fast-forward to today, an age when marketing is dominated by data-driven approaches, and marketing science has become a mainstream concept, too. Big customer data sets and emerging technologies like artificial intelligence (AI) enable more competitive value. Marketing science now stands for the intelligent use of data in business.

How can you apply marketing science effectively, not just talk about it? This book explains marketing effectiveness from a science perspective. It's simply about understanding customers and delivering value. It's customer-centric and data-first.

By adopting this perspective, you'll see beyond standard marketing. You'll learn the relationship between marketing science and actual effectiveness. Get ready for a crystal-clear view of marketing!

THREE QUESTIONS TO ASK YOURSELF RIGHT NOW

1 What is your current understanding of marketing science?

2 How do you use data in your marketing strategies?

3 Are your marketing efforts producing measurable results?

Remember, marketing science isn't just about sounding smart. It's about making smarter decisions to drive business growth.

The contemporary growth of marketing science

Some people imagine marketing scientists as a group of geeks in lab coats trying to understand why the chicken crossed the road. But instead of chickens, we're figuring out why customers come into the store or don't, why they buy your brand or the competitor, and why they buy the competitor.

Every behaviour, click, emotion and purchase can tell a story. But for that story to be accurate, science must be summoned.

With small exceptions, there is widespread agreement that marketing is not a formal and precise science – quite the contrary. To me, science is the mental floss thread that can enable smarter marketing decisions. I believe in the power of data, science and engineering to make a better brand.

> Marketing science is the application of scientific principles to make better business decisions.

Popularized over the last decades in part due to the increased availability of customer data and the bubbling evolution of new technological platforms, marketing science is often conflated with data analytics. But it's more than that!

Marketing science is about the curiosity to identify the exact customer needs, intelligence to build the correct hypothesis, testing it using the scientific method and applying what is learnt to make better marketing choices for tomorrow.

Marketing science came to life in academia with peer-reviewed journals popularizing the concept. The journal *Marketing Science*,[2] launched in 1982, played a key role in evolving the practice. Its timing was perfect. The 1980s marked the start of a new era in quantitative marketing research. With new information technologies allowing better customer data capture at scale, quant methods reached new heights.

Another milestone in the history of marketing science was Byron Sharp's 2010 release of the book *How Brands Grow*.[3] The marketing manual destroyed traditional marketing beliefs and introduced evidence-based thinking to marketing practitioners. It revolutionized how some marketers approach their roles, and it certainly did so for me.

Marketing transformed from being synonymous with colourful, casual conformity and catchy advertising slogans to embracing scientific principles. This shift mirrored broader changes in business and technology and continues to have an effect today in different categories. As data became more accessible, marketers learnt to apply new tools to understand customer behaviours, which enabled better strategies and more precise tactics to provide accurately measurable results.

Marketing science is well established today, providing an evidence-based decoding of brand growth. Often seen as a set of rules, marketing science is not about stifling creativity or innovation but using evidence to guide and enhance marketing efforts.

The journey of marketing science from academic papers to established business practices demonstrates the power of combining theory with real-world application.

Marketing, science and engineering = Love

Let's first clarify the fundamental definitions before a deeper exploration of the practical applications of science in marketing. What do we mean by Marketing, Science and Engineering?

Marketing 101 – marketing is the brand growth algorithm

Confession time: I rarely think of myself as a marketing figure. I never completed any formal business studies during my academic years. I am a not-so-rare breed of purely practical marketer who learnt the basics of the trade and its advanced theories on the job while working for major global marketing brands. I was extremely fortunate to be dealt a great deck of career cards for my marketing game.

I see no better way to attempt my marketing definition than by reminding you how great minds think about it. Marketing gurus like Sharp, Kotler, Godin, Drucker, Ogilvy, Ritson and many more were my inspiration.

They think of marketing as a game of grabbing human attention, a scientific exploration and value creation for business purposes. Some see marketing as more significant than any other field of business. For some, marketing is the whole business, as viewed from the perspective of the product or the client.

With zero assumptions that I could ever better these great thinkers' perspectives, looking at marketing through my engineering lens, here is my definition:

Marketing is a value exchange algorithm between people.

Marketing is a transfer of value, an exchange of financial capital for a concept, an idea or a benefit. There is always a seller (a brand or concept owner) and a buyer (a consumer or a customer). In many cases, the concept is something the customers already wanted, but in some instances they have no clue they need it, and perhaps it will change their future lives... iPad, anyone?

The concept or idea is always a business proposition on the seller's side, often materializing in a product with a distinctive brand name. A brand. Physical or virtual, brands are the intrinsic repositories of value for the businesses that own them. At the same time, brands satisfy a customer's need.

A few friends with whom I shared the above definition were surprised by my use of the word 'algorithm'. The word has its origin in computer sciences. It describes a finite set of commands that a machine must follow to solve a specific problem. Similarly, an algorithmic approach in marketing can maximize the transfer of value from brand to consumer and vice versa without too much friction.

But a successful algorithm can only be built on robust engineering and scientific principles. Welcome to marketing science engineering, or how to better satisfy customer needs while systematically generating business value using science.

Marketing as a core business function

Marketing is widely recognized as one of a business's essential functions in large organizations, alongside research and development, operations, finance, human resources, sales and IT. In smaller or start-up organizations, marketing often overlaps with sales or product teams.

It is widely agreed that 'business' and 'marketing' are related but distinct concepts. We, marketers, sometimes use these terms interchangeably, which can lead to confusion. While marketing plays a crucial role, it's essential to recognize that it's just one part of a larger business ecosystem. Marketing contributes to overall business strategy and operations but covers only some aspects of the whole business.

The role of marketing is to ensure the customer's voice is heard in the boardroom, identify and build the brand's unique assets to support the product propositions and, when done well, orchestrate a business's internal growth processes. That's why marketing is the business's heart in brand-focused organizations, like consumer-packaged goods. Just as the heart pumps blood to energize the body, marketing provides customer insights, product strategies and communication plans, infusing the organization with the energy needed to succeed. Successful marketing creates a growth cycle that propels the entire business.

This contrasts with other sectors where marketing is viewed as a department that simply creates brochures. In many B2B companies, product or commercial roles typically take precedence over marketing. Traditionally, in tech, product is the primary department, often receiving all the accolades from Wall Street, at the expense of marketing's peripheral role.

Understanding these different perspectives is a nice-to-have for a versatile marketer. Doing so will help you position yourself more effectively within your organization now and in the future.

The golden circle of marketing and business

Peter Drucker, a renowned consultant and author, praised the role of marketing in a business. He famously stated that marketing is not only much broader than selling, it is not a specialized activity at all. It encompasses the entire business.[4]

While we can acknowledge that marketing can serve as the glue driving business results in successful organizations, it's important to reflect when marketing is not the entire business.

Yes, marketing extends far beyond advertising and communication, often the focus of today's marketers. It influences strategy through market orientation, business financials through pricing, operations through product development, and sales through promotions and advertising. In all these aspects, marketing is an integral part of the business, operating at a deeper level. But marketing is not the business.

Drawing inspiration from Simon Sinek's golden circle metaphor, popularized in his book *Start With Why*,[5] and his millions-of-times-viewed TED talk, we can apply this concept to understand marketing within a higher-level business context – see Table 1.1.

In winning companies, marketing and leadership teams share similar outcome metrics: revenue, profitability, market expansion and long-term growth. For you as a marketer, aligning personal objectives with the overall business objectives can only be beneficial.

TABLE 1.1 Marketing within a higher-level business context

	MARKETING	BUSINESS
THE WHY	Aims to drive profit and growth by building brands that attract new customers and retain existing ones.	Generate profit and sustainable growth for long-term business value.
THE HOW	Defines market positioning, guides product development and pricing, manages paid and organic advertising efforts and runs research to inform future decisions.	Is a more complex mix of activities, including management, operations, supply chain, finance, strategy, marketing and sales, all working together to ensure efficient production and delivery of products to customers.
THE WHAT	Initiates product strategy, communications and customer understanding.	Expands to overall operations: planning, organizing, staffing, directing and controlling to achieve objectives.

How Dove inspired communication beyond its product category

Dove, one of Unilever's most successful brands, provides a fantastic example of the power of marketing to impact beyond its product category.

Every marketer is likely aware of Dove's 'Real Beauty' campaign,[6] which was celebrating its 20th anniversary in 2024. The campaign challenges beauty stereotypes and promotes body positivity and self-confidence. The goal is to broaden Dove's consumer base and enhance the brand's reputation for addressing societal issues.

The campaign's effectiveness is evident in the numerous awards it has received and the positive press coverage. Its impact extends beyond the brand and the corporation, influencing culture.

When I was walking along Chicago's famous Magnificent Mile recently, I was blown away by the diversity of body types reflected in storefronts, echoing the idea that was at the core of Dove's campaign 20 years ago.

What better outcome for a shower gel brand than to be followed by every apparel brand, including Nike and Adidas?

Today, body inclusivity is a critical communication strategy for athleisure brands. That a shower gel and deodorant brand may have started shows the strength of marketing communications done right.

Dove's story demonstrates the power of marketing to create value across businesses, industries and society. It's a true example of the transfer of value between consumers and brand owners.

Science and engineering are the enablers of effective marketing

As a telecommunication engineer with a 20-year career in consumer marketing, I've found that a blend of science, engineering and marketing principles could boost your career at times. But your academic background doesn't have to define your marketing career success. I am conscious not everyone is an engineer, but just by reading this section you can grasp the basics. You will see that from a certain point of view, engineering and marketing are very similar in approach. Let's discuss the basics.

Science 101

First, science seeks to understand how things work: studying the natural and social worlds systematically and methodically. It's driven by curiosity, asking questions like, 'Why is the sky blue?' Scientists conduct experiments, gather data and build theories to explain natural phenomena. They aim to expand our knowledge of the universe, uncovering the underlying principles that govern our world.

Science is a rigorous discipline that builds and organizes knowledge through testable hypotheses and predictions about the world.[7]

Modern science is typically divided into three major branches (see Table 1.2):

- the natural sciences (e.g. physics, chemistry and biology), which study the physical world
- the social sciences (e.g. economics, psychology and sociology), which study individuals and societies
- the formal sciences (e.g. logic, mathematics and theoretical computer science), which study formal systems governed by axioms and rules

TABLE 1.2 The word science stands for natural, formal and social sciences

Natural Sciences	Formal Sciences	Social Sciences
Physics	Logic	Economics
Chemistry	Mathematics	Psychology
Biology	Computer Science	Sociology

Engineering 101

Engineering is the practice of using natural sciences, mathematics and the engineering design process to solve technical problems, increase efficiency and productivity and improve systems.[8]

Engineering focuses on making things work for us. It takes the knowledge gained through scientific inquiry and applies it to solve practical problems. An engineer might ask, 'How can we make a building the colour of the sky?' They use scientific principles to design and create inventions that serve real-world purposes, effectively building answers to the questions science poses.

The word *engineering* is derived from the Latin *ingenium*, meaning 'cleverness', and *ingeniare*, meaning 'to contrive, devise'.[9]

Engineering is to create, to bring something to life. Engineering is the creative application of scientific principles to design. It is used to develop structures, machines, manufacturing processes, or physical or digital works. It is essential to construct or operate the above with a complete understanding of their design, capabilities and potential flaws; to forecast their behaviours under specific operating conditions, all related to the intended function, operation economics, and life and property safety. See Figure 1.1.

We need to teach more science + engineering

Science asks questions. Engineering builds answers. They work together to understand and shape the world around us. Science and engineering are fundamental forces shaping our culture and way of living, with science providing the foundation for engineering's practical applications (see Table 1.3).

While all educational systems introduce scientific concepts early on through subjects like math, physics and biology, engineering education remains limited to higher education institutions. I find that our educational strategy overlooks a valuable opportunity to develop critical thinking skills earlier in life.

I love engineering because it cultivates a systemic mindset, offers tools to navigate complex problems with clarity and structure. This method of thinking extends beyond traditional engineering use cases, proving particularly valuable in business careers.

Engineers bring a unique viewpoint, understanding interconnected systems and applying structured tactics that could lead to innovative solutions and better efficiency.

Introducing engineering concepts earlier in education could foster a generation better equipped to tackle the omnipresent complex challenges in technology, business and society. This approach would benefit individuals and companies and drive broader progress and innovation.

Because engineering touches every aspect of our lives, from the infrastructure we use daily to the digital systems that power our modern world. Its influence extends to business operations and, notably, to marketing strategies. By recognizing engineering as the practical application of scientific knowledge to solve real-world problems, we can appreciate its role as a bridge between pure science and the practical needs of society and business.

This symbiotic relationship between science and engineering drives progress – it can be visualized in Figure 1.2. Science asks questions. Engineering builds the answers.

FIGURE 1.1 The interrelation between sciences, engineering, business and society is what shaped the modern world

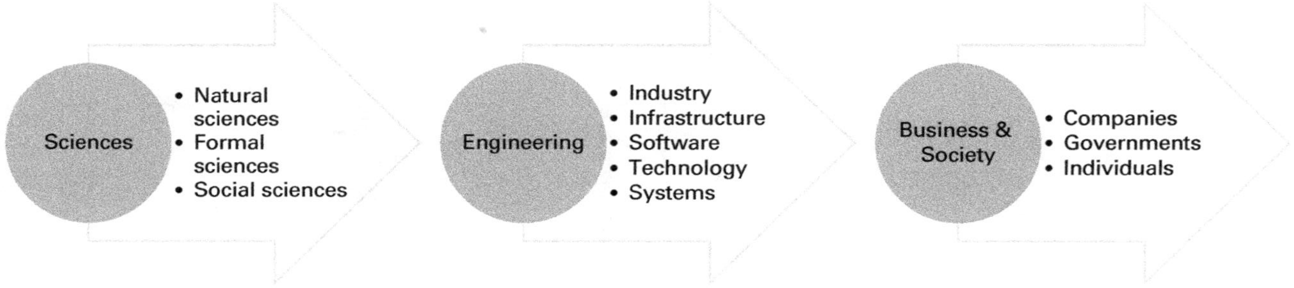

TABLE 1.3 A comparison of science and engineering using the WHY, HOW, WHAT and WHAT FOR framework

	Science	Engineering
OBJECTIVE (WHY)	Understand how nature and the universe works.	Build new technologies, products, and practical solutions to solve real world problems by applying scientific principles.
METHODS (HOW)	Systematic observations and the scientific method (hypothesis formulation, experimentation, observation, conclusion).	Problem-solving, designing, building, and testing to improve the output's feasibility, functionality and efficiency.
FOCUS (WHAT)	Discovery and expansion of the body of knowledge about the universe, from the microscopic level of atoms and molecules to the vastness of space.	Improving human life by addressing societal needs through innovation, functionality and design. From constructing buildings and developing transportation systems to creating medical devices and MarTech technologies.
RESULTS (WHAT FOR)	Principles and theories that explain certain phenomena or the behaviour of the natural world.	Tangible products, systems, or processes that serve specific purposes or address specific challenges.

FIGURE 1.2 The interrelation between sciences and engineering

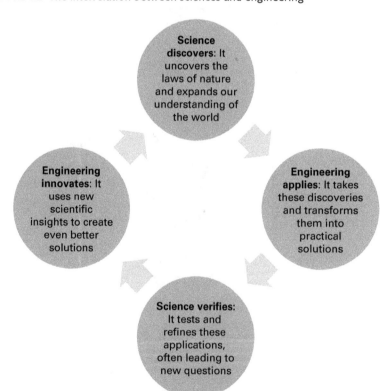

Science discovers: It uncovers the laws of nature and expands our understanding of the world

Engineering applies: It takes these discoveries and transforms them into practical solutions

Science verifies: It tests and refines these applications, often leading to new questions

Engineering innovates: It uses new scientific insights to create even better solutions

The power of engineering and science in shaping our world

Throughout history, engineering and scientific discoveries have driven human progress, reflecting our ingenuity and accelerating societal advancement. From ancient innovators to modern visionaries, countless individuals have left their mark on civilization by solving existing problems and anticipating future challenges.

Consider the impact of figures like Thomas Edison, Henry Ford, Nikola Tesla, Leonardo DaVinci, James Watt, Alexander Graham Bell and, more recently, entrepreneurs like Jeff Bezos and Elon Musk. These innovators have addressed immediate needs and often revolutionized industries, sometimes solving problems we didn't even know we had.

Engineering's influence spans from the ancient world to our modern era. The Roman aqueducts and the invention of the wheel are prime examples of how engineering solutions have shaped societies, improved living conditions and driven economic growth. Today, engineering continues to be at the forefront of addressing global challenges, from sustainable energy production to environmental protection.

Engineering is crucial in developing technologies that enhance our quality of life and foster global connectivity in our interconnected world. The internet, advanced medical technologies and sustainable energy solutions are just a few examples of how engineering pushes the boundaries of what's possible, profoundly impacting the course of human civilization.

Why not bring this engineering mindset into other fields, including marketing? By incorporating analytical thinking, scientific decision-making and ethical considerations into marketing practices, we can elevate the field from purely academic discussions to practical, impactful applications.

The evolution of marketing sciences should mirror the trajectory of engineering, moving from theoretical concepts to daily practical usage. This shift would allow marketers to harness the power of data, analytics and systematic problem-solving to create more effective, efficient and responsible strategies.

By embracing an engineering-inspired approach, marketing can become more innovative, precise and aligned with societal needs. This fusion of engineering principles with marketing expertise has the potential to drive progress, not just in business outcomes but in how we understand and meet the needs of consumers and of society at large.

The Engineering Marketing Framework (EMF)

As we have learnt, scientific principles are general laws explaining how something happens or works in nature. What if we could discover a similar set of tools inspired by science and engineering that can help marketing across all dimensions of our activity?

There are many similarities between engineering and marketing. Often, engineers and marketers use different tools for the same output. While engineers build machines or software, marketers build brands. Both design, test, refine and launch (one with steel, one with stories) and both create something of value.

This is why marketing can be engineered.

Here is how. The fundamental building blocks of any marketing strategy are like a continuous spinning wheel. In real-time, the marketing levers are constantly in motion, sequencing tactic after tactic while continually improving.

Jim Collins introduced the flywheel concept in his fantastic book *Good to Great.*[10] I've used its constant positive motion to inspire my own Engineering Marketing Framework concept (Figure 1.3).

FIGURE 1.3 The Engineering Marketing Framework: How the nine engineering marketing tools apply to the four areas of the marketing process

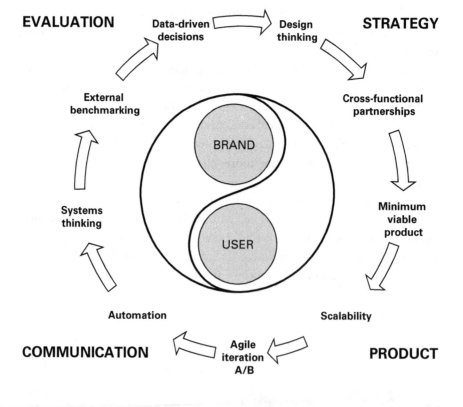

But how does a flywheel work? Like a fidget spinner, a flywheel seems to gain momentum instead of slowing down. In marketing, the flywheel effect creates a competitive advantage by harnessing a fundamental law of physics to influence human behaviour. A good decision fuels another, compounding into sustained effectiveness. Success is a series of smart choices, building unstoppable momentum. It's that simple.

To engineer marketing is to use scientific principles and spin this wheel of decisions faster than your competitors.

THE FOUR AREAS OF THE MARKETING PROCESS

1 Strategy – defining the market opportunity and the brand strategy that will help choose the tactics and ultimately guide execution.

2 Product and price mix – developing the product, including packaging, price positioning and distribution channels.

3 Communication – using media vehicles to communicate to customers the brand proposition.

4 Evaluation – measuring success and ensuring corrective actions are taken immediately.

The brand, the consumer, the user, the customer or your business's value proposition should always be at the centre of this wheel, never forgotten and always considered first.

Launching your brand successfully, diagnosing performance or continuously building your brand requires attention to all four quadrants of the flywheel.

Think of this wheel as your reminder to have the correct conversations on the topics that matter to diagnose your brand growth trajectory. The engineering principles will be the enablers of those conversations and subsequent actions.

You can start improving your brand proposition in every quadrant, but most marketers will begin brand assessments with STRATEGY. Then continue to tackle the product, communication and evaluation or measurement of impact. Once the circle is completed, you can revise the strategic plan, scale or launch a new product innovation, improve communication and continue to assess marketing effectiveness. The circle will then go on like a fidget spinner with close to zero friction.

Across the four areas common to any marketing strategy, I discovered nine engineering tools that come to help you better diagnose and plan. These tools symbolize the core idea of this book: using engineering tools to diagnose marketing growth.

While we will expand on their use in each chapter, let's quickly summarize how these principles work in both engineering and marketing domains.

Tool 1: Design thinking – applicable to marketing strategy

Every marketing strategy starts on the right track if you exhibit customer empathy. The famous customer-first thinking. By focusing on the user's needs, you create innovative business solutions that resonate with the addressee. That's what design thinking is. In engineering, user-centric research informs the design of various products, such as more efficient road toll booths, electronic devices for the elderly, or even hospital paths.

In marketing, one way to build a brand is to draw a customer journey map, learn user pain points, run more profound exploratory interviews and design prototypes that can address those needs. The design thinking method is highly flexible. It helps you create audience personas and rapidly test the concepts you develop (see Figure 1.4).

WATCH OUT

Be careful when you prioritize features or solutions that excite internal stakeholders at the expense of customer needs. Would Apple have launched the iPhone if it had run design thinking processes?

Find out more about design thinking and its practical applications in Chapter 3: The role data plays in shaping your marketing strategy.

Tool 2: Cross-functional partnerships – applicable to marketing strategy

The best marketing teams work well across all business departments and orchestrate collaborations with internal and external partners. Never underestimate the power of cross-collaboration (see Figure 1.5).

In aerospace engineering, for example, a new engine project involves inputs from different types of engineers, designers, pilots and materials scientists building a new engine in collaboration.

FIGURE 1.4 Design thinking

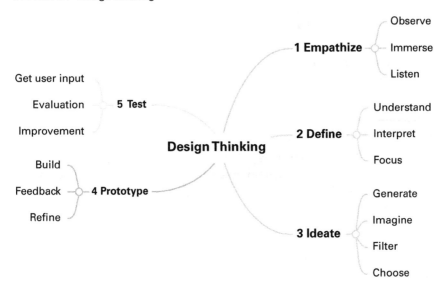

FIGURE 1.5 Cross-functional partnerships

In marketing, the best brands bring together various team members from sales, finance, design and analytics, all working on the same goal and bringing their expertise. It starts with acknowledging that $1 + 1 > 2$.

WATCH OUT!

When you disperse responsibility, it can lead to a lack of clear accountability. Should anyone other than the marketing director be blamed if the campaign fails?

Find out more about cross-functional partnerships and their practical applications in Chapter 3: The role data plays in shaping your marketing strategy.

Tool 3: Minimum viable product (MVP) – applicable to product mix

MVPs are key to product development for both physical and non-physical products. MVPs are the simplest product versions that can be launched and tested before scaling up (see Figure 1.6).

In software engineering, a basic app that fulfils the core functionality requirements is often used for initial testing and user validation. This is often called an alpha prototype, giving users enough functionality to understand what the final product will be like.

In marketing, a basic product version could be launched to test customer interest in a restricted distribution simulated test market. By measuring performance against action standards, the product can be further developed or launched at scale.

FIGURE 1.6 Minimum viable product

4. ITERATE		1. BUILD
	MVP	
3. MEASURE		2. LAUNCH

WATCH OUT!

An MVP that's too basic might fail to impress or engage customers. What is a good enough version of your brand's product?

Find out more about minimum viable product and its practical applications in Chapter 4: Product and pricing effectiveness.

Tool 4: Scalability – applicable to product mix

I learnt early that scale is a magic trick in the business world. A product that has the ability to scale grows more easily without diminishing performance or cost advantage.

In tech engineering, scalability can refer to choosing cloud computing resources that quickly expand with your business's demands instead of investing in physical storage systems.

In brand marketing, scalability is using brand core distinctive assets to create new product offers in adjacent categories. See Figure 1.7.

FIGURE 1.7 Scalability

4. Reap the benefits ———   ——— 1. Leverage the core

Scalability

3. Stay consistent ———   ——— 2. Expand in adjacencies

WATCH OUT!

Scaling too quickly can dilute brand messaging or sometimes quality. What is the benefit of scaling your brand quickly? What is the disadvantage?

Find out more about scalability and its practical applications in Chapter 4: Product and pricing effectiveness.

Tool 5: Agile iteration (Kaizen) – applicable to product mix and communication

A/B testing is a fantastic method for refining product designs and advertising communication by repeatedly testing and improving outcomes.

This tool can be found in engineering in the iterative nature of software developments using sprint cycles or the sequential assembly line efficiency enhancements in automotive.

In marketing, A/B testing is the best method for understanding advertising effectiveness. It offers a causal link between the stimuli and the effectiveness metric. We will look at this more in Chapters 5 and 6. My favourite ones.

WATCH OUT!

Continuous changes to products and communication may lead to shifting goalpost syndrome. Ask yourself, what can you A/B test for your brand today?

Find out more about agile iteration and its practical applications in Chapter 5: Media channels.

FIGURE 1.8 Kaizen is a Japanese philosophy focused on continuous, incremental improvement, emphasizing small, consistent changes that collectively lead to substantial progress over time

4. Act ———   ——— 1. Plan

Kaizen

3. Check ———   ——— 2. Do

FIGURE 1.9 Automation requires little human intervention

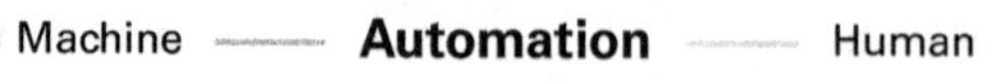

Machine ──── **Automation** ──── Human

Tool 6: Automation – applicable to communication

Automation is a desire to use technology to perform tasks with limited human intervention.

Automation in automotive engineering often refers to automated machine tooling along car assembly lines.

In marketing, it can be found in the programmatic media buying system, where impressions are traded automatically with little human oversight.

WATCH OUT!

Over-automation can lead to overemphasizing cutting costs at the expense of quality. The promise is significant, but staying connected to your brand is even more significant.

Find out more about automation and its practical applications in Chapter 5: Media channels.

Tool 7: Systems thinking – applicable to communication and evaluation

Systems thinking combines multiple discrete components into one coherent system with interconnected features.

In civil engineering, one example could be designing an integrated power grid considering the interplay between electricity generation, transmission and distribution.

In marketing communication, systems thinking could involve integrating sales, marketing and customer analytics data into a robust advertising delivery and measurement system.

FIGURE 1.10 The components of systems thinking

WATCH OUT!

Complexity sometimes hides a break in progress. What two internal systems or processes could be merged tomorrow?

Find out more about systems thinking and its practical applications in Chapter 6: Creative.

Tool 8: Benchmarking – applicable to evaluation

A classic way of looking at performance is by comparing processes and outcome performance metrics to your company's past performance or that of industry-leading competitors. This is benchmarking.

In automotive engineering, benchmarking could be about analysing the fuel efficiencies of competitive car models before deciding the distinctive feature of your motor.

In consumer marketing, brand benchmarking is often used interchangeably with a market share analysis or competitor benchmarking on product quality. It's about ensuring you win the category game.

WATCH OUT!

Too much external benchmarking may lead to strategy imitation rather than innovation. The certain path to no distinctiveness is to get too much inspiration from your competitive set.

Find out more about benchmarking and its practical applications in Chapter 7: Research.

Tool 9: Data-driven decision-making – applicable to evaluation

Often referred to as evidence-based marketing, this tool prioritizes data to inform and optimize all decisions. Not gut-feel.

FIGURE 1.11 Benchmarking: a comparison tool

Your competitors —— **Benchmarking** —— Your brand

FIGURE 1.12 Data-driven decision-making

In aerospace engineering, precise sensor data helps optimize a plane's engine performance and enables pilots to consistently make correct judgements in smooth flight conditions and in emergencies. Experience matters, but data from sensors takes precedence.

In marketing, prioritizing evidence-based decisions at the expense of gut-based choices is a no-brainer. We are lucky to live in a data-rich world; ignoring it would be a sin. As a bonus, this tool enforces another important marketing principle: you are not the consumer. Data-driven decision-making keeps you neutral and unbiased.

WATCH OUT!

Too much quant might kill the art. Marketing is not 100 per cent science; people behave unpredictably, so embrace the unexpected. Find out more about data-driven decision-making and its practical applications in Chapter 7: Research.

I look at these nine tools as conversation starters, guiding your meetings and, in essence, helping you build better brands. If anything resonates so far, I promise you'll get so much more value if we continue to unpack these with practical tips.

INDUSTRY EXPERT CONTRIBUTION
Academic entrepreneur: Dr Karen Nelson-Field

Attention science is a science

Just as marketing science has uncovered fundamental laws governing consumer behaviour, we have discovered similar 'laws of attention' that reveal how human attention operates in predictable ways. Marketing science, championed by Andrew Ehrenberg, showed that patterns such as the Double Jeopardy Law and the Duplication of Purchase Law consistently shape brand growth. These insights are not based on isolated case studies but on repeated observations across large data sets, making them reliable and replicable across different markets and conditions. In the same way, the study of attention has evolved from anecdotal evidence to rigorous, data-driven science that allows marketers to make more accurate predictions about how attention is captured and sustained.

The 'laws of attention' are emerging as we analyse scaled human attention across a range of media platforms, formats and devices. These laws demonstrate that attention behaves predictably depending on the context in which it is delivered. For instance, the Hierarchy of Attention explains that the interplay of media elements – such as platform, format and device – dictates how much attention an ad can generate. Similarly, Attention Elasticity describes the potential range of attention that can be achieved, depending on the media environment and user behaviour. Each platform or format has its own upper limit for attention – what we call its 'ceiling' – and even the most compelling creative cannot exceed that inherent limit.

These attention laws are now challenging traditional brand growth strategies. Ehrenberg's marketing laws emphasize growing penetration by reaching as many people as possible, but the laws of attention reveal that simply reaching people via an ad served isn't enough – capturing and maintaining their attention is the real challenge. While reach is still a vital component of brand growth, errors in measuring and delivering attention can significantly reduce the effectiveness of reach-based planning. For instance, you may purchase a million impressions, and so might your competitor, yet the actual amount of attention generated from those impressions could differ dramatically. This discrepancy has serious implications for key strategies like building mental availability or using share of voice (SOV) and share of market (SOM) in budgeting.

Advertisers can no longer rely solely on increasing market share through broad reach alone. Sustained attention is now crucial for long-term success, and the shift emphasizes the need to balance both reach and attention. Ultimately, the laws of attention are transforming how we approach not just media strategies but the entire framework of brand growth, highlighting that success depends on both reaching people and holding their attention in meaningful ways.

DR KAREN NELSON-FIELD

Dr Karen Nelson-Field, a prominent media science researcher, has helped transform media measurement on a global scale. An adviser to major media agencies and global brands, she's a sought-after speaker and author of best sellers *Viral Marketing: The Science of Sharing*,[11] *The Attention Economy and How Media Works*[12] and the latest category guiding book *The Attention Economy: A Category Blueprint*.[13] Her work has featured in top publications such as *The New York Times*, *Bloomberg Business*, *CNBC*, *Forbes* and *The Wall Street Journal*. As founder of Amplified Intelligence, she leads in omnichannel attention measurement, offering innovative solutions in attention collection, media planning and in-flight measurement, guiding the industry through the complexities of media measurement.

FIVE IDEAS TO TAKE WITH YOU AFTER READING THIS CHAPTER

1 Marketing is a value exchange algorithm between people and businesses.

2 Marketing science is the application of scientific principles to make better business decisions.

3 Science is the core of engineering; engineering is the core of business and society.

4 Science asks questions. Engineering builds answers.

5 The Engineering Marketing Framework is one proven method to bring more science to every aspect of your marketing plan.

Marketing science 101: a final reflection

Remember, marketing science isn't just about using any data to make any verdict but about identifying the most robust data, crystallizing the business hypothesis and action standard, and applying the scientific method to test. Surprisingly, in most cases, the data's quality, not quantity, matters most.

The purpose of this first chapter was to equip you with the basics of how science and engineering can impact current marketing thinking. I've made a case for the benefits of an engineering education for all business careers.

The nine tools in my Engineering Marketing Framework will also help you make robust, replicable and evidence-based business decisions.

Below are three questions to help you make the most of this chapter. Ask them often to make more effective decisions for your brand. As always, there are no right or wrong answers. Simply thinking about these concepts more will help you internalize them better. And for an added learning boost, consider discussing them with a colleague or a friend.

THREE QUESTIONS TO MASTER MARKETING SCIENCE

1 What percentage of business decisions that I make are customer behavioural data-based?

2 On a scale of 1–5, how confident am I that my hypothesis and following action generate business value?

3 How close am I to conducting an A/B test for each measurement project?

ONE MORE THING...

Want to stay effective and ahead of the curve? Scan this QR code to access extra content and updates online.

Notes

1 Kotler, P (2001) *Kotler on Marketing*, Simon & Schuster, New York

2 *Marketing Science* is a bimonthly peer-reviewed academic journal, https://pubsonline.informs.org/journal/mksc (archived at https://perma.cc/Y2DZ-UPDW)

3 Sharp, B (2010) *How Brands Grow – What Marketers Don't Know*, Oxford University Press, Oxford, UK

4 Drucker, P (1954) *The Practice of Management*, Harper & Row, New York

5 Sinek, S (2011) *Start With Why: How great leaders inspire everyone to take action*, 15th anniversary edition, Penguin Books, Harlow, UK

6 Unilever (2024) 20 years on: Dove and the future of Real Beauty, https://www.unilever.com/news/news-search/2024/20-years-on-dove-and-the-future-of-real-beauty/ (archived at https://perma.cc/8UDB-84MA)

7 Britannica (2025) Science, https://www.britannica.com/science/science (archived at https://perma.cc/9XTQ-JHF3)

8 Britannica (2025) Engineering, https://www.britannica.com/technology/engineering (archived at https://perma.cc/LRN9-86BP)

9 Shervin, J (2021) Where do science and engineering words come from? Part I, https://www.mub.eps.manchester.ac.uk/science-engineering/2023/01/18/ where-do-science-and-engineering-words-come-from-part-i/#:~:text=And%20 'engineering'%3F,manufacture%20or%20bring%20into%20being (archived at https://perma.cc/U9LL-UTKT)

10 Collins, J (2001) *Good to Great: Why some companies make the leap... and others don't*, HarperBusiness, New York

11 Nelson-Field, K (2013) *Viral Marketing: The science of sharing*, OUP Australia, South Melbourne

12 Nelson-Field, K (2020) *The Attention Economy and How Media Works: Simple truths for marketers*, Springer, Singapore

13 Nelson-Field, K (2024) *The Attention Economy: A category blueprint*, Springer, Singapore

02

Marketing effectiveness: the holy grail of business today

Introduction to marketing effectiveness

Marketing effectiveness is the Holy Grail of marketing today. The content of this chapter is probably the reason you are holding this book. You won't regret reading it.

After completing this chapter, you will have a clearer understanding of what marketing effectiveness means for various business functions, the concept's past, present and future, and, finally, how to navigate the confusion that often arises in marketing circles regarding effectiveness.

A key feature of this chapter is the Engineering Marketing KPI Framework I will introduce. This framework outlines a pathway to making your brand famous and effective by equipping you with tools that improve your understanding of the success of all your marketing initiatives.

Marketing effectiveness is a process for measuring the success of marketing activities based on the desired business outcome. It's simple: it's a linear relationship between input and output variables. Despite this perceived simplicity, marketers often confuse the meaning of marketing effectiveness with something more complex.

During the past decades, I have had the privilege of helping Mars, the global business active in the petcare, snacking and food sectors, establish its culture of marketing effectiveness and continuously measure marketing performance against solid business objectives. While this Mars experience was the highlight of my career so far, marketing effectiveness isn't out of this world. Let's discover it together.

Marketing effectiveness – the past, present and future

According to member research[1] commissioned by the WFA (World Federation of Advertisers – an industry association with over 150 brand members), marketing effectiveness is a top priority for major advertisers and companies focused on growing global brands.

Why is it so important for the world's largest organizations? How do they measure and approach the topic?

Marketing effectiveness is the link between what marketers do daily and the organization's higher goals. It keeps us grounded in the business process and, at the same time, offers us a seat at the executive table.

Marketing effectiveness measures a company's success in reaching its business goals through its marketing activities.

Through the recent history of corporations, the way businesses set their ultimate goals has evolved, influenced by prominent thought leaders and the surrounding culture.

Back in the 1970s, economist Milton Friedman published his much-quoted essay on the role of businesses in *The New York Times*.[2] He stated that the role of businesses is to increase profits. He argued that companies exist only to serve shareholders and that social responsibilities are outside their scope. This share price-centric view dominated corporate boardrooms for several decades, influencing business approaches in the Western world.

Jack Welch, the former CEO of General Electric, evolved Friedman's perspective, focusing this time on profit rather than stakeholder value as its north star. Welch believed a company's primary responsibility was to its investors, once stating, 'Shareholder value is the dumbest idea in the world.'[3] He championed the pursuit of financial performance to the extreme. The products of this approach are well known today: aggressive cost-cutting and strategic acquisitions, solidifying a business thinking where profitability was the main driver of corporate actions.

In recent years, modern business approaches have evolved towards a 'Triple Bottom Line' or 3P model – Planet, People, Performance. Many companies today increasingly consider their broader impact, recognizing that long-term success requires more than just profits.

This approach reflects the sentiment of contemporary business leaders like Paul Polman, former CEO of Unilever, who led the company to pioneer strategies that he calls 'net positive' in his book of the same name.[4] Other modern strategies today bring together environmental sustainability (Planet), social impact (People) and financial performance (Performance). This illustrates a growing recognition of significant global challenges not just as a moral imperative but as fundamental to enduring business. Companies like Mars, Patagonia and PepsiCo are often quoted as visionaries in this field, and they all champion multi-level impacts in their strategies.

It's not for me to judge which of these theories you are most aligned with. However, one thing stands out when attempting to understand them. Whether it is share price, profit or 3P, we always have an effective transaction in the middle of a hypothetical Venn diagram of business models. Without a financial exchange between a business and a customer, there is no shareholder value, profit or 3P.

The role of the marketing function is fundamental in that exchange. Marketing effectiveness is like a report card for your marketing team, showing how effective your strategies and tactics are and how effective your contribution to the business goals is.

I don't think this concept applies only to large organizations with big marketing budgets. Marketing effectiveness is just as crucial for small owners and even non-profit organizations (NGOs). Every brand desiring to reach an audience and achieve its specific business objectives must measure and improve its marketing effectiveness.

But here's where things get interesting – and a bit confusing.

In most marketing minds, marketing effectiveness is synonymous with advertising effectiveness. Why is that?

Marketing effectiveness isn't just about creating catchy slogans or viral videos. It's a complex concept that touches on all aspects of a brand-building process, from how well you craft your initial growth plan to how you achieve product superiority or pricing power, how impactful your media and content approaches are, and how robust your measurement of total effectiveness is.

Marketing effectiveness is a concept that touches all marketing levers.

The present state of marketing effectiveness

Marketing effectiveness seems to be in the spotlight almost everywhere around our marketing bubble.

Marketing professors, agency experts and consultants have made crucial contributions to challenging established marketing myths and building a culture of evidence over gut feeling.

Marketing research organizations and various industry bodies have fostered this enthusiasm by supplying the appropriate data and, consequently, the platform to discuss the evolving theories of marketing effectiveness.

Here are four big ideas that shaped my thinking in the effectiveness space.

1 How brands grow

To drive brand growth, focusing on acquiring new buyers is more effective than cultivating customer loyalty. Despite the long-held belief that nurturing a small, loyal customer base fuels success, recent evidence shows that expanding reach leads to better results.

Marketers should prioritize maximizing mental and physical availability, ensuring the brand is top-of-mind and widely accessible to potential buyers, rather than investing heavily in loyalty programmes and niche targeting.

The best resource to dive into this theory is the seminal work from Byron Sharp, *How Brands Grow*.[5] The author is building his insights on an extensive set of quantitative sales data sets from numerous product categories. I learnt that focusing on reach and broad audiences widens the pie.

2 Balanced, fundamentals-driven marketing

In a marketing world often distracted by the latest digital trends, it's easy to lose sight of what a marketer should do. Mark Ritson reminds us of the marketer's core role. His advice? Focus on the fundamentals and separate strategy, tactics and execution.

Focusing on strategy involves careful market segmentation, targeting appropriate customer groups and establishing strong positioning. Rather than pursuing every new channel, successful marketers prioritize these essential fundamentals.

Ritson's *Mini MBA in Marketing* was undoubtedly the best marketing class I've ever taken. He achieved a cult-like status in the marketing industry by providing accessible, high-quality academic specialized education. I **learnt** that marketing is much more than just communication tactics and laughed a lot while learning.

3 The 60/40 rule for effective communication

The 60/40 rule is a key principle in effective brand communication, recommending a 60 per cent investment in long-term brand building and 40 per cent in short-term sales activation.

Extensive research shows that brands prioritizing long-term growth through emotional campaigns achieve sustainable success, while short-term tactics may offer brief spikes but risk undermining long-term brand health.

This balance ensures brands don't fall into the trap of chasing quick wins at the expense of lasting value.

This essential framework comes from Les Binet and Peter Field, whose work has become foundational for marketers aiming for balanced, results-driven advertising. With access to data from the IPA (the Institute of Practitioners in Advertising) they were able to draw conclusions based on hundreds of winning case studies. I **learnt** that a balanced view on investment choices is always best.

4 The value of attention in advertising

In a cluttered digital landscape, consumer attention is one of the scarcest resources in advertising. Not all media platforms are equally effective at capturing and holding this attention; clicks or impressions alone don't reflect true engagement. Quality of attention matters more than quantity.

Effective advertising today requires understanding where meaningful engagement happens – placing ads where they're likely to be noticed and remembered rather than just seen.

This approach reshaped my thinking, prompting me to prioritize behavioural measurements of effectiveness over superficial metrics. Karen Nelson-Field's groundbreaking research, published in *The Attention Economy and How Media Works*,[6] drives this framework for media effectiveness. I **learnt** that focusing on real consumer behaviour is the key to success in ad research.

Debates about marketing effectiveness are flourishing online, particularly on platforms like LinkedIn. However, these conversations often lack a crucial perspective: the voice of the advertiser.

While academics, researchers and consultants offer valuable insights, their views rarely reflect the challenges marketers face in real-world settings. Budget constraints, internal pressures and rapidly evolving markets demand practical solutions that go beyond theoretical frameworks.

Marketers on the front lines fight with balancing long-term brand building with the immediate need for sales, often under intense scrutiny from their senior stakeholders. Their unique experiences and nuanced perspectives are essential for a comprehensive understanding of marketing effectiveness.

That's why I decided to write this book and provide my brand-side point of view.

A brand-side perspective on effectiveness

Like with every other domain of the marketing practice, in effectiveness, the challenge remains for all marketers to move beyond theory to action. To fully adopt evidence-based strategies while acknowledging the complexities of real-world brand management.

The tools, data and insights are out there. It is time for advertisers to step into the conversation about marketing effectiveness and lead it. After all, we are the ones who genuinely live marketing effectiveness every single day.

The future of marketing effectiveness is bright

I am not a futurist, but zooming into the implications of current industry trends, ongoing debates about measurement and the emphasis on upskilling marketing teams in terms of marketing effectiveness, the future of this practice can only be bright.

Gaining increased traction, marketing effectiveness will become a standard element in all marketing academic curriculums. But first, the industry needs to reach a common understanding.

After the advent of Big Data and AI, it's true that we are living in the golden era of marketing. Outside marketing, if you only glance at the S&P 500 index over the last two decades, you perceive a story of relentless 6× growth from 1.200 in 2005 to 6.000 in 2025.

But should we expect this growth to follow indefinitely? We might be in a lucky business cycle that has stopped by the time this book is in your hands. During this business cycle, for most organizations the growth objective was non-negotiable. But should it be so in the future?

Why do we expect all organizational problems to be solved if only we grow relentlessly? Some businesses have already recognized this and are pivoting their narrative towards newer topics like Sustainability, Diversity and Inclusion (Representation). While these tend to steal the attention of the markets, the importance of how brands allocate marketing budgets to generate financial results is never overlooked. Whatever business objectives companies choose to pursue in the future, the need to be more effective will always be there.

Technological progress has been constant over the last decades and the capability growth probably won't stop. If today we think we live in the golden age of data-driven marketing analytics, imagine how well we will understand consumers in the future with evolved technology.

By then, the winning organizations will have built a culture of effectiveness. This culture of effectiveness will be the sum of artifacts and practices that live on after people move on to other careers. This will provide competitive edge and a focus on robust decisions.

A bit of empathy – marketing effectiveness is a story of different perspectives

Marketing effectiveness means different things to different colleagues in your organization. Understanding these diverse viewpoints is key to aligning strategies and fostering business empathy.

We often think about effectiveness from our singular marketing role perspective, where brand and consumer are elevated at the highest level. However, the effectiveness story has diverse human perspectives; almost always, inside organizations, the conversation quickly becomes an interpersonal story of power and preconceptions.

Building awareness of the different perspectives and attempting to find the overlap is a sign of a highly successful marketing effectiveness culture.

For the chief executive officer (CEO), effectiveness represents how marketing aligns with the company's strategic goals. It's about driving market share, growth and brand equity (value) to enhance shareholder and stakeholder value. Because the CEO looks at high-level performance indicators like market position, customer lifetime value and return on investment (ROI) from marketing, their question is often, 'How is marketing boosting the overall business?' For example, when a marketing campaign successfully launches a new product line, the CEO sees it as a win for the brand's long-term positioning and future revenue streams but also looks for short-term (quarterly) benefits.

The chief financial officer (CFO) zeros in on the financial returns. For them, it is not just about growth; it's about cost efficiency and sustainable growth. The CFO most often scrutinizes marketing budgets, playing an essential role in the measurement and ROI of marketing activities. They ask, 'How do these efforts improve our financial shape?' Metrics like cost per acquisition, marketing ROI and revenue growth matter here. If a campaign fails to show clear financial gains, the CFO is the one who will push back, challenging the chief marketing officer (CMO) to justify further spending. This perspective often feels disconnected from brand building, but it is essential since it speaks the board's language and prioritizes the business's fiscal health. The CFO usually thinks of ROI first and brand building later.

Then there's the CMO, who lives in the marketing tactical trenches. For the CMO, effectiveness spins around customer engagement, conversion rates and brand value. High conversion rates and positive brand equity metrics trends are signs of success. These focus on the impact of marketing activities. The CMO asks, 'How do we drive customer acquisition and retention? How are we building the distinctive brand assets for the future?' It's about using data and market insights to generate growth. The CMO often thinks of the brand first and the business second.

The CTO (chief technology officer) adds another different layer to the effectiveness conversation. From their viewpoint, marketing effectiveness hinges on how well digital channels and marketing technologies are utilized. The CTO considers metrics like website performance, user experience and data analytics integration. They ask, 'Are we leveraging technology to enhance customer experiences and gather insights effectively?' A successful campaign improves lead generation and provides valuable data for future marketing activations, aligning with the CTO's focus on innovation and technological advancement. The CTO often thinks of technology first and brand later.

The Head of Sales has yet another complementary perspective. For them, marketing effectiveness is about how well marketing efforts generate quality leads that convert into sales. Their primary concern is, 'Are these campaigns effectively driving customers in stores or down the funnel?' They monitor metrics like lead conversion rates and sales cycle lengths. When marketing launches a campaign promoting a new product feature, sales look for immediate impacts on velocity and even contract negotiation closures. The Head of Sales thinks of activation first (boosting sales) and brand building later.

The blue-collar worker in logistics, production or customer service sees marketing as a critical factor in job stability and belonging. When marketing drives product demand, they translate that into company growth, which in turn translates into job security. An effective product that becomes a best-seller keeps production lines running and works schedules full. A strong brand boosts morale, creating pride in being part of a company that customers recognize and trust.

Though often overlooked in this conversation, HR (Human Resources) professionals have their own take on marketing effectiveness. They focus on how marketing shapes employer branding and attracts top talent. Their key concern is, 'Does our external brand image align with our internal culture?' A well-regarded brand brings in customers and draws job applicants who want to work for that company. Therefore, effective marketing helps build a motivated workforce that believes in the company's mission.

As we can see, each role's perspective on marketing, though different, is correct. CEOs think strategically, CFOs focus on financials, CMOs concentrate on engagement, CTOs focus on technology utilization, Heads of Sales target conversions, blue-collar workers focus on job security and HR focuses on employer branding.

Despite these differences, everyone recognizes that effective marketing drives business success.

Building your own awareness of these varied viewpoints fosters a culture where marketing strategies are embraced across all levels of the organization. This alignment is what transforms marketing from a simple department into a driver of the business strategy.

EXPLAIN MARKETING EFFECTIVENESS TO A FIVE-YEAR-OLD

When my kids, Emma and Sebastian, asked what I do at work, I explained marketing through the lens of their street project: the lemonade and cupcake stand from last summer. It was a perfect example of the decisions and continuous improvement involved in marketing.

I reminded them how they had decided on the right amount of lemon for their lemonade and picked colourful decorations for their cupcakes. Those choices – what goes into a product and how it looks – are similar to decisions companies make to create appealing products. Then there was the price they set for each item and the sign they made to catch people's attention. Each choice, I explained, was a marketing tactic.

But my job, I told them, is about *marketing effectiveness* – figuring out whether these choices work. Did people like their lemonade enough to buy more? Was the price correct? Did the sign make people stop? If something isn't working, it is a signal to make changes.

They quickly got it. Emma suggested that if people thought the lemonade was too sour, they could add more sugar next time. And Sebastian thought a more colourful sign would help. They understood that success depended on *continuous improvement* – trying new things, learning from results and adjusting.

This simple experience reminded me that marketing is about being flexible and focusing on results. Just as my kids kept testing and refining to sell more lemonade, brands must stay adaptable, constantly testing and refining their offers and messages to meet customers' evolving needs.

Marketing effectiveness is all about finding what works best. It's about making small adjustments to ensure people are excited to 'line up for your lemonade'.

The three big ideas about marketing effectiveness

- Marketing effectiveness is much more than advertising effectiveness.
- Marketing effectiveness often gets confused with efficiency.
- Marketing effectiveness is about the long- and short-term impacts.

Marketing effectiveness means more than advertising effectiveness

One of the most prevalent misconceptions in marketing is the oversimplification of marketing effectiveness to mere advertising effectiveness. This confusion is so widespread that even seasoned professionals, myself included, have fallen into this trap. Reflecting on my career, I recall holding the impressive title of Senior Director of Marketing Effectiveness. Yet, in retrospect, I realize that an overwhelming 95 per cent of my efforts were devoted to helping colleagues create better ads. *Mea culpa* indeed!

It wasn't until I explored marketing theory more deeply, particularly during my Mini MBA class with Mark Ritson, that I began to understand why this reductive view is so widespread in today's marketing landscape.

The root of this issue lies in the evolving nature of marketing roles within large organizations. Over recent decades, the scope of the typical marketer's responsibilities has gradually eroded. Especially in brand-centric companies, like those in the consumer packaged goods (CPG) sector, we now see dedicated departments for strategy, pricing, product development and even product placement in 'perfect stores'. As a result, many marketers find themselves branded with a narrow focus on advertising and communications. They've unconsciously transformed from holistic marketing managers into de facto communications managers, constantly tinkering with ad campaigns to justify their pay cheques.

However, it's vital to note that this phenomenon isn't universal. In smaller organizations or businesses where marketing plays a less central role (think product-focused companies), the marketing function often retains a broader, more holistic scope. These companies can sometimes offer a more authentic marketing experience, free from the artificial constraints imposed by overly segmented corporate structures.

In summary, true marketing effectiveness encompasses far more than just successful advertising campaigns. It involves a comprehensive understanding of market dynamics, consumer behaviour, product development, pricing strategies, distribution channels and, yes, communication strategies. By recognizing this broader perspective, marketers can reclaim their strategic role and drive genuine business value beyond the confines of advertising metrics.

As we continue to explore marketing effectiveness, it's essential to keep this broader context in mind. Effective marketing is about orchestrating all marketing mix elements to create, communicate and deliver value to customers while achieving business objectives.

The delicate balance of effectiveness vs efficiency

Understanding the interplay between effectiveness and efficiency is crucial for making the right decisions for your business. I am shocked at how often I hear the two terms used interchangeably. These two concepts represent distinct aspects of marketing performance that require careful consideration and balance (see Figure 2.1).

EFFECTIVENESS: THE IMPACT DRIVER

Marketing effectiveness is the quantitative measurement of the impact driven by a business decision, most commonly assessed in dollars. It answers the fundamental question: 'What results did our marketing efforts achieve?' While the typical measure is incremental sales, there are often cases when brand awareness or even click-to baskets are considered measures of effectiveness.

EFFICIENCY: THE RESOURCE OPTIMIZER

Efficiency introduces another critical element into the equation – the cost of a business decision. It's not just about what was achieved but how resourcefully it was accomplished.

Efficiency (ROI) is typically calculated as Effectiveness divided by Cost, commonly referred to as return on investment. This metric is highly dependent on both the effectiveness of the marketing efforts and the resources invested. Maximizing effectiveness improves the return on investment at the same cost levels. Let me repeat that: maximizing effectiveness improves the return on investment at the same cost levels.

FIGURE 2.1 Effectiveness–Efficiency relationship: Efficiency, often confused with effectiveness, is actually Effectiveness divided by Cost

$$Efficiency = \frac{Effectiveness}{Cost}$$

There is a significant difference in internal decisions between focusing primarily on effectiveness and on efficiency. While both are important, prioritizing effectiveness can often lead to greater efficiency.

A positive ROI is a condition to play. But the trap is to centre too much focus on an optimized ROI. The first steps are to reduce investment and solve ROI, which is detrimental to long-term growth.

While efficiency should not be ignored, prioritizing effectiveness in marketing efforts can lead to more sustainable and impactful results. Effectiveness fosters a culture of continuous learning and improvement, aligns marketing goals with broader business objectives and positions the marketing function as a critical driver of business growth.

Efficiency is often a natural consequence of being effective first and then implementing well-optimized, impactful marketing tactics.

The long and short of marketing effectiveness

Popularized in the industry by esteemed authors Les Binet and Peter Field following the publication of an IPA release titled *The Long and the Short of It: Balancing short and long-term marketing strategies*,[7] the concept is fundamental to any conversation about marketing effectiveness today.

Short-term marketing effectiveness is all about fast results. It's like sprinting in a race – aiming for immediate impact. This includes:

- Examples: performance-driven activities like sales promotions, click-to-action advertising, email campaigns and time-limited offers
- Objective: spark immediate customer behaviour and generate quick revenue
- Measurement: using easy-to-execute metrics like click-through rates, conversion rates, sales volume and return on ad spend (ROAS)
- Timeframe: results will be visible within days or weeks
- Advantages/Risks: there is little risk as you can quickly see what's working and adjust on the go. However, there could be a slippery slope towards discounting and eroding brand perceived value

Long-term marketing effectiveness is more like a marathon. It's about building something that lasts, like a brand, for example:

- Example: brand-building marketing executions
- Objective: build distinct memory structures and equity

- Measurement: tracking long-term sales impact, brand value, customer lifetime value and market share
- Timeframe: results develop over months or even years
- Advantages/Risks: builds the brand for the future, but can feel riskier due to delayed results attribution and complexity in measurement

Binet and Field advocate for a balanced approach. They even venture into a numerical split – the 60/40 Rule. This suggests allocating about 60 per cent of the marketing budget to long-term brand building and 40 per cent to short-term sales activation. But beyond the exact formula, the 'and' vs 'or' mindset was what sparked my curiosity when reading their work. After all, without a short-term impact, it is highly unlikely that there will be a long-term impact too.

By blending short-term and long-term strategies, businesses can boost immediate sales while creating a brand that stands the test of time. This seems like common sense until it isn't. In real life, when push comes to shove, most companies consciously choose to prioritize short-termism to make up quarterly numbers.

Marketing effectiveness engineering

Apply the engineering marketing framework– demystify, define, simplify

Too often, we want to answer a complex question like the effectiveness of marketing using a single number. It's like making conclusions on geopolitics using a political map instead of a geological map.

I know it's complicated, but don't despair. I am here to help (see Figure 2.2). I am here to guide you through the complex marketing effectiveness decision framework step by step, chapter by chapter.

A different metric and definition can be applied to marketing effectiveness for each marketing lever. To better understand the complexity, Table 2.1 provides an example of how marketing effectiveness works across a set of marketing processes.

The list in the table is by no means exhaustive. It's just a sample of what you can expect when measuring effectiveness. Know that sometimes, a more complex answer is a better answer than one size fits all.

But this is just a teaser – find out more in the chapters dedicated to each marketing lever.

FIGURE 2.2 The complexity of marketing effectiveness across all levers: a list of key performance indicators to measure effectiveness

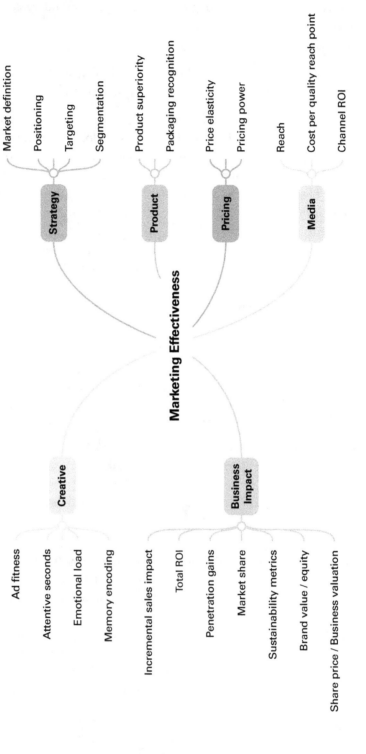

TABLE 2.1 A limited list of measures contributing to different marketing effectiveness areas

Marketing Lever	Process	Measure	Description	Considerations
Strategy	Market Definition	Market Penetration Rate	Percentage of customers who have purchased in the category vs. total population.	There is art and science in finding the right balance between size of market and product fit.
Strategy	Market Segmentation	Segment Penetration Rate	Percentage of customers within each identified segment who have purchased the brand.	Good segmentation criterias are often based on past behavior and not only demographics.
Strategy	Brand Positioning	Brand Awareness	Combined measure of brand recall and recognition.	Needs consistent tracking especially in launch phases.
Pricing	Pricing Strategy	Pricing Power or Elasticity	Change in quantity demanded resulted from a change in price.	Analysis of historical sales data and competitor pricing strategies.
Product	Product/Service Superiority	Customer Satisfaction Score and Net Promoter Score (NPS)	Direct comparison of product performance vs. competitors & customer satisfaction score and the likelihood of customers recommending the service.	NPS - for services. CSS - for products.
Media	Media Channel	Channel ROI	Return on Investment per media channel per 1000 impressions.	Independent and comparable source of channel impact attribution is key.
Creative	Advertising Impact	Ad Fitness	Content compliance with platform best practices (Y/N).	AI solutions offer automatic checks and prevent low impact creatives to be placed online.
Business Impact	Sales Incrementality	Incremental $ captured	Measures the dollar impact of exposure to the campaign, vs. non-exposure.	Randomized control tests are the golden standard for incrementality.

INDUSTRY EXPERT CONTRIBUTION
Business strategy: Joe Zawadzki

Five steps connecting goals to results

Data is at the core of marketing strategy, or at least it should be. Yet, too often, marketers lose sight of the obvious: *marketing exists to sell products*. Not to drive clicks. Not to win awards. Not to chase the latest tech innovation. Marketing's job is to deliver sales, whether moving units today, nurturing long-term loyalty or driving word-of-mouth evangelism tomorrow. Let's start with the basics. Marketing strategy boils down to one clear loop – see Figure 2.3.

Everything else is noise. A great strategy doesn't just aim to 'move the needle'; it proves it. It aligns your team around shared goals, makes trade-offs obvious and ensures you're spending money where it drives real outcomes. If your strategy can't answer 'How does this lead to more revenue or better margins?', you're probably doing it wrong. I always think about marketing strategy in five steps.

Step 1: Define the goal first

For the first question: What are we trying to achieve? Here's my multiple-choice answer:

1   Reach new customers. If they don't know you, they can't buy from you.

FIGURE 2.3 The five steps of an effective strategy

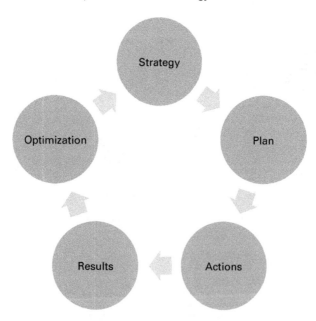

2 Grow wallet share. Cross-sell, upsell or renew offerings to trusted customers.

3 Fuel word-of-mouth. Satisfied customers are your unpaid sales team: activate them.

I once bought an Oura Smart Ring. I heard about it through influencer ads and searched for reviews. Then, I researched its benefits and got hooked. I bought one, subscribed to the app, upgraded it twice, purchased several as gifts and consistently recommend it to others. That's just an example of a complete customer lifecycle, and a solid marketing strategy should guide every step of this process. Goal first.

Step 2: Build a plan

Once the goal is clear, design an execution plan that answers the goal. Execution is always about making disciplined trade-offs. I like the rule of thumb of 70/20/10 on budget allocation:

1 70 per cent to proven tactics (think online video, social, email).

2 20 per cent to experimental tactics (new platforms, influencer campaigns).

3 10 per cent to moonshots (AI-based predictive ads, immersive AR experiences).

A good marketing plan feeds directly into product and customer-facing functions and vice versa. I love the example from Capital One. They claim that Capital One's strategy was a 'marketing and analytics company that happened to issue credit cards' with product, distribution and operations in service to their ability to reach and communicate to customers.

Step 3: Take action

Here's where strategy meets execution. Marketing isn't just about the big picture, it's about doing the basics right, day after day:

1 Target the right audience. Determining your ideal customer will always involve intuition. Start there, but test with small-scale experiments. Scale using lookalike models that deliver broad reach efficiently.

2 Deliver the right message. Don't just tell people your product exists, show them why it matters. A strong offer, personalized messaging and seamless user experiences always win.

3 Iterate on the creative. Whether it's ad visuals, landing pages or product descriptions, creativity is your multiplier. Make ads so good that people will pay to see them.

Step 4: Measure results

Marketing without measurement is like driving blindfolded. Metrics are your map: good ones show you where you're winning and where you're lost. Ground your measurement and analysis in:

1   Channels: how's email performing compared to paid social?

2   Funnels: are you optimizing for awareness, conversion or retention?

3   Product lifecycle: what works for a mature product won't work for a new launch.

And then remember that all models are wrong even if some are useful. Step back from the silos and the stages with some mix of Ferris Bueller's 'if you don't stop to look around every once in while you might miss something'. Can you identify a new product that you can launch different or identify a test market that develops playbooks for other markets? Australia is popular, though Canada is where the smart money is going for this.

Step 5: Feedback and optimization

Here's the dirty truth: no strategy survives contact with the real world. The market shifts, customer needs evolve and competitors respond. Feedback loops are your lifeline. Use real-time data to make minor tweaks and analyse quarterly trends to pivot bigger plans. Always be ready to scrap what isn't working and double down on what is.

Marketing is inherently elastic, both as a department and as a profession. Why would the strategy be different? Marketing thrives on shiny objects and is compelled to market them to the world. This blend of art and science has shielded marketing from the intense scrutiny of other corporate cost centres. Everyone has an opinion on marketing, so how can marketing stay strong?

Remember the one thing that won't change: *marketing exists to sell*. It's not about fancy ads, viral campaigns or innovative screens. It's about connecting your product to the right customer in a seamless, valuable and human way.

So, keep it simple:

Goals → Plan (Audience, Offer, Messages) → Actions → Measurement → Feedback and start again.

And while the tools will change – faster than ever – your focus shouldn't.

Sell the product. Make people happy they bought it. Rinse and repeat.

JOE ZAWADZKI

Joe Zawadzki is a General Partner at Aperiam, a visionary team shaping the future of AdTech. He is the founder and former CEO of MediaMath, the industry's first demand-side platform. With a notable background in co-founding, and serving on the boards of the IAB, MMA and DMA, he has played a key role in shaping the digital advertising landscape. He is a graduate of Harvard University and was a Teaching Fellow in cosmology, set theory and the history of science.

Building a marketing effectiveness culture: a roadmap for success

Maximizing marketing ROI and driving sustainable growth requires a strong marketing effectiveness team and business culture. This goes beyond measuring selected campaigns. It's about proving how *all* marketing activities impact sales, profit, market share and price sensitivity. This transforms marketing from a cost centre into a strategic business driver, and a partner for the C-Suite.

Inspired by how I approached the roadmap at Mars, here is how I would do it again.

First, get everyone on board. Secure buy-in from your CEO and CFO. They should publicly champion marketing's impact. When they mention it on earnings calls, it signals a strategic priority across the company. It goes without saying that your number one sponsor should be your CMO. Help them demonstrate the commercial impact of marketing.

Second, establish a robust measurement and evaluation framework. Regularly review and update your foundational research to incorporate new metrics and emerging techniques. This forward-thinking approach keeps you ahead of the curve and provides an edge to your team's reputation. Build a dedicated team to drive the effectiveness agenda. In larger organizations, this may involve a global structure with clear reporting lines, preferably outside of the traditional business units. This team must work closely with finance to communicate progress effectively to leadership.

Third, develop a common language around marketing effectiveness. Use standardized terms, metrics and rating systems that everyone understands. Extract from your company's marketing philosophy the right artefacts to explain marketing-led growth to make it accessible to non-marketers.

Fourth, aim to develop proprietary insights. Create a learning agenda, an internal testing database and scale learnings. This gives you a competitive edge. Build effective partnerships with your agency partners early on. Treat them as collaborators, not just vendors. Use the same language and evaluation scales to ensure seamless integration and alignment of goals.

Fifth, but not least, don't forget to celebrate successes and share what you have learnt widely. Initiate internal effectiveness awards contests to motivate the organization and further promote the approach. Share campaign wins with the entire company to build buy-in. As this culture takes root, its influence can extend beyond marketing. Apply these effectiveness principles to areas like customer experience and product innovation.

This five-step approach – leadership alignment, robust infrastructure, a common language, effective partnerships and a culture of celebration – can create a powerful engine for marketing effectiveness and drive sustainable business success.

Go ahead and build your culture!

FIVE IDEAS TO TAKE WITH YOU AFTER READING THIS CHAPTER

1 Marketing effectiveness is the holy grail of marketing and business.

2 Marketing effectiveness means different things for different business functions, but identifying the shared link will help you position your organization more effectively for the future.

3 There was never a better time to be in marketing effectiveness; the abundance of quality customer data enables better measurement and accountability.

4 Confusion still exists in marketing effectiveness, but don't forget:

   a Marketing effectiveness is much more than advertising effectiveness.

   b Marketing effectiveness shouldn't be confused with efficiency.

   c Marketing effectiveness is about both the long- and short-term effects.

5 A holistic measurement solution powered by the Engineering Marketing Framework might help you measure the success of your total marketing efforts.

Demystifying marketing effectiveness: a final reflection

This chapter aims to equip you with a helicopter view of marketing effectiveness, the number one concept modern advertisers are passionate about today. For me, marketing effectiveness is about balancing various marketing lever decisions to achieve the best business outcomes. It is about more than just advertising; it requires a short- and long-term mindset approach to brand building and, lastly, being agile and acting on the subsequent research results.

The rest of the book will explore the effectiveness concepts associated with each marketing lever: strategy, pricing, product, media, creative and research. But before jumping into the details, I have one suggestion.

Below are three questions to help you make the most of this chapter. Ask them often to make more effective decisions for your brand. As always, there are no right or wrong answers. Simply thinking about these concepts more will help you internalize them better. And for an added learning boost, consider discussing them with a colleague or a friend.

THREE QUESTIONS TO MASTER MARKETING EFFECTIVENESS

1   How do you measure the effectiveness and efficiency of your marketing activities? Are those two terms used for the same process? They shouldn't be.

2   What is your right mix of short-term and long-term approaches to building your brand? Are you thinking long-term but acting short-term?

3   What internal narrative do you tell your stakeholders about the impact of marketing? What are some artifacts of marketing effectiveness in your organization? What can you change today?

ONE MORE THING...

Want to stay effective and ahead of the curve? Scan this QR code to access extra content and updates online.

Notes

1   Green, M (2023) World Federation of Advertisers – Creating a global culture of marketing effectiveness, https://wfanet.org/knowledge/item/2023/08/23/Creating-a-Global-Culture-of-Marketing-Effectiveness (archived at https://perma.cc/ZQE2-4L63)

2   Friedman, M (1970) A Friedman doctrine – The social responsibility of business is to increase its profits, https://www.nytimes.com/1970/09/13/archives/a-friedman-doctrine-the-social-responsibility-of-business-is-to.html (archived at https://perma.cc/RB95-KV2V)

3 Welch, J (2009) Welch condemns share price focus, https://www.ft.com/
content/294ff1f2-0f27-11de-ba10-0000779fd2ac (archived at https://perma.cc/
A3NF-GUJT)

4 Polman, P (2021) *Net Positive: How courageous companies thrive by giving
more than they take*, Harvard Business Review Press, Brighton, MA

5 Sharp, B (2010) *How Brands Grow: What marketers don't know*, OUP
Australia, South Melbourne

6 Nelson-Field, K (2020) *The Attention Economy and How Media Works: Simple
truths for marketers*, Springer, Singapore

7 Binet, L and Field, P (2013) *The Long and the Short of It: Balancing short and
long-term marketing strategies*, Institute of Practitioners in Advertising, London

03

The role data plays in shaping your marketing strategy

Introduction to marketing strategy

Strategy is what turns marketing from a shot in the dark into a disciplined, results-driven machine. Marketing strategy is the driving force behind every successful brand campaign.

Strategy is a cocktail of right-brain creativity and left-brain analytics, synthesizing data to enhance understanding and translate ideas into action. Contrary to the common belief that marketing is mostly about creativity, a solid strategy comprises a thorough analysis of customer data, maps competitive landscapes and establishes straightforward tactics to inform the execution of your idea.

Developing a marketing strategy is all about making choices. It's about defining your market orientation, identifying and segmenting your audience, selecting the target customers who matter most and uniquely positioning your brand in the marketplace. All following decisions regarding channels, tactics and budgets flow from these four core elements – the engine driving your brand's growth.

Too often, marketing strategy is confused with tactical execution. A clever copy tagline or high-profile campaign might grab attention, but without a well-defined initial strategy behind it, such efforts risk being short-lived. An authentic marketing strategy is about crafting opportunities for mental and physical availability and ensuring you build a consistent and reliable presence in the market that influences future purchase decisions and drives long-term growth.

Authentic marketing strategy is all about using data to steer your brand in the effectiveness space.

This chapter will cover the essential ideas to fuel your much required marketing strategy conversations. First, we'll examine how to choose a market orientation that aligns with your business's strengths. Then, we'll discuss how to balance mental and physical availability, the importance of segmentation, positioning, targeting and even loyalty. We will conclude with the foundational principles and marketing engineering tools that will help you assess your decisions with data, debunk common myths and replace intuition with practical, evidence-based strategies.

By the end of this chapter, you'll have a toolkit to enhance your future marketing strategies to stand out. Dive in to explore how science can assist you in developing an effective strategy.

The strategy–tactics trap: why we keep getting it wrong

Let's be honest, fellow marketer, how often do we say we're 'working on a strategy' when in fact we get buried in tactical decisions? From debating which media channels to use to obsessing over colour choices in our ads, we often become lost in the details. Important as they are, these elements aren't strategy.

Strategy is about the bigger picture: setting your brand's North Star and charting a course to get there.

A good strategy defines where your brand is heading and, significantly, where it is not going. It's about clarifying the type of relationship you can build with the market, identifying your most valuable customer segments and positioning your brand effectively within the competitive landscape. Tactics, such as media choices, creative colour schemes and potential discounts, serve as tools to implement this vision, not the vision itself.

Here's the truth: a robust strategy shapes every tactic, giving significance to each detail. Dedicate enough time to a carefully crafted strategy and you're laying the foundation for your brand's long-term success. But don't stay in strategy mode forever. For new brands, crafting a strategy requires a dedicated period of market analysis, customer discovery and positioning. Once that's in place, you transition to tactical execution mode. For more established brands, the strategy shouldn't change frequently; it serves as a stable guide, revisited only occasionally when market conditions shift.

Your daily tactical work must not be confused with strategy. Most commonly this happens when tactics lack a guiding strategy and execution is all there is. Spend time and enjoy all the elements of the marketing journey.

When you start into strategy mode, begin by asking the right questions. These questions will ensure your team gets aligned on the big picture.

THREE QUESTIONS TO ASK YOURSELF AT THE START

1   What type of business do you want to build?

2   How do you want to build that business?

3   Do you prioritize the short-term or the long-term?

The story of the three little pigs (or marketers)

The following story is about creating sustainable brands for the long term. It is funny to sometimes think of marketing through the perspective of the famous fable of the three little pigs. Each character in the story symbolizes a different type of marketer.

The first marketer is like the pig who quickly builds his house of straw. He focuses on whatever comes first to hand. He skips both strategy and tactical conversations entirely. He tosses up quick solutions, mostly copying the competition and hoping for immediate results. But when the wolf of competition arrives, this pig's straw house collapses, leaving the business vulnerable or bankrupt. *No strategic thinking is dangerous.*

The second marketer is like the pig building with wood. He understands the value of tactics in planning execution but overlooks strategy. He jumps into action with short-term tactics, such as promotional activities or narrow targeting. His wood house stands for a while, but when the market's winds change, it can't withstand the pressure, revealing the weaknesses in his approach. *Short-term thinking is dangerous.*

The third marketer, however, builds with bricks. He knows that success requires strategy, tactics and execution to work together. He invests time in crafting a comprehensive strategy, thinking through market dynamics, positioning and customer behaviour. He carefully selects the tactics aligned with that strategy and executes them precisely. His brand stands firm when the wolf howls or the economic winds blow. *Long-term thinking is winning.*

Reflecting on the story, I recognize the cultural value of building with a sustainable mindset in your organization. This is often expressed in building an internal culture of 'brick behaviours' that emphasizes thoughtful strategy, strong tactics and effective execution. Strategy is time-consuming, but it prepares the terrain for long-term success. Only the 'brick' marketer who covers all three – strategy, tactics and execution – creates a business resilient enough to weather any storm, proving that building for the future is the sustainable path to success.

Your employees' internal business behaviours (and culture) strongly predict your company's long-term success.

The four topics at the core of any effective strategic marketing process

When I think of an effective marketing strategy, I think of four questions that you should discuss and get precise answers to:

1 What is the focus or orientation of my business? (Are we oriented towards the market, the customer, our product or on becoming famous through advertising?)

2 Which key customer segments make up the targeted market? (Which are the largest groups of potential buyers in my market?)

3 How will I position my product or products to best appeal to each segment I want to target? (What best aligns my offer with what each group needs?)

4 What is my targeting strategy for each golden customer segment and how will I implement it? (How do I plan to reach each golden segment and what steps will I take to make it happen?)

See Figure 3.1. Let's examine each area one by one. Consider the above questions as conversation guidance, not just a tick-the-box exercise. Spending enough time debating them will be crucial for the effectiveness of your strategy.

Business orientations

Deciding which business orientation to follow is a deliberate choice when starting your business. Traditionally, this is done based on a understanding

FIGURE 3.1 At the core of any marketing strategy process are reflections on the four key strategic areas: Orientation, Segmentation, Positioning and Targeting

The 4 Strategy Areas

Orientation	Segmentation	Positioning	Targeting

of your brand's strengths, the external context and future business objectives. The first question your strategic work must address is:

'What type of orientation will my business have?'

There is no right or wrong answer as long as the strategic choice is supported by quality data and followed by excellent tactics and execution. The four most common business orientations are market, product, advertising and sales (Figure 3.2).

Let's explore the various methods to help you see how they influence your future.

FIGURE 3.2 The four orientations: most businesses choose between a market, a product, a sales or an advertising orientation

Market Orientation	Product Orientation
Sales Orientation	Advertising Orientation

MARKET ORIENTATION

When choosing a market orientation, you focus on *listening to understand the market*. Stay tuned to current and emerging trends, existing customer behaviours and potential shifts in their needs. Instead of creating products in an isolated lab, your brand should develop solutions that respond to market needs, ensuring your offerings align with current demand. In my view, this seems to be the most common type of orientation. Any business that prioritizes marketing research can be a potential example of a market orientation approach.

PRODUCT ORIENTATION

Choosing this path means committing to creating the best product possible and expecting the market will embrace it accordingly. Companies with this mindset believe that a strong product will naturally attract a following, regardless of current market conditions or customer needs. Think of brands like 3M or Tesla, which introduced innovative products that effectively shaped their markets and created a demand for new concepts, like Post-It Notes or electric cars. However, the downside of this approach is the potential neglect of changing customer needs. A common bias, survivorship bias, is often existent in business. We hear about successes overlooking the numerous great initial product ideas that ultimately failed.

ADVERTISING ORIENTATION

This orientation prioritizes advertising and brand fame. The goal is to capture attention through creative campaigns, sometimes, though rarely, at the expense of product substance. You seek to be seen everywhere, dominate the conversation, win awards and capture the market through aggressive communication. The belief is that if you control the narrative and consistently capture attention, market success will follow since you'll remain top of mind. Once again, due to survivor bias, we only hear about successful brands that embrace this orientation and hear less about those that don't succeed. For me, Burger King and Pepsi are examples of brands where advertising is crucial but is extensively complemented by a popular product.

SALES ORIENTATION

This orientation focuses on maximizing sales through effective persuasion tactics and prioritizing direct conversion efforts. The primary objective here is not necessarily to align with market demands or create the best product or brand but to sell what you already have in the most effective manner possible. Sales-oriented companies often emphasize short-term sales goals over long-term brand building. In my view, car dealerships and insurance companies are typical examples of this segment.

While these four types of orientations are the most common in the world of brands, combinations of orientations or even new orientations emerge in importance. Purpose- and sustainability-focused orientations have become core choices for guiding various business operations and brand positioning.

For example, Patagonia, Unilever and Danone have adopted this route over the last few years. In my opinion, the success of these strategies is additive to initially choosing one of the main types of orientations.

Simply selecting one orientation over another does not guarantee success. Building a strong brand requires a strategy that incorporates market understanding, deep customer insights, product excellence and effective communication.

How can data science help? The availability of customer data for your business will often guide your initial marketing orientation choice. The core of marketing orientation effectiveness lies in using customer insights, market trends and performance metrics to align products and strategies with customer needs while outpacing competitors. Investing in consumer insights will nudge your strategic positioning towards a market-oriented approach.

Surprisingly, for some businesses, the choice is less data-driven than one might think – it's often already part of the company's ethos or founders' beliefs, the organizational culture built over the years, or the idea the owner posted about on an emerging social media platform.

How do competitors influence your strategy? Understanding the competitive landscape is crucial, regardless of your approach. For me, the following three proven research methods have been valuable frameworks for gaining competitor insights:

- SWOT analysis to understand competition orientation.
- Duplication of purchase to identify gaps in the market.
- Share of Voice, Share of Shelf and/or Share of Search to benchmark versus competition.

THREE METHODS TO UNDERSTAND COMPETITORS

1 SWOT analysis is a valuable tool for understanding a competitor's orientation and position in the market. Strengths and weaknesses reveal what's effective (and what's not). Opportunities and threats examine external factors: market trends, competitors and risks. A thorough SWOT can identify gaps in competitor strategies you can capitalize on. Remember to perform a SWOT analysis on your brand from the same perspectives.

2 Duplication of purchase analyses how customers share purchase occasions in the market among the set of brands available. High-competitive categories typically show how customers aren't loyal to a single brand but to a repertoire

of brands. The data helps spot overlaps to potentially inform your positioning change or discover gaps your future product propositions could fill.

3 Share of Voice/Shelf/Search/Large Language Models are metrics similar at first to market share, a description of output, but in contrast focus on input variables of your marketing mix. It's how much your brand 'speaks up' compared with competitors, how much space it occupies in-store on the shelves, or how often people search for it. Always be curious about how this data is captured and ask yourself how representative this metric is for total market behaviour.

Segmentation

Market segmentation is the process of dividing a company's customer base into meaningful subgroups of current and potential customers. This enables the development of more targeted marketing strategies with distinct products and communication messages that can better address each group's needs.

The segmentation approach is widely debated in the marketing academic space. Diverging points of view range from 'no segmentation is needed' to 'data-driven marketing unlocks the treasure of segmentation'. Regardless of which side you take in this debate, the ideas below will help you be smarter in strategic segmentation conversations and make better choices for your brand.

Your strategy work should now answer the second question:

'What distinct segments make up the market?'

THREE METHODS TO IMPROVE YOUR SEGMENTATION

Ditch trendy demographic labels and explore behavioural data if you want segmentation that drives predictable growth. Unlike age or gender, behaviours reveal real buying intent. By prioritizing your customer actions, you align your strategy with what truly impacts the bottom line rather than relying on a proxy. Here's how to enhance segmentation to improve your effectiveness.

1 Prioritize behavioural data over demographics

Avoid trendy labels like 'millennials' or 'Gen Z' in your segmentation. These tags oversimplify diverse customer groups and yield generic insights. Your segmentation should not aim to sound fashionable; it must accurately represent your entire customer base. So, don't shy away from segment labels like 'Unemployed', for instance. Every customer segment can contribute to your growth.

Since most demographic approaches lack precision, prioritize behavioural data that reflects consumer actions. As a bonus, by not using demographics you could also avoid potential racial or gender biases that can hurt your corporate image.

2 Fewer segments reduce complexity and increase efficiency

Effective segmentation should simplify your strategy and enhance execution. 'Over-segmenting', driven by superficial criteria, results in unnecessary complexity that drains resources and overwhelms marketing teams' workloads. Therefore, I believe that often, less segmentation is better than more. When defining the number of segments, consider: will this grouping make execution more manageable and effective? Frequently, fewer segments provide better focus for your team's resources.

3 Segmentation is probabilistic, not deterministic

Segmentation is a probabilistic tool, not a crystal ball. Even well-defined segments won't perfectly predict behaviour. Understand that segmentation offers guidelines, not certainties. For example, a segment labelled 'high spenders' may include outliers. Rather than strictly adhering to segments, treat them as a flexible framework that allows for variability and unexpected behaviours. Like everything in marketing, you are forecasting the future, not guaranteeing it. So relax, and don't be too rigid about it.

THE IN-MARKET EFFECTIVENESS OF SEGMENTATION

Just because you segment the market on paper doesn't mean that, in real life, you will precisely reach all those customers making up the segments.

It's important to understand that defining your customer segments is just an initial step. Activating this segmentation in the real world requires careful planning and constant adaptation. The mental and physical availability channels you select and your available budget will influence how accurately you can target the defined segments.

The probabilistic nature of segmentation makes the exact addressability of your campaign a likely event in practice. There is a strong correlation between the quality and cost of the data you use for activation and the validity of the process. However, don't assume that reach occurs automatically for 100 per cent of customers just because you created a segment.

Imagine targeting a segment of customers who have previously purchased health-related brands through the following media channels: Instagram, YouTube and Spotify. You've likely used purchase data to create a 'past health-purchasers' segment and compiled a list of attributes to help identify them. However, each platform's interpretation of that target group is probabilistic. The playlists they listen to on Spotify or the posts they like on Instagram are never 100 per cent accurate predictors of what they bought in the past, even less so for what they might be willing to purchase in the future. So, while segmentation enhances relevance, precise execution isn't guaranteed on every platform.

The effectiveness of segmentation can be measured by how well it targets specific audiences and how adaptable it is to the behaviours of customers outside those groups. Continuously monitoring customer behaviours and conducting experiments to understand the impact of segmentation can enhance your marketing strategy. Consider various segmentation options, test and control them, and adopt an adaptive learning mindset. How can AI assist you?

THE INCREASING ROLE OF AI IN MODERN SEGMENTATION

AI is revolutionizing segmentation. Advanced generative models and synthetic data sets now allow marketers to identify customer behaviour patterns with unprecedented speed and accuracy, moving from insights that once took months to source to insights that now can be generated in minutes.

My experience with Evidenza,[1] a pioneer company in AI-powered segmentation, showed me how synthetic AI agents can predict new customer segments that traditional research might overlook. Their approach enables brands to identify sources of growth faster than traditional methods, where data might lag months behind the market shifts.

Synthetic data, an increasingly important tool in AI segmentation, offers a scalable and efficient alternative to traditional customer research. In a rapidly changing market, an 80 per cent accurate result today is often more valuable than a near-perfect one six months from now.

Segmentation is a continuous and adaptive process. AI-driven tools enable marketers to monitor real-time consumer behaviour, embracing its probabilistic nature. As AI and synthetic data continue to evolve, brands that use these innovations will shape the future of dynamic segmentation.

Positioning

Positioning is the third essential element of an effective marketing strategy. It demands creating a unique and memorable identity for your brand in the minds of your target audience. This goes beyond catchy slogans or attractive visuals; it's about clearly communicating how your brand better fulfils customer needs compared with the competition.

When positioning is done effectively, your brand cuts through the marketplace noise, providing you with a competitive advantage and ensuring that your brand is the first choice for most customers. Your strategic work continues if you answer the third question:

How will I position my offer to achieve the greatest success for the segments I target?

Effective positioning starts by deeply understanding your target audience and what matters most to them. By focusing on how your brand solves specific problems or meets desires in ways that others can't, you can create messages that resonate deeply personally. This approach informs every aspect of your marketing execution, from campaigns to product development, ensuring consistency across all the touchpoint mix.

DIFFERENTIATION VS DISTINCTIVENESS

Standing out on a congested retail shelf can mean the difference between a rockstar brand and insignificance. But should brands focus on being different or simply more recognizable? Understanding the distinction between differentiation and distinctiveness is essential for building a brand that stays top of mind. As a bonus, you can now participate in the never-ending online debate about the two concepts:

- Differentiation is about making a product or service unique through features, benefits or technology, offering a specific reason for consumers to choose your brand. However, differentiation is often short-lived, as competitors can quickly replicate or improve upon these aspects.

- Distinctiveness, in contrast, is about making your brand memorable and recognizable in ways that competitors can't easily copy. This involves consistently using distinctive brand assets, such as colours, logos and design elements, that create mental availability, ensuring your brand is top of mind when customers are ready to buy.

For example, Pepsi-Cola's iconic logo makes brand communication instantly recognizable. McDonald's uses its golden arches and red-and-yellow scheme, ensuring its brand is memorable even from a distance. These brands succeed not because their products are different but because their brand assets are unforgettable.

Distinctiveness is critical to long-term brand success. Differentiation is essential when you start. While differentiation may create initial interest, distinctiveness builds brand equity and keeps customers returning. The takeaway for marketers: invest in building distinctive brand assets that make your brand instantly memorable and recognizable.

Targeting

Targeting is the process of identifying and focusing on the most valuable market segments to ensure your marketing efforts generate the highest possible ROI and future growth opportunities. Targeting is often about saying no to specific low-growth opportunities, to focus resources on key wins. The fourth and last question your strategic work should answer is:

What is my targeting strategy for each golden customer segment and how will I implement it?

MAXIMIZING IMPACT THROUGH PRECISION

In marketing, precision can make the difference between campaigns that engage and those that miss the mark completely. Targeting the right audience with the right messages, offers and media channels isn't just an advantage. You can uncover what motivates your audience and their behaviours by leveraging the explosion in customer data analytics.

For instance, a luxury brand seeking affluent consumers may invest in exclusive media channels such as high-end lifestyle publications, invite-only events or premium social media content to highlight quality and exclusivity. In contrast, a budget brand aimed at price-sensitive shoppers would concentrate on mass media channels, with messages focused on affordability and value. Precision targeting enhances relevance in both scenarios, ensuring that the right message reaches consumers. Precision targeting is essential.

When targeting is executed well, it delivers a dual payoff: immediate results and long-term gains in sales and equity.

TARGETING FOR MARKETING EFFECTIVENESS

Ultimately, the effectiveness of targeting can be assessed by how well it generates both short-term and long-term success. Running analytical models that forecast business outcomes based on various targeting strategies is an excellent approach to balancing your initial targeting options.

Investing in data-driven targeting and continually refining your approach ensures your campaigns are more impactful, cost-effective and profitable.

The first goal of marketing is to provide a solution to an existing or future opportunity in the market. It is not to identify ways to better sell an innovative product to a market that doesn't need it yet. If your marketing strategy work could be summarized in five words, I would use the following: YOU ARE NOT THE CONSUMER.

Everything you do at every stage of the marketing strategy process is to understand better the market, the customer and your own brand proposition. Keeping a humble view on all this will guide you in building a strategy that puts them, your customers, not you, at the centre point.

You are not the consumer.

How brands really grow

Brands grow by increasing penetration

Professor Byron Sharp explains in his amazing book *How Brands Grow*[2] that building market penetration is the most effective way to grow your brand. Long-term brand growth is achieved by constantly increasing the number of people who buy your product, even if they buy infrequently. Conversely, the author dismisses customer loyalty, shocking many traditional marketers. Multiple data sets showcased in his book prove that loyalty varies little between brands. Thus, the likelier driver of growth is expanding your buyer base, not making your existing buyers buy more.

WHAT IS BRAND PENETRATION? DON'T YOU LOVE A SIMPLE MATH FORMULA?

Penetration is the ratio between the number of brand buyers and the number of total category buyers over a set time period (see Figure 3.3). The commonly used period is one year to avoid any periods with seasonality of sales.
Expressed as a percentage, penetration is a measure of the power of your brand in the category.

FIGURE 3.3 The equation of penetration: penetration is the ratio between the number of brand buyers and the number of total category buyers

$$\text{Brand Penetration} = \frac{\text{Number of Brand Buyers}}{\text{Total Category Buyers}} \times 100$$

Compared with other outcome metrics, penetration is a reliable predictor of future growth. For example, compared to value share, it removes the price impact from the equation. The maximum penetration for your brand is 100 per cent: when everyone active in the category buys your product at least once. Yet, as 100 per cent penetration brands are rare in non-monopolistic industries, the only way is up for your current brand penetration.

To measure penetration, use sales data from a nationally representative panel or any other comprehensive and complete purchase data set. If you own all your sales data already, measuring penetration becomes kids' play.

Sharp's theory has influenced numerous brands to pivot towards broader segmentation groups, mass targeting and a focus on distinctiveness, often at the expense of brand differentiation. Building on extensive evidence-based data from various categories, he advises brands to prioritize all category buyers instead of focusing on niche segments. This approach translates into tailoring messages for broad appeal and creating simple, memorable branding that enhances both mental and physical availability.

Improving physical availability is a critical, often overlooked driver of market penetration. Physical availability refers to how easy it is for consumers to find and buy your brand when buying into the category. This involves optimizing distribution channels to ensure your products are widely accessible, whether online or offline. Expanding your presence in more retail outlets, ensuring sufficient shelf space and reducing out-of-stock situations are practical ways to accelerate physical availability. Additionally, partnering with e-commerce platforms and exploring new retail channels can significantly enhance it. Brands that are easier to find and buy will naturally attract more buyers, thereby increasing penetration.

Mental availability complements physical presence. By utilizing reach-based advertising, you can ensure your brand is at the top of mind when purchase decisions are made. Broad reach advertising doesn't necessarily mean avoiding segmentation in your messaging, it means using segmentation wisely. Craft messages tailored to specific segments within your larger market, but ensure you still reach a broad audience. For example, different creative executions can resonate with various consumer needs while all contributing to the same overarching campaign.

Reach-based advertising affects both brand penetration and the purchase frequency of existing buyers. I often receive the question: what type of creative elements drive the highest penetration gains? I don't know! The quest for this elusive golden nugget, the campaign that solely drives significant penetration, is a favoured distraction for marketers. Unless you know you're always incredibly lucky, you should focus your efforts on creating a strong, effective ad that resonates with a broad audience. This will, by default, drive more penetration compared with a less effective creative.

Bonus: if you deploy a reach-based strategy, you don't need to advertise directly to your brand buyers. They will be exposed to your communication message, and on top of that they are already exposed to your real product and experience it firsthand, which is more important than the one second they pay attention to your message on social.

Byron Sharp's leaky bucket metaphor is an excellent analogy for the quest to build penetration continuously. As time passes, due to regular buying patterns, most buyers become lapsed buyers. In a world where all media impressions are costly, choose wisely and reach everyone who could purchase your brand. Keep building penetration and measure it using real sales data, not declarative data.

Action steps: use segmentation to shape your communication messages, but don't limit your targeting to just one or two segments. Reaching as many potential buyers as possible within the category ensures consistent penetration growth. To further validate this strategy, examine your brand data. Look at how often your products are in stock, where they are sold and how widely they are distributed. This will reveal opportunities to improve physical availability and extend your market reach.

Physical and mental availability: the twin columns of brand growth

These two fundamental concepts shape a brand's success story: physical and mental availability. While distinct, these pillars work harmoniously to elevate a brand's presence in the market and in consumers' minds.

THE ESSENCE OF PHYSICAL AND MENTAL AVAILABILITY

Physical availability is all about finding your product when shoppers are in the market for the category across the various channels they shop. Think of it as a brand's footprint in the real world.

PepsiCo exemplifies this concept in B2C with its ubiquitous presence in places where drinks are bought and consumed worldwide, from small rural shops to sprawling supermarkets to concert halls and nightclubs. As of 2023, PepsiCo products were available in over 200 countries.[3]

In the B2B space, consider how cloud services like Amazon Web Services (AWS) achieve physical availability through their expansive global server network. As of 2024, AWS operates in 99 availability zones within 31 geographic regions worldwide, ensuring businesses can readily access its services with limited lag.[4]

Mental availability, meanwhile, focuses on building the brand in the customer's mind with the clear intent to elicit a recall when a purchase occurs. Mental availability is the likelihood of a brand coming to mind when a relevant need arises. This cognitive presence is crucial for influencing purchase decisions, especially in low-connection categories like detergent and candy.

While distinct, these two concepts are most potent when working in tandem. Strong physical availability reinforces mental availability and vice versa. When a brand is easily accessible and top of mind, it creates a powerful synergy that drives customer choice.

STRATEGIES FOR ENHANCING PHYSICAL AVAILABILITY

Optimizing physical availability requires a multifaceted approach. Expanding distribution into new channels relevant to the target audience is crucial, but ensuring consistent stock levels across all points of sale is equally important.

Leveraging technology can significantly enhance physical availability in today's digital age. Real-time inventory tracking systems can help prevent stock-outs, while omnichannel strategies can bridge the gap between online and offline experiences.

Visibility is another critical aspect of physical availability. In physical stores, this might mean negotiating prime shelf positions. Online, it translates to optimizing for search engines and e-commerce platforms. The goal is to make the brand easily discoverable wherever potential customers look.

BOOSTING MENTAL AVAILABILITY

Enhancing mental availability is about creating strong, positive associations with your brand in the minds of your audience. This starts with consistent brand messaging. Developing a clear, unique brand voice that resonates across all touchpoints helps create a cohesive brand image in consumers' minds. Memorable taglines and distinctive visual identities play a crucial role in this.

Creating emotional connections with customers is another powerful way to enhance mental availability. Brands that tell compelling stories can create more profound, more lasting impressions in B2C and B2B, too. Emotional ties can influence purchase decisions, especially in busy B2B markets with minimal functional differences between products.

THE SYNERGY OF SHELF AND MIND

The magic happens in the interplay between physical and mental availability (see Figure 3.4). Mental availability drives desire, while physical availability enables action. For example, Nike's[5] latest ad campaign might strongly influence a customer, but if they can't find Nike products in their local stores or on preferred online platforms, the brand's mental availability won't translate into sales.

Conversely, a product might be widely available, but without strong mental availability, it risks not being noticed. Imagine a new soft drink with excellent distribution but no brand recognition – it might sit on shelves untouched despite its physical presence.

This synergy also plays a crucial role in building long-term brand value and equity. A consistent presence in both the physical and mental realms reinforces a brand's position in the market and in consumers' minds.

FIGURE 3.4 Growth strategies: physical and mental availability are recognized strategies for how brands grow – the sweet spot is activities that engage both at the same time

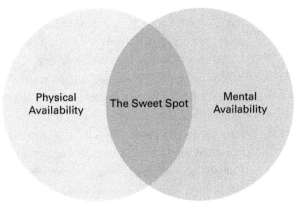

Growth Strategies

THE BALANCING ACT: ADVERTISING VS. PROMOTIONS

Both advertising and promotions can contribute to physical and mental availability, but they serve different purposes and require careful balancing.

Advertising primarily builds long-term mental availability and brand equity. It creates associations and emotional connections that keep a brand in consumers' consideration. Meanwhile, price promotions drive short-term sales and can enhance physical availability by encouraging retailers to stock and display products prominently.

The challenge for marketers lies in finding the right balance. Over-reliance on promotions can erode brand value over time, training consumers to buy based on price rather than brand preference. Conversely, neglecting promotions entirely might lead to missed sales opportunities and reduced physical availability if retailers are less inclined to stock the product.

The key is strategically using promotions while maintaining a solid focus on brand-building advertising. This approach helps maintain both short-term sales performance and long-term brand health.

REAL-WORLD EXAMPLE
Snickers – how to activate the sweet spot

In 2016, Snickers faced the challenge of capturing the attention of millennials, a demographic increasingly vital for every product category, especially chocolate. Collaborating with Clemenger BBDO Melbourne, the Snickers team developed an innovative solution: Hungerithm. This algorithm monitored Twitter sentiment, dynamically adjusting the price of Snickers at 7-Eleven stores according to the internet's mood. The angrier people were online, the lower the price of Snickers.[6]

The target segment of this campaign was well known for their less-than-average consumption of traditional advertising vehicles like TV. Hungerithm was a fresh approach, bridging mental and physical availability strategies in digital. The real-time Twitter behaviour drove a different price in physical stores. By analysing over 14,000 tweets daily, Snickers adjusted prices to 10 times daily, dropping Snickers prices as low as AU$0.50 (US$0.30) when Twitter was especially 'angry'.

The results were impressive. In just five weeks, Snickers reached over 4 million millennials in Australia, doubling the initial target of 2 million. The campaign generated 71 million impressions, with more than half coming from earned media, thanks to widespread media coverage and organic buzz on platforms like Reddit, Gizmodo and Mashable. Millennials connected with the dynamic pricing, with one in eight visitors to the Hungerithm website claiming a barcode to redeem Snickers at their local 7-Eleven. The real win was in sales: Snickers saw a 20 per cent increase in sales at 7-Eleven, surpassing the 10 per cent goal and reversing its previous decline.

Beyond sales, the campaign significantly strengthened Snickers' relationship with 7-Eleven. By combining in-store signage and point-of-sale displays, and leveraging the retailer's own channels, Hungerithm increased foot traffic and earned Snickers valuable shelf space. The collaboration boosted the overall self-consumption category within 7-Eleven, solidifying a partnership that benefited both the brand and the retailer.

Ultimately, Hungerithm is an outstanding example of how mental and physical availability can work together. The campaign kept the brand top of mind, ensuring strong mental availability. This seamless integration of a clever digital strategy and strong retail execution allowed Snickers to capture attention, drive sales and deliver a powerful lesson in how brands can activate physical and mental availability simultaneously.

MEASURING SUCCESS

To assess the effectiveness of physical and mental availability strategies, marketers have to monitor various outcome metrics. For physical availability, these metrics might include distribution coverage, stock-out frequency, share of shelf space and online visibility metrics. Mental availability can be assessed through brand recall of distinctive assets and brand awareness, share of voice measurements and brand association strength.

Remember, physical availability without mental availability means a product may be ignored on the shelf. Mental availability without physical availability leads to frustrated consumers. The intersection of shelf and mind is where brand magic happens. It's where consumer needs meet brand solutions, where awareness transforms into action.

REAL-WORLD EXAMPLE

McDonald's – the power of physical availability

Every time I travel to the United States, I am puzzled by the omnipresence of fast-food restaurants. They are everywhere. My curiosity made me wonder how far one can be from a McDonald's in the US. To my surprise, I was not the only person asking this question. Irrespective of the answer, McDonald's ubiquity in the US stands as a major example of the power of physical availability.

I've learnt that McDonald's has over 13,000 points of sale in the United States alone.[7] It feels like you could toss a stone and hit one of those iconic golden arches from anywhere. But how far would you need to throw? To nurture my curiosity, I turned to Google and discovered, to my surprise, some interesting facts about the distribution of its restaurants.

Only one state capital has no McDonald's: Montpelier, Vermont. Going west is the only way you can partially 'escape' the fast-food giant. What the data geeks call the 'McFarthest Spot' in the United States can be found in northwest Nevada, an unfamiliar wilderness area. It's just 120 miles from the nearest McDonald's – if you could fly in a straight line. On a normal road, the distance to grab a Big Mac is about 135 miles. However, this McFarthest Spot is somewhat variable and changes over time. Initially identified in 2009, the original McFarthest Spot was in South Dakota.

Blog writer Stephen Von Worley uncovered this point by playing with online data that captured the geographical coordinates for all 13,000 McDonald's outlets nationwide. Unsurprisingly, both McFarthest Spots are situated in the western US, where South Dakota has a relatively sparse population of under 1 million residents. While home to 3 million people, Nevada has much of its land dedicated to remote desert areas. The shift of the McFarthest Spot occurred due to a McDonald's closure in Nevada, which increased the distance to the nearest restaurant by 13 miles. This relatively short distance highlights McDonald's overwhelming presence and focus on physical availability.

What does this mean for us in marketing? It shows the power of physical availability and its importance for a continuously evolving company in a competitive environment. It also shows how the distribution of your products should follow the geographical distribution of your target audience. In the case of McDonald's, I assume the target was close to the entire human population.

The power of loyalty: lessons from hospitality and transportation

F. Scott Fitzgerald famously wrote: 'The test of a first-rate intelligence is the ability to hold two opposing ideas in mind at the same time and still retain the ability to function.' Let's demonstrate our intelligence and construct an argument for loyalty, even after previously asserting that it is less critical vs a light buyers' focus.

In the heated debate about focusing on market penetration or customer loyalty, some business sectors with high involvement and large purchases have been building loyalty programmes for decades. The two industries that first come to mind are hospitality and transportation, particularly airlines. They both provide cases on how loyalty can drive sustainable revenue and growth.

When loyalty wins: the case of airlines

For traditional airlines, particularly those that depend heavily on business travellers for revenue, loyalty programmes have become impactful in retaining customers. Frequent flyers encounter significant switching costs, both financial and habitual, making them less inclined to consider alternatives. Airlines take advantage of this by providing elaborate loyalty programmes that include frequent flyer miles, elite status tiers and exclusive benefits.

Academic research[8] confirms that these programmes create a sense of exclusivity and perceived value, directly influencing customer retention. Who doesn't value benefits such as priority boarding, lounge access, extra baggage allowance and seat upgrades? They enhance the travel experience and create a strong incentive for customers to stay loyal.

Name any airline and you'll find a loyalty programme gamifying frequent business travellers to raise or maintain their status. The accumulated benefits and personalized experiences often outweigh considerations of brand availability or mass appeal in purchase decisions. And this choice gets an extra boost when corporate expenses are part of the equation.

Hospitality loyalty programmes[9] positively influence customers' emotional and behavioural commitment, increasing repeat rates. This loyalty is built through consistent, superior service, personalized offers and recognition, creating a strong brand–customer relationship that market penetration alone cannot achieve.

I am not arguing that a reach-based strategy is not crucial for an airline's overall revenue growth; I believe that repeat purchases are sensible for certain customer segments where the lifetime value is higher. It's true that, ultimately, some customers are more significant than others in services.

Lessons for brands that don't believe in loyalty

While loyalty tactics may not be universally transferable in packaged goods, for example, many brands can learn valuable lessons from the successes seen in hospitality and transportation:

- Personalization and data utilization: both airlines and hotels use extensive customer data to personalize offers and experiences. Your brand can adopt this approach by using first-party customer segment data to tailor interactions with look-a-like segments. This could only enhance your penetration efforts.

- Tiered benefits structure: the tiered loyalty system creates aspirational goals for customers. Your brand can implement similar structures, offering increasing benefits for higher levels of engagement or purchase volumes. After all, collect-and-get tactics are often a way this comes to life in grocery stores.

- Experiential rewards: beyond traditional discounts or points, brands can offer unique experiences related to their products, creating deeper emotional connections with customers. How would you do this?

As markets become increasingly competitive, the ability to build and maintain customer lifetime interactions is a defining factor in long-term business success. The hospitality and transportation industries' examples provide valuable insights for brands looking to strengthen their customer relationships and drive sustainable growth.

A step-by-step guide to craft an integrated customer journey

Creating a seamless and integrated customer journey is an ambition aimed at delivering memorable brand experiences to your customers. An integrated approach unites your internal teams around a common goal, aligning their efforts to consistently reinforce the brand's message across every touchpoint. This transcends traditional, siloed marketing efforts, offering a cohesive experience that builds brands and drives measurable outcomes.

In large organizations, different departments often handle customer interactions, with diverging objectives, which can lead to inconsistency. From a customer's perspective, brands should deliver consistent, integrated experiences, increasing the likelihood of engagement and conversion through familiarity. But that's not as easy on the brand side.

To craft an integrated marketing strategy, your first step is the brief. Cover these elements:

- Crystallize the ultimate goal.
- Define the target audience.
- Clarify the core message.
- Specify the role of each touchpoint in the customer journey.

Rather than setting separate key performance indicators (KPIs) for each department, brands benefit from establishing a single measure of success, such as Incremental Sales, Penetration Points Increase, Contribution to Customer Lifetime Value, Share of Wallet, or a combination. This is where the internal negotiation of metrics and KPIs should focus.

Aligning budgets and resources under a single, integrated marketing budget is essential for building a unified brand experience. This approach enables a flexible allocation of budgets based on real-time performance and shifting market conditions.

A dedicated brand orchestrator must play a central role in making this integration effective. This person:

- maps the (most common) entire journey across all touchpoints
- identifies critical moments and potential pain points
- coordinates content and offers across channels
- ensures consistent messaging and branding
- optimizes the journey based on real-time data and feedback

Next is a cohesive content strategy. Creative messages should be adapted for each channel while maintaining consistency, which can be achieved through modular content that is flexible across channels, a central content management system (CMS) and clear guidelines for how content translates across platforms to ensure the brand's message remains unified.

A unified tracking system should span all touchpoints for measurement, offering a complete view of the customer journey. Essential tools in this process include:

- multi-touch attribution models for tracking customer interactions across channels
- AI-powered analytics and regression to provide real-time insights
- customer data platforms that unify data from various sources

Success lies in dismantling internal silos, promoting cross-functional collaboration and maintaining an unwavering focus on the customer. With these principles in mind, marketing initiatives can transform from a collection of disconnected tactics into a cohesive strategy that provides genuine value.

Applied engineering for marketing strategy

Engineering concepts can enhance your marketing strategy. Starting in this chapter, I will describe the tools and idea generators I utilize to integrate science into each marketing lever.

Let's get started with the first two tools: design thinking and cross-functional partnerships.

FIGURE 3.5 The design thinking process

Design Thinking Process

EMPATHIZE	DEFINE	IDEATE	PROTOTYPE	TEST
Understand users' needs through research and observation.	Identify and articulate the core problems based on user insights.	Generate a wide range of ideas and potential solutions.	Creat tangible representations of ideas to explore their viability.	Get feedback on prototypes to refine and improve solutions.

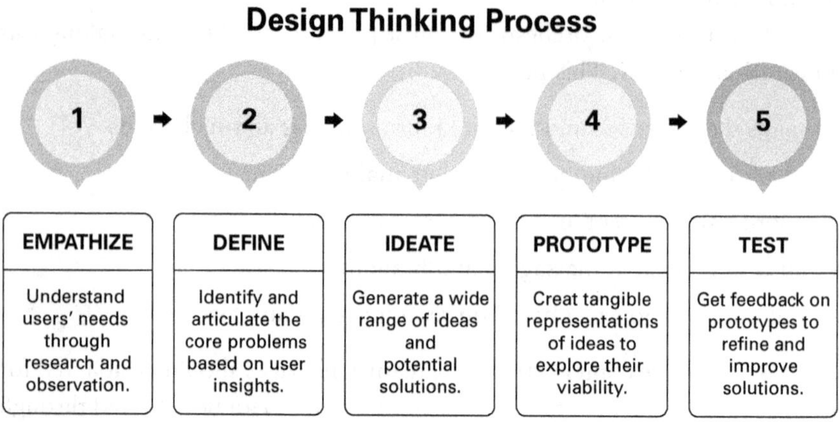

Engineering Marketing Tool 1: Design thinking – precision in marketing strategy choices

Design thinking is a structured process for solving complex problems by putting the user at the centre. It acts as an algorithm for innovation, eliminating guesswork and driving data-informed decisions. Applying design thinking to early marketing strategy development has shown how it transforms insights into action.

Rather than relying on assumptions, design thinking enables teams to collect customer data, formulate hypotheses and experiment with ideas. Originating in the mid-20th century for architecture and engineering, its principles now inform business strategy and innovation.

Today, design thinking aligns human needs with business objectives. By fostering curiosity and structured experimentation, it enables teams to create impactful solutions that drive growth and differentiation.

THE FIVE PHASES OF DESIGN THINKING

The five distinct phases of a design thinking project mirror the scientific approach: hypothesize, test and iterate. Here is a practical way to apply it to marketing:

1   Step 1 – Empathize: Forget your intrinsic assumptions. External customer insight is the answer. Marketers must gather deep insights from their

audience through research, analytics and user observations. This is about identifying realistic, unmet needs, not relying on your gut instincts or focus groups alone. Empathizing with your customers is one way to define your market orientation.

2   Step 2 – Define: In the same way that engineers must solve problems they have defined clearly, marketers should do the same. This step distils your research into a precise, actionable problem statement. Is your split of the market segmentation offering you the best coverage? Does the targeting match the segmentation you defined?

3   Step 3 – Ideate: This isn't about throwing random ideas around, or sometimes it is. In theory, it's a disciplined approach to generating possible solutions. Looking at the problem from different perspectives (think Six Thinking Hats)[10] and brainstorming for the best or the worst possible idea can help. Remember to tie each idea back to your defined problem.

4   Step 4 – Prototype: In engineering, you don't build the final product until you've tested mock-ups. Marketers should do the same. Define the physical attributes of your product and embrace design irrespective of whether you are building a physical product, a service or an intangible solution. Try to get to the core of it.

5   Step 5 – Test: Testing isn't just about gathering feedback, it's about validating your initial assumptions and using A/B testing or other scientifically proven data-driven methods to make decisions. Adjust and refine your strategy based on real-world performance. If it doesn't work, iterate.

Successful companies like IBM and PepsiCo[11] have publicly stated that design thinking has helped them improve their marketing and product development. PepsiCo, under Indra Nooyi, integrated design thinking into everything from product design to marketing. By prototyping new packaging designs and getting real-time feedback, the company saved millions on failed launches and optimized its product presentation.

IMPLEMENTATION: BRINGING DESIGN THINKING TO YOUR MARKETING TEAM

Don't look at design thinking as a one-time exercise. It should become part of your operational DNA. Begin by involving cross-functional teams that include data scientists, engineers and marketers. These teams concentrate on continuous iteration, utilizing data to refine every aspect of your marketing, from segmentation to customer retention.

Design thinking brings engineering precision to the marketing process. It allows marketers to think like scientists. Brands that adopt this approach systematically eliminate risk and increase their chances of delivering ideas and products that truly resonate.

Ultimately, by centring on the customer – user – consumer, design thinking can impart a very personal lesson that I believe every marketer should have printed and displayed on their desk:

You are not the customer!

Engineering Marketing Tool 2: Build cross-functional partnerships – creating a collaborative machine

An esteemed academic I greatly admire is renowned for stating that, in most cases, new and successful ideas are not generated in isolation but rather at the intersection of business domains or among individuals who choose to collaborate.

Cross-functional partnerships are the engine that drives successful marketing-led collaboration inside your business. Like aerospace projects, where engineers, designers and material scientists must collaborate, top-performing marketing campaigns rely on seamless collaboration between sales, finance, design and analytics teams.

Imagine an orchestra where musicians play without coordinating. The result? Chaos. The same goes for marketing projects: cross-functional collaboration is necessary for brands to perform.

THE CORE OF BUILDING STRONG CROSS-FUNCTIONAL TEAMS
Successful cross-functional partnerships create cohesive work decisions where each department contributes its expertise:

- Empower diverse expertise: Every marketing campaign involves input from multiple teams. Sales offers insights into customer behaviour. Finance ensures creative ideas stay within budget. Designers bring the vision to life, while analytics teams keep efforts data-driven. Each function brings critical insights. And when combined, magic is unleashed.
- Leadership and accountability: Collaboration is vital, but accountability is essential. If a campaign fails, it shouldn't be blamed on just one team or individual, like a pilot in a plane crash. Each team must own its role.

The marketing director acts as the conductor, ensuring all departments play their part and are responsible for their portion of the process.

• Shared responsibility, continuous improvement: Cross-functional teams must share success and failure. When campaigns succeed, celebrate as a team. When they fail, learn together. This approach fosters a culture of transparency and constant improvement, like engineering teams refining their processes after tests.

There are many ways to build effective collaboration in your organization, but from my experiences I've learnt that three are the most effective:

• Define clear roles: Each team must understand its function and its responsibilities. You can plot this down as a RACI matrix with Responsible – Accountable – Consulted – Informed. Define who makes the brand positioning decision, who manages the budget, how the budget is controlled and who tracks marketing effectiveness. Clear role definition ensures that no one works in a vacuum and that every team knows its responsibilities.

• Establish open communication: Communication is critical. Set up regular status meetings and open channels to keep everyone informed. When challenges arise, an open forum ensures quick pivots, similar to how pilots adjust course based on real-time data.

• Celebrate success together: Recognize achievements as collective wins. When finance delivers the budget and design brings the vision, it's a team success. Acknowledge it together to reinforce the value of collaboration. There will always be another project after the celebration.

You'll build innovative and well-executed brands by nurturing open communication, defining clear responsibilities and continuously improving. Cross-functional teams are critical to your success.

INDUSTRY EXPERT CONTRIBUTION
On strategy: Fergus O'Carroll

I have to admit to having a love/hate relationship with data in marketing strategy. I love how it can be used but hate how it can be abused.

I've come to see both its value and its faults. Conventional wisdom sees data as the magic elixir in marketing. That it solves the unseen problems and brings clarity to the task at hand. But conventional wisdom is a dangerous anchor. It reflects an acceptance of assumptions. It rejects the idea of fluid markets, mindsets and preferences. It's a crutch for the less curious, the shackling of the inquisitive mind.

Don't get me wrong, data is necessary, but it's not sufficient. Rory Sutherland, vice chairman of advertising agency Ogilvy UK and established marketing author, famously claimed that marketing is a domain that craves the illusion of certainty. We desperately want marketing to appear to be factual and predictable. But data without correct interpretation or context can mislead. Without a strong, talented, human hand at the rudder, everything can stray.

The weaving together of stories based on data found in various studies that may or may not be related, or may or may not have the same sample, is too common a practice. Unqualified interpretation is data's greatest enemy. We must question it, interrogate its origins, understand how it was collected and the questions or environments it was derived from.

The challenge for brands is that, in general, people are not truth seekers. They survive by being cooperative, by not disrupting the hierarchy, by not questioning assumed authority.

So truth seekers are what data needs. Highly qualified, curious and questioning minds versed in objectivity.

As Einstein is quoted as saying, 'Not everything that counts is being counted and not everything that is counted, counts.' So it's only the curious, qualified human mind that can make that determination.

When at its best, strategy is informed intuition, the ability to make decisions based on a combination of instinct, knowledge AND trusted data.

So let's not lose our hunger for detail and questioning.

Let's not sacrifice strategy to a desire for speed, convenience or consensus.

Let's not let right get into the wrong hands.

FERGUS O'CARROLL

After 20-plus years as an agency strategist, Fergus O'Carroll started the industry podcast *On Strategy Showcase*. It's where marketers and agencies share the stories behind the strategies that led to amazing, successful campaigns. It's for those in the industry who love to learn continuously and those generous enough to share. Brand marketers and agencies from around the world have appeared on the show. With more than 250 episodes, Fergus has interviewed the best of the best. It is the most successful show of its kind in the industry.

FIVE IDEAS TO TAKE WITH YOU AFTER READING THIS CHAPTER

1   Marketing strategy is the critical work you do before discussing tactics and executions.

2 Business orientation, segmentation, positioning and targeting are the core elements of any marketing strategy.

3 For most product brands, penetration is the most trusted strategy for growth. Loyalty programmes are omnipresent for service brands, but reach is as important.

4 The best brands seamlessly integrate mental and physical availability strategies with a high impact on the final customers.

5 The single best tool to design your next marketing strategy is design thinking.

The art and science of marketing strategy: a final reflection

Congratulations on completing another chapter tackling marketing strategy's essential elements.

Marketing strategy is an intentional fusion of creativity and data-driven insights. It involves mastering the art of product storytelling and the precision of data analytics to deeply understand the market's needs.

Effective strategies position your brand to address customer and market needs more compellingly than your competitors. A good strategy is a prerequisite for choosing the tactics that guide execution. Don't skip essential conversations about brand positioning, targeting, segmentation and market orientation decisions.

Below are three questions to help you make the most of this chapter. Ask them often to make more effective decisions for your brand. As always, there are no right or wrong answers. Simply thinking about these concepts more will help you internalize them better. And for an added learning boost, consider discussing them with a colleague or a friend.

THREE QUESTIONS TO MASTER THE ROLE OF DATA IN YOUR MARKETING STRATEGY

1 Can you describe your brand strategy without mentioning tactics? Consider aspects such as orientation, segmentation, positioning and targeting.

2 For your brand, what takes precedence: mental or physical availability? What is the ideal balance when both work in harmony?

3 Think of three ways you can run a design thinking session and ensure that a mixed cross-functional team is invited to help you strategize the next significant evolution of your brand or product.

ONE MORE THING...

Want to stay effective and ahead of the curve? Scan this QR code to access extra content and updates online.

Notes

1   Evidenza (no date) Better plans, bigger budgets, https://www.evidenza.ai/ (archived at https://perma.cc/Y7UJ-Y29Z)

2   Sharp, B (2010) *How Brands Grow: What marketers don't know*, OUP Australia, South Melbourne

3   PepsiCo (2024) PepsiCo releases its 2023 global ESG summary, https://www. northerneurope.pepsico.com/our-stories/press-release/pepsico-releases-its-2023-global-esg-summary-highlighting-pepsico-positive-pep-results (archived at https://perma.cc/NL6Q-Z8S3)

4   AWS Global Infrastructure (2024) https://aws.amazon.com/about-aws/ global-infrastructure/ (archived at https://perma.cc/45NN-TKHR)

5   Nike (2025) https://www.nike.com/ (archived at https://perma.cc/MT9B-FELQ)

6   Snickers Hungerithm case: CNBC (2016) Snickers bars get cheaper the angrier the internet gets... in Australia, https://www.cnbc.com/2016/05/24/snickers-bars-get-cheaper-the-angrier-the-internet-getsin-australia.html (archived at https:// perma.cc/5VQ4-5BTQ); Campaign Brief (2019) Australian Campaigns of the Decade: Snickers 'Hungerithm' (2016) via Clemenger Bbdo Melbourne, https:// campaignbrief.com/australian-campaigns-of-the-decade%E2%80%88snickers-hungerithm-2016-via-clemenger-bbdo-melbourne/ (archived at https://perma.cc/ J9JH-8A53)

7   Loboy, J (2021) https://www.wytv.com/home/the-mcfarthest-point-explained/ (archived at https://perma.cc/WAK7-F662)

8   Magatef, S G and Tomalieh, E F (2015) The impact of customer loyalty programs on customer retention, *International Journal of Business and Social Science*, 6(8), 78–93

9   Yoo, M and Bai, B (2013) Customer loyalty marketing research: A comparative approach between hospitality and business journals, *International Journal of Hospitality Management*, 33, 166–177

10 De Bono, E (2016) *Six Thinking Hats*, Penguin Life, London

11 Ignatius, A (2015) How Indra Nooyi turned design thinking into strategy: An interview with PepsiCo's CEO, https://hbr.org/2015/09/how-indra-nooyi-turned-design-thinking-into-strategy (archived at https://perma.cc/8N24-H3V2)

04

Product and pricing effectiveness

The balance of product and pricing

Now that we've covered the fundamentals of a marketing strategy in the previous chapter, it's time to unpack the effectiveness of product and pricing. These are the first of the four marketing Ps (product, price, place and promotion) that need careful attention because they establish the foundation for how a brand can create mental and physical availability and ultimately determine its success.

Starting with definitions is always wise. A product serves as a physical embodiment of the brand you offer. It includes everything from the essential physical ingredients to design and packaging, delivering a complete brand experience to customers. For non-physical brands and services, a product represents the intangible offerings available to customers, such as an experience (e.g. a hotel stay), expertise (e.g. a consultancy project) or a digital solution (e.g. software).

Price refers to the value exchange between a brand and the customer for a product or service. But it means much more than the number on your price label. It's an artifact of your strategic decision that signals the product's value relative to competitors and plays a crucial role in shaping perceptions, positioning and, ultimately, your long-term business performance.

Price and product have a symbiotic relationship, providing customers with the two variables to solve the brand value equation. Customers evaluate what they receive against what they pay. Offering a premium product at a bargain price confuses customers and undermines the brand. Conversely, value pricing lacking quality cannot sustain long-term success. IKEA exemplifies this relationship: its model combines well-designed, affordable furniture. Simple, functional design with accessible pricing maintains perceived value. Affordability and design demonstrate a well-defined pricing and product strategy in harmony. Balance is part of the fundamentals of product and pricing.

In this chapter we'll explore key ideas, such as the FIP (Function, Innovation and Packaging) framework for product strategy, best practices for managing product line extensions, and the critical role consistency plays in building brand identity. We'll then dive into elements of pricing architecture and methods for evaluating price effectiveness. I will also introduce two new engineering marketing tools designed to tackle the everyday challenges of product appeal and scalability.

By the end of this chapter you'll see how getting the product and pricing right sets you up for success ahead of tackling the mental and physical availability strategies.

The science of product effectiveness

Product management through a systematic framework

Have you ever wondered how to understand if your product offer is genuinely compelling? I did. As an engineer with a strong passion for design, I have always looked for a framework to assess product performance beyond the obvious indicators like sales volume or preference.

Recognizing the complexity of covering all aspects of a customer's experience with a product, I developed the FIP framework early in my marketing career. Throughout the years, I've depended on this straightforward yet effective tool to clarify product decision-making in marketing. The FIP framework has three key elements, shown in Figure 4.1.

FIP is an acronym for Function, Innovation and Packaging. Each of the three elements guides your choices towards a more effective product. Buckle up – let's examine them one by one.

FIGURE 4.1 The FIP Framework for product: Function, Innovation and Packaging – three elements that help you assess the power of your product

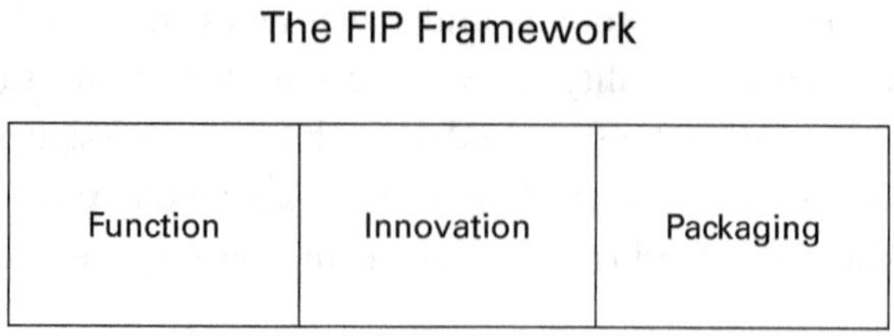

The FIP Framework

Function	Innovation	Packaging

F STANDS FOR FUNCTION

Product function revolves around addressing user needs. It's the reason your product exists. Does it perform as intended? Is it user-friendly? These are the questions you must answer through research. Functionality is the foundation of product effectiveness, directly affecting the customer experience.

One method of getting answers directly from consumers is to use a Customer Satisfaction Score (CSAT). CSAT measures how happy customers are with a product or service. It's a simple survey asking for a rating from 1 to 5 or 1 to 10. A high CSAT is a possible golden ticket, proving the product meets its core promise and satisfies users. While effective, CSAT is often paired with metrics like NPS (Net Promoter Score) or CES (Customer Effort Score) for a fuller picture of customer experience.[1]

One tip to boost your CSAT is to ensure your respondents have tested your product recently. Get category users to familiarize themselves with your product. Listen to their feedback, both verbal and non-verbal. Think about the competitive set offer. Ultimately, listen and make iterative improvements based on what you learn. Remember that a good CSAT is only one element contributing to your business success. If you sell a service, your next best bet is to explore NPS.

I STANDS FOR INNOVATION

Product innovation is all about staying ahead and keeping your product offerings exciting. It's not just about introducing a new line extension, flavour or package format to the market, it's about delivering incremental value to attract new customers. But here's the catch: not all product innovations are perceived equally by your customers. Research can help you once more.

One proven method to assess the performance of your innovation is to track your New Feature Adoption Rate (NFAR) – see Figure 4.2. This

FIGURE 4.2 NFAR: the new feature adoption rate formula is a ratio between users that adopted the feature vs eligible users

$$NFAR\ (\%) = \left(\frac{\text{Number of Users Who Adopted New Feature}}{\text{Total Number of Eligible Users}} \right) \times 100$$

metric reveals how many customers are adopting your latest features and innovations, providing direct insight into whether they resonate. Understanding NFAR allows you to identify which features contribute to customer growth and where your focus should lie for ongoing innovation success.

One tip to increase adoption is to ensure that the new features of the product line extension are intuitive and provide incremental value, demonstrating to customers how these features address their problems. Additionally, make sure to promote your innovations enthusiastically! Effective communication, especially near the point of purchase, is the other half of the battle.

P STANDS FOR PACKAGING

Product packaging: Your product's wrapper or outer package is your first communication tool with brand users. For non-brand users, beyond its functional role of protecting the product, packaging tells your brand story and grabs attention, whether on a store shelf or online. But how do you know whether it's effective?

One method you can try is measuring the Shelf Standout Score. This metric measures how well your product catches the eye in a crowded store layout, like the one your brand competes in daily. It captures how easily consumers notice your product on the shelf. Tracking this metric can help you understand how visual elements impact consumer behaviour and guide design decisions to improve your product's standout.

One tip to boost your packaging perception is to think hyper-visually. Use bold colours or distinctive shapes that stand out in your category. Ensure your packaging communicates your product's value proposition. And don't overlook sustainability – it's good for the earth and your brand's appeal and reputation.

FIP: FUNCTION, INNOVATION, PACKAGING

This simplified FIP framework provides a holistic approach to various product-related effectiveness discussions. The framework balances current functionality with future innovation, introducing the first communication layer in packaging. You can begin with research that supplies data supporting the metrics I've outlined, but don't stop there. These metrics are intended to stimulate thought, help identify improvement areas and track your progress over time. So, the next time you evaluate your product offering, think FIP.

A truly effective product excels in all three areas: function, innovation and packaging.

Like many areas of marketing, product development is another field where a magic formula for success has yet to be found. There are no magical guidelines for creating a great product; however, there are established principles for failing to build one. In the following pages I will discuss three common pitfalls I've encountered as a marketing practitioner in product development.

In line with the elements of the FIP framework, these are the common pitfalls of product parity, the mistakes to avoid with product line extensions and the potential harm caused by altering your packaging. I aim to assist you in sidestepping these pitfalls.

The common trap of product parity

Once you implement a product framework like FIP, any marketer will ask the classic question: How does my brand compare to the competition? This question is crucial, but don't make it the sole focus of your product research. It's common for businesses to fall into a product parity trap, where products across competitive sets are nearly indistinguishable, often leading to brand blandness.

BLANDNESS

Blandness in branding indicates a lack of unique elements and differentiation within a category. It implies something uninspired, generic or forgettable in both products and messaging. A bland brand or campaign typically fails to attract attention or evoke an emotional response, often fading into the background instead of standing out. Reject blandness!

This trap often happens when marketing teams prioritize matching their competitors' basic features, fonts and functions instead of innovating to develop a truly distinctive product offering.

FIGURE 4.3 Branding homogenization in premium fashion: a selection of premium fashion brands exemplifies blanding in font choice

YveSSaintLaurent   ⟶   **SAINT LAURENT**

BALENCIAGA   ⟶   **BALENCIAGA**

BURBERRY   ⟶   **BURBERRY**
London, England   LONDON ENGLAND

Berluti   ⟶   **BERLUTI**
Paris   **PARIS**

BALMAIN   ⟶   **BALMAIN**
PARIS   **PARIS**

SOURCE What is 'blanding' and why are so many brands doing it?[2]

When all brands within a category share similar appearances and product benefits, they blend together on shelves and in consumers' minds. This lack of differentiation could drive every brand in the category into a downward spiral of price competition, a race to the bottom that diminishes profitability and transforms brands into commodities.

Seek differentiation, not blandness.

Relying on product parity weakens your ability to establish emotional connections and brand value. Consumers will perceive your brand as interchangeable with others, making it more difficult to stand out and capture attention. Without distinctiveness, customers have little reason to choose you over the competition.

To escape this trap, focus on your unique value propositions, innovation and crafting an emotional appeal that distinguishes your brand. Avoid becoming overly focused on what the competition is doing.

A mindset of product superiority in all dimensions is something you should build into your arsenal of tools.

The hazards of poorly executed product line extensions

Product line extensions are to brands what oxygen is to fire, a potential source of more growth but not the ignition.

Extending your brand beyond its core products is a common growth strategy, but it can also be dangerous if not executed thoughtfully.

For most brand managers working on respectable brands, altering any feature of the core brand is forbidden territory. You can't play with the master product recipes, packaging or distinctive assets. When nothing is left to do, an often-used growth strategy, especially in fast-moving consumer goods, is to piggyback on the brand name of the core product and launch another variant with a twist (e.g. a different flavour, pack size, better feature(s)).

We call that line extension or, more fancy, product innovation. What is the role of product line extensions in a brand's growth trajectory? Typically, we use them to generate incremental brand sales, upsell existing customers to higher-margin propositions, or increase opportunities to build mental availability for the brand.

In categories where power is concentrated in the distribution channel of your brand (think limited-assortment retailers), not launching innovations is like fracturing the ongoing conversations with your retail partners.[3] Retailers seek novelty, promotional appeal and buzz to bring more value to the end customer. Product innovation is a standard request from retailers. That's after the retailer margin conversation was settled. In other product categories, the competitive pressure is so high that you can't avoid playing this game.

Product line extensions are typically built on the equity of the core brand. However, I am still puzzled by how marketers constantly fight to position the extensions as differentiating. These line extensions or innovations fail to register in customers' minds when, at best, they will only remember the master brand.

Positioning a line extension or new product in customers' minds can feel like pushing water uphill. From my experience, a more straightforward growth strategy is to focus on driving the growth of your main product rather than investing resources in creating something new. The established proposition often benefits from the scale of the supply chain, distribution channels and well-defined memory structures. This often translates into a better margin for your business compared with a new product extension.

Product line extensions' better role could be to contribute to building brand equity that could generate halo effects on the core brand and support its growth further.

It's hard to admit for many of us, but your customers don't think much about your product innovation and all the efforts you've put into it. I don't think most customers really care about your brand, either. They probably are curious to try but don't want to over-intellectualize their choice and build new memory structures. In my mind, any marketing choice is a game of minimizing risks.

Here are three tips on approaching a new product innovation launch to enable increased chances of growing your total brand:

- In communication, ensure the line extension uses the same tone of voice as the established brand and uses the brand's distinctive assets to the maximum to complement established memory structures.

- In pricing, be mindful not to undercut your current price points by over-using promotional discounts or a permanently lowered price point for your innovation. This decision will negatively halo into your core brand.

- Stop expecting your customers to fall in love with your product line extensions. At best, they will try it and continue to consider your brand in their repertoire of products.

A PRACTICAL GUIDE ON HOW TO THINK ABOUT A PRODUCT LINE EXTENSION

Launch a product line extension only after carefully evaluating the risks and opportunities. Here's my go-to list of three questions you should have in mind:

- Do I have the right to play in this new product category? First, ask if your brand's existing mental availability can be translated into a new category. Customers should immediately understand why your brand belongs in this category, otherwise the product may feel disconnected. Would you buy an Audi toothbrush?

- Do I have the credentials and if so, can it be profitable? Second, consider whether your company can create a high-quality product that stands out and is profitable in the new category. Entering a category without adjacent expertise might be possible, but failing to make a profit with your extension is a risk. Would you buy an Audi truck?

- Is there a risk of diluting the overall brand margin? Consider whether this new extension could harm your brand's reputation or financial standing. A poorly differentiated product can confuse or alienate existing customers, ultimately impacting sales of your core product. Ensure the new product doesn't dilute your brand image and, more importantly, that it at least matches your current margin. Would you buy an Audi bike?

Stop playing with packaging: a lesson from the frontlines

Back in my days as a brand manager for British American Tobacco, the most awaited marketing activity of the year was the annual limited-edition pack redesign. However, strict legal communication restrictions destroyed the marketing dreams of any newcomer in the industry. As tobacco marketers, we had few levers to play with: no consumer advertising, no product sampling, no pricing discounts, no product differentiation. This naturally led us to turn to packaging, viewing it as our marketing playground.

Each year as marketers, we brainstorm new designs and test them with consumers to identify the winning routes. We launch them into the market, hoping to spark excitement among consumers and, let's be honest, to keep ourselves busy as marketers.

But looking back, I can't help but wonder if consumers truly asked for a brand-new look every year. Did they really crave the refreshed colour palettes and updated typefaces we so eagerly crafted? I doubt it now. Most of the time, our packaging changes reflected our own boredom more than any real consumer demand. And while we believed we were 'innovating', we were likely confusing our loyal customers in front of the shelf, making it harder for them to locate their go-to product.

The reality is that playing with your packaging designs is a bad idea unless the market tells you to change them. Good advice is never to do so unless you're forced to do so for legal reasons, like plain packaging laws in the tobacco industry. Apart from those exceptions, in almost all cases a packaging change is often an internally driven initiative that keeps brand teams busy and risks the brand's future.

Packaging is more than a wrapper: it's your distinctive asset. It's how consumers recognize your brand in a sea of choices. Every time you alter it, you risk disrupting the memory structures customers rely on to quickly identify your product. Remember the Tropicana disaster?[4] It changed the packaging, thinking it would modernize the brand, but it confused customers who suddenly couldn't spot their favourite juice on the shelf. Sales plummeted and created one of the most quoted case studies in packaging.

> *Altering your distinctive assets frequently is a recipe for confusion and is rarely needed.*

The same applies to limited-edition packaging. While it may seem clever to create buzz, it often does more harm than good. Limited-edition designs can confuse buyers, leading them to believe the product is different from what they typically purchase, or, worse, making it less noticeable on crowded shelves. What you might consider a fun way to celebrate a holiday or event could ultimately lead to lower sales because your customers can't find their preferred product.

The bottom line is this: stop toying with your packaging just for the sake of it. Leave your distinctive assets intact unless the market demands it or you're legally obliged to. Packaging is one of your brand's most excellent communication tools. Think twice about playing with your brand identity.

Differentiation vs distinctiveness

In the last decade, a lively debate has unfolded in the marketing industry over what truly drives brand growth from a product communication perspective: differentiation, distinctiveness or a combination of both.

My personal challenge with differentiation is based on the experience that big brands need to reach broad appeal to capture a wide consumer base. Trying to be truly 'different' from every competitor in the category can narrow the brand's reach and make the reach objective difficult to achieve. Distinctiveness is seen as a more inclusive approach, ensuring the brand appeals to as many potential customers as possible without alienating any specific group.

Is there a middle ground, combining distinctiveness and differentiation? Some academics, like Professors Mark Ritson and Koen Pauwels, argue for a balanced approach that combines both distinctiveness and differentiation. It's an AND, not an OR, decision. Ritson believes brands need distinct cues for quick and easy recognition, but they also require elements that set them

TABLE 4.1 Differentiation vs distinctiveness[5,6,7,8]

The Case for Distinctiveness	The Case for Differentiation
On one side, experts like Byron Sharp argue that *distinctiveness* is all that matters. **Distinctiveness** refers to a brand's unique, recognizable characteristics – such as colours, logos, slogans, and other 'cues' – that make it easy to notice, remember, and choose. Research shows consumers make most decisions on autopilot, using fast, subconscious processes (System 1 thinking), where familiarity and ease play a central role. People don't need to acknowledge differences in brands, especially in very competitive categories; they just need to purchase them, mentions the author of *How Brands Grow*.	Conversely, research companies, some academics and various marketing practitioners argue that distinctiveness alone isn't enough. They advocate for *meaningful differentiation* which goes beyond being memorable and easy to recall.
	Differentiation is the extent to which a brand offers something unique or leads the way in a way that sets it apart, making it less substitutable. This approach taps into System 2 thinking, where customers process information more thoughtfully and choose brands consciously because it represent something unique and valuable to them.
Focusing on distinctiveness, marketers ensure that their brand stands out enough to be top-of-mind when making purchase decisions.	For differentiation advocates, brands need to stand for something that isn't just recognizable and resonates on a deeper level. It's not about being unique in every attribute but about offering specific product-based, experience-based, or emotionally-driven qualities that make the brand irreplaceable to its target audience.
Research suggests that salience (being noticeable and memorable) correlates strongly with market share	
True distinctiveness isn't as easy as it sounds; in my view, very few of a brand's assets become distinctive. Creating a memorable logo, slogan, or product design that intuitively cues consumers to remember the brand requires thoughtful, consistent branding exercises. Beyond logo-tag-line-packaging, building distinctive assets is a complicated business.	As research company Kantar notes, seeking 'difference' opens up a world of advantages. True differentiation may be difficult to achieve, but it can create a pathway to long-term growth by making the brand meaningfully different, rather than merely distinct.

apart in a meaningful way. This dual approach aims to strengthen brand memory while ensuring that the brand possesses specific, valuable qualities that make it more than just another option in a crowded marketplace. Differentiation and distinctiveness are equally essential and complement each other to enhance marketing effectiveness.

THE UNDERLYING DEBATE: SYSTEM 1 VS SYSTEM 2 THINKING

At the heart of this debate is a fundamental difference in how people believe consumers make decisions:

1 Supporters of distinctiveness rely on System 1 thinking, which leads to quick, intuitive customer choices based on familiarity.

2 Differentiation advocates, meanwhile, argue that brands must engage System 2 thinking, where customers assess options more carefully and are drawn to brands that offer a distinct, meaningful difference.

Ultimately, the debate raises a crucial question for marketers: can brands achieve sustainable growth by relying on a single approach or is there true strength in integrating both? It's best to consider your brand's life stage as an essential factor in developing an effective marketing strategy. For a newly launched brand, you can formulate strategies that emphasize both differentiation and distinctiveness. Conversely, an established brand can focus more on refining distinctiveness, depending on the differentiation it has already established to maintain effectiveness.

Pricing effectiveness: the link between marketing and the board room

Pricing as an indicator of brand value

Many marketers are curious about how to enhance their brand's pricing effectiveness. Given that a business's ultimate strength lies in its pricing power, pricing remains a hot topic in numerous executive circles.

Pricing is more than just setting the correct number. It reflects brand value, influences customer perception and defines market positioning. It connects marketing and the C-suite by directly affecting a business's revenue, profit and brand equity.

An effective pricing strategy is engineered so customers see enough value in your product to pay a premium. It also reveals whether your brand can withstand future market pressures without sacrificing profitability.

To start, here are three ways to think about the value of pricing:

- First, price communicates value. It's a signal to consumers about the return they can expect from your product. Too low and you risk being perceived as low quality (Shein); too high and you may alienate potential customers (Tesla). It's not just about cost, it reflects your brand's worth and positioning.

- Second, pricing affects competitiveness. It's a silent salesman that tirelessly influences consumer choices and messes with loyalty. Effective pricing can create a competitive edge, drawing in customers looking for value that aligns with their expectations.

- Third, a strategic pricing approach allows for market adaptability. The only constant in business is change. An adaptive pricing strategy can help you navigate economic shifts and changes in consumer behaviour, ensuring your brand remains relevant and competitive.

Pricing elasticity is brand power

A brand's ultimate objective is to have the ability to up-price with a marginal impact on its growth. However, marketers often forget that pricing is one of the strategies available in their growth toolkit. On the contrary, they might deploy short-term price reductions more often than necessary and negatively impact the health of their brand.

Promotional pricing becomes reference pricing when overused. Do you know the retail price of a detergent brand? It isn't very easy.

It is a widely acknowledged fact that marketers' comments are often overshadowed by finance colleagues in boardrooms worldwide. To speak the language of CEOs, marketers have to change their verbiage. Awareness or consideration conversations are pleasant, but when boards only care about revenue generation and customer acquisition costs, marketers need to find another vocabulary of impact.

Introducing price power – an economic concept that can bridge the gap between marketing efforts and overall business objectives and offer you a valued seat at the board table. Price power, defined as a brand or business's ability to raise prices without significant demand or market share loss, is an underutilized concept in marketing strategy. It is simple to measure, easy to benchmark with competitors and less fuzzy than ROI.

Price power should get more of your attention. Why? Famous investor Warren Buffett famously said that pricing power is the most crucial consideration when assessing a company.[9] And based on his track record, Warren Buffett is one business personality I would take investing advice from.

FIGURE 4.4 Formula of price elasticity: price elasticity is the ratio between the change in sales and the change in price

$$\text{Price Elasticity} = \frac{\text{Change in Sales (\% or Units)}}{\text{Change in Price (\% or Value)}}$$

At the heart of price power is the price elasticity of demand. This measures how sensitive your customers are to price changes.

Let's take an example. A coffee shop sells 100 cups per day at $3 each. After raising the price to $3.50, it now sells 90 cups per day. Change in Price: $0.50 increase. Change in Sales: 10 cups decrease.

$$\text{Price Elasticity} = 10 / 0.50 = 20$$

This means for every $0.50 increase in price, sales decrease by 20 cups. When you check the revenue impact: before 100 cups × $3 = $300; after: 90 cups × $3.50 = $315. Even though they're selling fewer cups, revenue increased by $15. This shows good price power.

So, instead of overthinking brand equity metrics, why don't you simplify and try to understand how your brand pricing power impacts equity?

Others have done it with success:

1 Apple: Despite premium pricing, Apple maintained a global market share of 16 per cent in Q4 2023,[10] showcasing remarkable price power. Few phones are more expensive than iPhones.

2 Coca-Cola: An older academic study found that Coca-Cola's brand equity allowed it to charge a 28 per cent price premium over private labels.[11] In a hypercompetitive and high-volume market, every penny counts.

3 Nike: The company's focus on brand-building resulted in an industry-leading gross margin of 44.3 per cent in 2023.[12] Despite recent hiccups in share performance, no one can threaten its #1 place in the global sports apparel market today.

What can you do for your brand? To manage price power, do these three things: run regular price sensitivity analyses, invest in brand-building advertising at the expense of short-term promotions, and emphasize value creation in marketing communications.

By focusing on price power, you will demonstrate the direct impact on profitability to your leadership team and gain a stronger voice in boardroom discussions.

Building a price architecture

Pricing is a powerful yet often overlooked marketing lever that defines your brand, shapes customer perceptions and, when executed effectively, can work wonders for your profitability. However, in many companies, pricing is not a marketing decision. Instead, it is controlled by finance or sales departments, focusing on immediate revenue or volume rather than on a long-term brand-building strategy.

I firmly believe that marketing must control a brand's price architecture. Marketing is the department that best understands customer value, brand positioning and market dynamics. Without marketing in command, pricing decisions can quickly derail profit potential and dilute brand equity.

Pricing decisions should not be made in isolation. That's why price architecture is a structured approach in which every price point across your product range supports the total brand's positioning and aims to meet customer expectations. Think of it as a blueprint communicating value rather than just setting prices based on costs or market trends.

Consider the mobile device category: Apple and Samsung each use distinct price architectures, but both are effective. Apple has clear pricing tiers – from mid-level to super-premium – communicating value and exclusivity. Samsung offers a broader range of price points to appeal to different customer segments, ensuring market reach and diluting a bit of brand quality perception for reach. Both strategies align with each company's brand value positioning and customer expectations.

When marketing controls the pricing strategy, it often ensures that pricing does more than compete on cost – it communicates value. And when done correctly, a solid price architecture guides how your entire portfolio is perceived, from entry-level products to premium offerings.

Rather than a random collection of price points, marketing must establish clear tiers that resonate with different customer segments. Price tiers should reflect more than just the product's features – they should embody the experience and value you want associated with each tier. Entry-level products should invite newcomers to the brand without devaluing it, while premium options must signal luxury or exclusivity. This segmentation allows you to cater to diverse customer groups without diluting your brand message.

Your pricing strategy defines your business's freedom to innovate, grow value and reinvest.

Price = Profit = Freedom

How can you implement this in your business?

1 Start with perceived value, not costs: Understand your product's value better and how existing customers perceive it. Are you selling innovation, quality or exclusivity? Your price should reflect that value, not just cover costs with a standard markup percentage.

2 Develop clear pricing tiers: When your brand targets multiple customer segments, establish pricing tiers that cater to each segment. Entry-level products should attract new buyers without cheapening the brand, while premium offerings should signal higher quality and be aspirational.

3 Let price tell a story: Pricing could reinforce your brand's unique selling points. Whether it's craftsmanship, sustainability or advanced technology, each price point should reflect your brand's core values and communicate them clearly to customers.

In conclusion, pricing is too crucial a lever to assign to departments that do not fully grasp your brand's long-term strategy. Marketing must take ownership of the pricing architecture to guarantee alignment with brand goals and values. When you get your pricing strategy right, you'll maximize profits and unlock the freedom to grow, innovate and potentially lead your industry.

The three ways to measure price effectiveness

Pricing is a vital consideration for most brands as it directly impacts business profitability, market share and customer perception. Recently, the range of tools available for assessing pricing effectiveness has grown significantly. If you're feeling overwhelmed by your choices, a solid starting point is to focus on three complementary methods that offer unique insights: price elasticity, customer willingness to pay (WTP) and gross margin analysis:

• Price elasticity examines how customer demand responds to different price levels. By modelling historical data, it helps determine whether a price increase or decrease will significantly impact future sales volume. A key advantage is that it illustrates how price adjustments influence future revenue and market share. This information enables you to identify the optimal price level based on your specific goal, whether it's maximizing profits, increasing volume or finding a balance between the two. However, price elasticity requires significant historical data to ensure accuracy. It works best in stable markets for well-known products. Unfortunately, it does not account for external factors such as shifting customer preferences or competitive actions.

- Customer willingness to pay analysis gathers direct customer feedback, typically through surveys or experiments, to identify the maximum price they are willing to pay for a product or service. This method helps to understand customer price sensitivity and the perceived value of an offering. It provides direct insight into customer perceptions of value, enabling you to set prices that match real customer expectations. However, customer bias can distort WTP data, as people often underestimate what they would pay. The way questions are framed can also result in inaccurate responses. This is a common limitation of survey-based research.

- Gross margin analysis is a straightforward metric that measures the difference between the cost of goods sold and the selling price. It provides a clear view of product profitability per unit. The key advantage is its ease of calculation and tracking. It offers a simple yet insightful perspective on profitability over time, helping ensure that pricing covers production costs while delivering satisfactory profits. However, its limitation lies in focusing solely on cost and profitability, neglecting demand and customer perception. If used in isolation, it may result in suboptimal pricing decisions. Therefore, it should be combined with other analyses to develop a comprehensive pricing strategy.

All of these methods offer valuable insights into pricing strategies. However, the best approach is to integrate them to develop a comprehensive strategy that aligns financial performance priorities with actual customer behaviour in the marketplace.

USING BEHAVIOURAL SCIENCE TOOLS FOR PRICING

Behavioural sciences examine human behaviour, concentrating on how individuals make decisions, interact and react to stimuli. These fields encompass psychology, sociology, anthropology and behavioural economics. They rely on empirical research and observation to comprehend the patterns and motivations underlying human actions.

A primary focus is on understanding cognitive biases, common errors in thinking that affect judgement and decision-making. Biases such as confirmation bias and loss aversion help explain why people sometimes act irrationally.

I've found that behavioural science offers crucial insights into how consumers react to pricing strategies. Here are three practical applications:

1 The anchoring effect: As outlined in Daniel Kahneman's *Thinking, Fast and Slow*,[13] people rely heavily on the first information they see (the anchor) when making purchase decisions. Apple might be using this anchoring effect in its marketing strategy. After launching new iPhone models, I've observed that Apple consistently places the most expensive model (like the iPhone Pro Max) front and centre on its web pages or in communication materials. This sets a high anchor, making the other versions seem more affordable, even though they're still premium-priced.

2 Loss aversion: Derived from Kahneman and Tversky's Prospect Theory,[14] this shows that people prefer avoiding losses over acquiring gains. Amazon Prime potentially leverages this through its free-shipping benefits. Once customers get used to receiving free shipping with Prime, they are reluctant to go back to paying for shipping, seeing it as a loss. These can drive continued membership renewals, as customers feel they're avoiding the 'loss' of free shipping.

3 The decoy effect: Dan Ariely explored this concept,[15] which occurs when a third, less attractive option makes a simple two-way choice more appealing. *The Economist* is the most famous brand to use this in its subscription pricing. It used to offer three options: a digital-only subscription for $59, a print-only subscription for $125 and a print + web subscription for $125. The print-only option acted as a decoy, pushing customers towards the print + web option, as it appeared to offer the most value for the same price. At the time of writing, *The Economist* uses a newsletter as a decoy alternative to drive digital and print subscriptions at a more lucrative price point.

You, too, can apply behavioural science insights and get inspiration from how these global brands do it. This can significantly enhance customer decision-making and improve the effectiveness and profitability of your pricing strategies. Let me know how it goes.

Applied engineering for product and pricing

Engineering Marketing Tool 3: Minimum viable product

A minimum viable product is a product version with just enough features to be functional and valuable for early users, who can provide feedback for future improvements. This approach helps companies test product-market fit while avoiding extensive upfront investment. By focusing on essential features, MVPs allow teams to gather insights, validate early assumptions and iterate quickly based on real customer reactions.

I first encountered the term while reading Eric Ries' book *The Lean Startup*.[16] In a lean entrepreneurship context, MVPs minimize risk, time and costs by refining the product through validated learning. This iterative feedback loop helps businesses identify market needs and adjust before making significant financial commitments.

In marketing, MVPs solve complex product development cycles in physical and service brands. At its essence, an MVP is the simplest version of your product. It is a prototype that can be launched and tested before scaling up.

Launching an MVP, a product's basic version, is typically restricted to a smaller geographical market where businesses can gather critical data on customer interest, engagement and buying rates. For services, the same approach could apply to a set of trialists selected from the service's user base.

Be careful: an MVP that's too basic may fail to engage or impress your final customer. If it doesn't provide enough value or functionality, it risks losing consumer interest before a full product launch. A good question to ask yourself is: What's the minimum viable version of your brand's product that still delivers value and showcases its potential?

The four phases of implementing an MVP are:

- Build: Develop the core functionality or most essential features of your product.

- Launch in a test market: Introduce your MVP to a controlled environment, whether a niche customer segment or a limited distribution channel.

- Measure: Use action standards (e.g. customer engagement rates, purchase rates) to measure whether the product resonates with your audience.

- Iterate: Based on your findings, improve or pivot your product for a broader launch.

An MVP focuses on rapid learning and adaptation, which marketers require just as much as product engineers do. When executed properly, your MVP should reveal your product's potential for scaling. Which takes us to the next tool.

Engineering Marketing Tool 4: Scalability

Scalability is a powerful strategy for building brands to scale. From early on in my career, I understood scalability as a way to perform a magic trick on your brand. When executed well, scalability enables your brand to expand while maintaining present performance and tapping into cost efficiencies. The brand development cycle represents the natural progression following a successful MVP launch, evolving an initial product into a significant market contender.

In technology engineering, scalability often means using flexible systems like cloud computing that can expand alongside the business. Instead of investing heavily in physical servers, tech companies choose cloud solutions that grow as their user base does, maintaining efficiency without upfront costs. This adaptability ensures the business can handle growth without unnecessary strain on resources. What can you learn from this?

Scalability is not exclusive to tech, however. In brand marketing, it involves leveraging a brand's distinctive core assets – unique qualities, tone and identity – to expand into new categories or markets. For example, a beverage company could use the branding of its flagship product to launch adjacent products, such as snacks, under the same name.

Scalability comes with its challenges. One significant risk is dilution – expanding too quickly or into unrelated categories can confuse customers and dilute the brand's messaging. When a brand stretches itself too thin or launches products that don't match its core identity, it risks losing the essence that made it strong.

Furthermore, scaling too rapidly can affect product quality. Speeding up production to meet growing demand may lead to shortcuts or compromises, which could erode customer trust.

The three core phases of scaling a brand are:

1 Leverage core assets: Start by analysing what makes your brand distinctive. Whether it's a logo, colour scheme or unique message, these assets must be strong enough to carry over into other categories.

2 Expand into adjacent markets: Test the waters by launching complementary products that align with your brand's identity. For example, Apple transitioned from computers to smartphones using the same sleek design principles and branding.

3 Maintain consistency: As you grow, it is crucial to keep your messaging aligned across all products and markets. Scaling too fast without strategic alignment could dilute your brand's core value proposition.

The benefit of scaling quickly is clear: you can capture more market share and outpace competitors. But the downside can be equally severe: missteps in branding or quality can cost revenue.

Brands that scale successfully know how to strike a balance between growth and consistency. Nike, for example, expanded from shoes to apparel to fitness tech, all while maintaining its iconic brand messaging centred around performance and athleticism.

Scalability is essential for growing a brand, but it's a double-edged sword. Rapid growth without purpose or alignment can damage what you've worked hard to build. The secret is to expand thoughtfully, using your brand's distinctive assets to venture into new categories while ensuring that quality and messaging remain intact.

The next time you consider scaling, ask yourself: Is your brand ready to grow without losing what makes it unique?

Brand size provides an undeniable advantage in marketing. While the media loves stories of disruptive newcomers stealing market share, the reality is that few small brands grow big. Many fall victim to survivorship bias, where only the rare success stories are celebrated while countless failures go unnoticed. Much like venture capital, betting on small brands is a high-risk, low-probability game.

That's why scale matters. Marketing investments are often tied to sales, meaning smaller brands allocate a fraction of what larger competitors spend. With limited budgets, their reach is minimal, making significant growth difficult. The idea that small brands have an easier path to success is a myth – brands grow through sustained investment, not magic.

In the world of brands, size brings scale, reach and momentum. While exceptions exist, the reality remains: in most cases, Goliath wins against David.

INDUSTRY EXPERT CONTRIBUTION
Product marketing: Danilo Tauro

The word 'product' carries different meanings across industries. At P&G, I focused on marketing (B2C) consumer products. At Amazon Ads and Uber Advertising, my primary role has been building and growing (B2B) tech products that help marketers achieve efficiency and effectiveness.

While these industries may seem worlds apart, the process of conceiving and bringing products to market is strikingly similar. Some say, 'consumer is boss' while others call it 'customer obsession' – but the principle is the same. To build products that consumers and customers love, you must understand how they think, talk and operate.

Identifying pain points and addressing them through cost advantages or differentiation gives a product the edge it needs to win. Once this is achieved, the impact of your go-to-market (GTM) strategy improves dramatically. Product strategy and marketing effectiveness are deeply interconnected and companies that master both dominate their markets.

It's no surprise that product management (PM) has become one of the most sought-after and well-compensated roles in tech. Fun fact: P&G invented the role of PMs, although it called them brand managers (BMs). This approach transformed P&G into a brand-centric organization, laying the foundation for modern product management as we know it today.

In my experience with designing, building, testing, launching and scaling products across three organizations – P&G on the buy side, Amazon Ads on the tech side and Uber on the growth side – the work and challenges have been remarkably similar. Success in all three environments has required understanding customer needs, crafting a compelling vision and inspiring teams to deliver with excellence.

By driving marketing efficiency and effectiveness through cutting-edge adtech and MarTech solutions, I've seen first hand how impactful the right decisions can be when paired with the right talent, structure and incentives.

There were two areas where this approach paid off significantly: retail media (where product improvements directly drive higher sales) and creative tech (where optimized creative assets enhance marketing performance). Ultimately, the playbook remains consistent: be empathetic with your customer and build backwards from their needs.

DANILO TAURO

Danilo Tauro is an established marketing executive and partner at Aperiam Ventures. He was the general manager at Uber Eats Advertising, where he helped grow the company by working across product, sales, marketing, operations and delivery. Previously, he served as a product leader at Amazon Ads, where he built advertising technology products, and as global director at Procter & Gamble on the advertising buy side. Danilo is an expert in the digital, media, adtech and MarTech ecosystems and is an investor and adviser.

FIVE IDEAS TO TAKE WITH YOU AFTER READING THIS CHAPTER

1   Product and pricing are interlinked elements of your marketing strategy, making the foundation for brand success and value perception.

2   The FIP framework (Function, Innovation, Packaging) systematically evaluates product effectiveness and guides decision-making conversations.

3   Product parity is a trap that leads to commoditization; brands should push for distinctiveness and consistent emotional appeal.

4 Pricing is a powerful marketing tool that communicates value, affects competitiveness and indicates brand power. Price power is a crucial metric for understanding a brand's strength. Marketers should take control of pricing strategies and use price power in the boardroom.

5 Behavioural science concepts, such as anchoring, loss aversion and the decoy effect, can be leveraged to create effective pricing strategies.

Product and pricing: a final reflection

Congratulations on completing another chapter that introduced you to the essential concepts around product and pricing effectiveness.

Decisions regarding the first two Ps, product and pricing, require critical conversations that your marketing team should have with other departments in the organization – using customer analytics to align marketing strategy with the C-suite expectations and identify the valid drivers of future business growth.

Gaining expertise in product and pricing will set the stage for tackling better mental and physical availability strategies, which I know you'll find fascinating.

Below are three questions to help you make the most of this chapter. Ask them often to make more effective decisions for your brand. As always, there are no right or wrong answers. Simply thinking about these concepts more will help you internalize them better. And for an added learning boost, consider discussing them with a colleague or a friend.

THREE QUESTIONS TO MASTER PRODUCT AND PRICING

1 How does your current product strategy perform using the FIP framework and are there areas for improvement to enhance overall product effectiveness?

2 How are you leveraging pricing as a strategic tool to communicate your brand's value and position in the market rather than solely focusing on costs or competitor prices?

3 How are you balancing the need for product innovation with supporting the core brand product to meet changing customer needs?

ONE MORE THING…

Want to stay effective and ahead of the curve? Scan this QR code to access extra content and updates online.

Notes

1   Hyken, S (2023) Unveiling the ultimate secret to high CSAT and NPS scores, https://www.forbes.com/sites/shephyken/2023/09/17/unveiling-the-ultimate-secret-to-high-csat-and-nps-scores/ (archived at https://perma.cc/5LX9-4WWD)

2   Maxwell, K (no date) What is 'blanding' and why are so many brands doing it? https://fluxbranding.com/the-rise-of-blanding/ (archived at https://perma.cc/2K5X-GN92)

3   McKinsey (2020) Will innovation finally add up for consumer-goods companies? https://www.mckinsey.com/industries/consumer-packaged-goods/our-insights/will-innovation-finally-add-up-for-consumer-goods-companies (archived at https://perma.cc/XUV5-6CZ3)

4   Young, S and Ciummo, V (2019) Managing risk in a package redesign: What can we learn from Tropicana? https://www.packagingstrategies.com/articles/91264-managing-risk-in-a-package-redesign-what-can-we-learn-from-tropicana (archived at https://perma.cc/V32J-KN3Y)

5   Romaniuk, J, Sharp, B and Ehrenberg, A (2007) Evidence concerning the importance of perceived brand differentiation, *Australasian Marketing Journal*, 15(2), 42–54, https://doi.org/10.1016/S1441-3582(07)70042-3 (archived at https://perma.cc/WYF7-4EZX)

6   Romaniuk, J and Sharp, B (2004) Conceptualizing and measuring brand salience, *Marketing Theory*, 4(4), 327–342, https://doi.org/10.1177/1470593104047643 (archived at https://perma.cc/4BUM-AT29)

7   Hollis, N (2013) What makes your brand meaningfully different? in *The Meaningful Brand*, Palgrave Macmillan, New York, https://doi.org/10.1007/978-1-137-36559-0_3 (archived at https://perma.cc/4NST-RURH)

8   Guerrieria, M (2021) The pursuit of 'difference' unlocks a multitude of benefits, https://www.kantar.com/inspiration/brands/the-pursuit-of-difference-unlocks-a-multitude-of-benefits (archived at https://perma.cc/GP5H-X83M)

9   Frye, A and Campbell, D (2011) Buffett says pricing power more important than good management, https://www.bloomberg.com/news/articles/2011-02-18/buffett-says-pricing-power-more-important-than-good-management?embedded-checkout=true (archived at https://perma.cc/95YS-7D73)

10   Counterpoint (2023) Global smartphone market reaches its lowest Q3 levels in a decade; Apple's share at 16%, https://www.counterpointresearch.com/ insights/global-smartphone-market-reaches-its-lowest-q3-levels-in-a-decade-apples-share-at-16/ (archived at https://perma.cc/8ZHY-XTMT)

11   Counterpoint (2023) Global smartphone market reaches its lowest Q3 levels in a decade; Apple's share at 16%, https://www.counterpointresearch.com/ insights/global-smartphone-market-reaches-its-lowest-q3-levels-in-a-decade-apples-share-at-16/ (archived at https://perma.cc/8ZHY-XTMT)

12   Nike (2023) Nike Inc. reports fiscal 2023 fourth quarter and full year results, https://investors.nike.com/investors/news-events-and-reports/investor-news/ investor-news-details/2023/NIKE-Inc.-Reports-Fiscal-2023-Fourth-Quarter-and-Full-Year-Results/default.aspx (archived at https://perma.cc/H6YX-FGMP)

13   Kahneman, D (2011) *Thinking, Fast and Slow*, Penguin Books, London

14   Kahneman, D and Tversky, A (1979) *Prospect Theory: An analysis of decision under risk*, Econometrica, New Haven, CT

15   Ariely, D (2009) *Predictably Irrational: The hidden forces that shape our decisions*, HarperCollins, New York, Chapter 1

16   Ries, E (2011) *The Lean Startup: How today's entrepreneurs use continuous innovation to create radically successful businesses*, Crown Currency, New York

05

Media channels: effectiveness vs efficiency

The power of media

'Why can't Instagram just be free without all the ads?' a friend asked me over drinks, visibly frustrated by their cluttered social feed. I laughed and replied, 'Thanks to those ads, it is free.' What followed was a lively debate. They desired an ad-free, user-funded social media utopia, while I explained how advertising is the engine that keeps platforms running without users paying a fee.

One might say that our attention is the fee – the price we pay for the convenience and abundance of content we enjoy. That conversation got me thinking that what marketers call media may seem invisible to the average person. But we know that, inside our marketing circles, media is one of the most heated areas of debate. It stirs passions and splits marketing teams into opposing parties because the stakes are so high.

Brands use media as a path to reach their audiences. Let's better understand this marketing communication lever through the lens of effectiveness.

Effective media delivers measurable value to a brand by reaching the right audience at the right time with the right message.

An effective media strategy, tactic or channel provides measurable value to a brand by reaching the right audience at the right time and delivering the message. Ideally, this process generates a lasting long-term cognitive impact in addition to a short-term one. The discussion about media effectiveness is often linked with media efficiency. Efficiency emphasizes optimizing the media budget for maximum returns. To achieve this, media professionals aim to quantify the effectiveness of their media choices using sales lift and ROI.

The balance between media effectiveness and efficiency initially feels straightforward to quantify but not as simple to manage. During my years at Mars, I have witnessed how challenging it can be to find the right balance. In many marketing discussions, significant confusion remains about which of the two should take precedence: sales or ROI, and their inter-relationship.

In this chapter we will explore the media world, as brands call it, unpack the metrics and showcase examples of successful campaigns. We will also discuss the ecosystem players – advertisers, agencies and platforms – and how they interact to bring brand messages to customers. We will challenge common myths that often hinder effective planning, from the obsession with personalization to misconceptions about reach.

By the end, you'll better understand how to approach media effectively and efficiently. You'll also be equipped with two new engineering tools that might improve your future marketing efforts.

Media matters in marketing

Media is not just the pipeline through which advertising messages flow, it serves as a bridge connecting brands to consumers. As the top generator of mental availability, media functions like an engine that drives brand awareness, engagement and conversion.

Media carries your marketing strategy to your customers' minds.

Media includes all the platforms and channels through which a brand communicates with its customers. This communication occurs via various devices, most commonly a mobile phone, a TV, a desktop computer, a tablet, a printed magazine, a radio receiver or an out-of-home display. For each device, numerous platforms compete for media budgets and customer attention.

With the rise of mobile devices and widespread broadband internet, the number of platforms available to reach audiences has surged over the past 20 years. Communication channels have also evolved to become more complex and diverse regarding customer engagement. This increase in opportunities for competing for brand media investments presents one of marketing's most pressing effectiveness challenges.

For brands, media effectiveness is about making the right choices of platforms and formats to deliver better business results. For platforms, it is about improved engagement and a higher share of viewers' time.

An effective media investment builds brand value in consumers' minds and generates short- and long-term conversions.

Understanding the media ecosystem

An ecosystem is a network of interconnected players that depend on one another for resources, growth and sustainability. Originating in the natural sciences, ecosystems include living organisms interacting with each other and their environment in a balanced exchange. In business, ecosystems describe relationships that generate value for all members.

In media and advertising, the ecosystem includes brands, agencies, publishers, audiences and much more. Given its complexity, the media ecosystem is prone to create inefficiencies. A thorough understanding of the basics is the first step in maximizing the value it offers to all parties sustainably.

Media planning and activation rarely happen without human interactions. These processes typically involve a complex web of relationships between three key players: advertisers, agencies and publishers (see Figure 5.1):

- Advertisers (or brands): These businesses are entitled to pay for media in exchange for the communication of brand messages. Advertisers set the communication goals, allocate budgets and determine how effectiveness will be measured. They expect media to reach the right audiences in the right place at the right time with resonating messages. All of this is to maximize the effectiveness and efficiency of brand communication.

- Agencies (middleman): Media agencies act as intermediaries between advertisers and publishers. These business entities advise advertisers and plan, negotiate and buy media. They secure optimal placements and rates from publishers using their scale and expertise. By analysing audience behaviours, media consumption trends and platform performances, agencies build media plans that respond to the advertiser's objectives. Innovative agencies create plans using business outcome metrics, such as sales impact, over more superficial media metrics to build long-term relationships with both brands and publishers.

- Publishers (or platforms): These businesses sell the advertising space to generate revenue. Platforms like Google, Meta, radio stations and TV networks, to name a few, control how and where ads are delivered to audiences.[1] These companies operate with proprietary algorithms, a deep understanding of audience data and media formats to offer advertisers precise targeting, reach and customer access. Their influence stems from the vast number of users they engage and the data they manage. Each platform is distinct in how it interacts with its users and brands must tailor their media tactics accordingly. How you plan TV campaigns is very different from how you plan a TikTok campaign, for example.

FIGURE 5.1 The simplest chain in advertising: brand use agencies to reach platforms that provide a service to brands directly

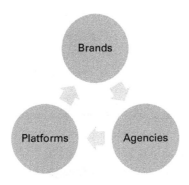

For most of marketing history, media space was transacted directly using contracts with a precise relation between cost and ad space. The progressive transition from direct media transactions to programmatic media transactions was probably the largest shift impacting this three-party relationship in just the last decade. Today, most media transactions are completed through a complex programmatic supply chain, a system that automates the buying and selling of advertising using technology.

Programmatic advertising leverages algorithms and data to instantly bid for ad space and target specific audiences across platforms with minimal human intervention. This process speeds up and refines ad placement, ensuring that brands reach their ideal audience more efficiently.

Facilitating interactions between brands, agencies and publishers for smooth activation, message optimization and various types of measurement requires a never-ending set of third-party businesses that offer added value. Here are the most important ones, at the time of writing:

- Ad networks – aggregate available advertising space from multiple publishers and offer it to advertisers or agencies, allowing for more efficient buying across multiple websites or apps. Examples include Google AdSense, Amazon Publisher Services, Youmi and many more.

- Ad exchanges – facilitate real-time bidding (RTB) for media inventory by tapping into multiple ad networks. Examples include AppLovin, Google Ad Manager, InMobi, OpenX and many more.

- Demand-side platforms (DSPs) – technology platforms used by advertisers or agencies to buy ad impressions from ad exchanges or networks in an automated way. DSPs offer real-time bidding and data integration for targeted ad placements. Examples include The Trade Desk, Google DV360, Amazon DSP, Criteo, Adform, iPinYou and many more.

- Supply-side platforms (SSPs) – technology that allows publishers to manage, sell and optimize their ad inventory programmatically. SSPs work in tandem with DSPs to enable automated media buying and selling. Examples include PubMatic, Verizon Media, Magnite, Xandr and many more.

- Data management platforms (DMPs) – solutions that collect, organize and activate data from multiple sources to enable more precise audience targeting and campaign personalization in programmatic advertising. Examples include Adobe Audience Manager, BlueKai, Lotame, NielsenIQ and many more.

- Content delivery networks (CDNs) – optimizing media content delivery by saving the same version of content across multiple physical server locations globally, reducing the time required for users to download the content. Examples include Akamai, Cloudflare, Fastly, ChinaCache and many more.

- Ad verification and measurement – platforms to verify the ad placement accuracy and integrity, measuring audience viewability and brand safety and monitoring potential fraudulent impressions. Examples include DoubleVerify, Moat (Oracle), Integral Ad Science (IAS) and many more.

- Third-party analytics and attribution – tracking the effectiveness of campaigns, ensuring accurate reporting on metrics such as clicks, views, conversions, customer journeys and ultimately media ROI. Examples include Nielsen, Circana, Comscore, Kochava and many more.

- Ad tech providers – offering specific technologies or tools to enhance the ad experience or optimize the buying process, such as dynamic creative optimization (DCO) tools, personalization and audience segmentation tools. Examples include Sizmek, Innovid, Flashtalking and many more.

If you thought that, in theory, the media path from a brand's content to a customer screen should be simple, think again. Figure 5.2 is my attempt to illustrate the possible sequence of interactions between different players in media delivery. It is by no means comprehensive as the solutions are constantly evolving. I only wanted to give you a basic understanding of how complex media works in the programmatic age.

FIGURE 5.2 The programmatic media supply chain: the complex value chain of programmatic advertising

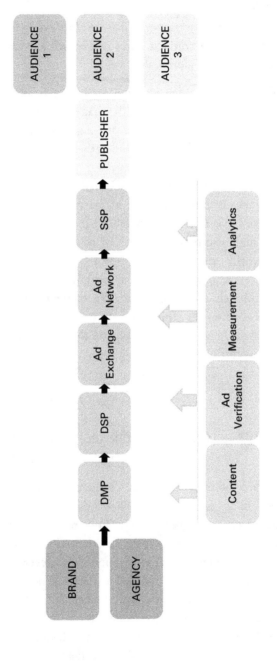

The advertising market is simultaneously a collaborative and immensely complex system. Advertisers rely on agencies for expertise, while agencies depend on platforms for reach and placement.

The advertising market is a massively multiplayer game in which thousands of players compete and work together to extract value from the brand–customer relationship.

With collaboration comes tension, too. For example, agencies must balance their activation recommendations with what is also profitable for them, and publishers may prioritize their interests (e.g. displaying more ads to my friend who complained about ad load rather than prioritizing experience with content).

Estimates of the total scale of the annual global advertising market are difficult to pinpoint, but they range between US$400 billion and US$700 billion.[2] Any of those two numbers is difficult to comprehend. To give some context, the highest-grossing film of all time, *Avengers: Endgame*, made $2.7 billion worldwide.

While I understand the confusion around industry jargon, remember that businesses ultimately aim to provide value to themselves. The media landscape is indeed complex, but with some clarity it can become more manageable. A good lens to seek clarity on the ecosystem players' priorities and decisions is this: Are you building long-term relationships or are you in for the quick wins? Choose wisely.

The perception gap between time spent on media and advertising opportunities

One of the prime points of confusion I've faced in my attempt to decode the media opportunities for brands is the wrong association of time spent on devices with advertising opportunities. Many marketers wrongly assume that if people spend more time on their devices, they will automatically have more chances to be exposed to ads. This assumption, however, can cause brands to overestimate their opportunity for media effectiveness.

In the old days, when TV was the dominant channel in advertising, more time spent watching TV directly equalled more advertising exposure opportunities. TV breaks were an integral part of scheduling and while viewers did not always enjoy them, they tolerated them. Whether viewers used ad breaks to restock their snacks, make a quick trip to the bathroom or just sit through the ordeal and be entertained by 30-second stories, more breaks translated into more reach and frequency. Opportunity was simple, at least, to quantify.

Today, however, this dynamic has shifted radically. Even as overall media consumption has skyrocketed,[3] particularly on mobile devices, I don't feel ad opportunities have grown at a similar rate. Just check your device screen time statistics and you might be surprised. A significant amount of time on devices is spent in ad-free environments. Messaging apps like WhatsApp or Telegram and ad-free streaming services like premium versions of Netflix and Disney+ consume substantial daily media time without any opportunities for traditional ad exposure.

A media consultancy conducted a survey to understand teens' behaviour. The results show that overall screen time increased from 2019 to 2021, outpacing growth in the previous four years. Average daily screen time rose for tweens (ages 8 to 12) from 4 hours and 44 minutes to 5 hours and 33 minutes, while teens (ages 13 to 18) saw an increase from 7 hours and 22 minutes to 8 hours and 39 minutes.[4]

My experience shows that my media consumption tends to focus on content rather than advertising. On YouTube, I may watch hours of cat videos, but only a fraction involves ads. While pre-roll or mid-roll ads appear, my attention is on the videos, not the ads. Consequently, the divide between media use and advertising opportunities widens (see Figure 5.3), along with the rise of ad-skipping and YouTube Premium subscriptions.

Media experts must understand this distinction between time on devices and ad opportunities. Despite the dramatic rise in overall media consumption,

FIGURE 5.3 The evolution of time spent with media: despite an increase in time spent with media, the ad opportunity hasn't captured the same pace

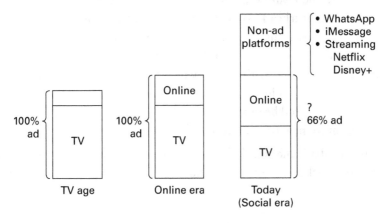

the genuine opportunity for ad placements might be shrinking. Check your numbers. The next time you are exposed to data about media usage, ask yourself: Who is presenting this data? What do they have to sell? What would my agency guide me to do?

How to think about paid, owned and earned media

Open any marketing magazine website today and I bet you will find a marketing opinion leader preaching that a brand's success in this era centres on building strong influencer content that earns you free media impressions. Does it?

My experience taught me that while this desired tactic is possible, it is unlikely to scale. I am a bigger fan of leveraging a balanced mix of paid, owned and earned media instead. These distinct media types uniquely influence marketing plans and drive healthy debates. Let's unpack them:

- Paid media is the most controllable form of brand communication. Brands pay to place their messages on platforms and media channels like TV, online video, social media or podcasts. The advantage of paid media is the ability to control timing, placement and audience targeting precisely. However, maintaining efficiency and effectiveness is a big challenge. Compared with owned and earned media, paid media brings significant costs and increased competition for placement. Reach is a key metric for paid media; high-quality reach is the next level.

- Owned media refers to the media channels a brand fully controls, such as its website, blog, social media organic pages and email newsletters. These channels are typically lower in reach but are important for long-term brand building because they offer an opportunity for two-way communication with the brand users. Owned media is not free media. Beware of the internal overhead costs of managing owned media and also the opportunity costs missed while focusing on owned. My experience tells me that driving scale traffic to these channels typically requires paid or earned media support. Keeping owned media up to date and engaging demands significant investments in non-working media (content development and increased headcount internally). Owned media, typically, rarely reaches future new brand buyers.

- Earned media is the cool kid on the block, a desired but less predictable form of marketing communication. It covers organic PR and press coverage, word-of-mouth activations, social media amplification, customer reviews, influencer executions and user-generated content. Audiences might appreciate earned media because it feels more authentic, coming from third parties rather than directly from the brand. However, good luck predicting its scalability. Once again, many marketers rely on paid and owned media to stimulate earned media, desiring to create shareable, buzz-worthy content that encourages more attention.

Choosing where to focus your attention and media efforts is not easy. In an ideal world, brands might adopt a holistic approach that integrates all three types of media: paid, owned and earned – paid media for immediate reach, owned channels for depth and earned media for credibility. But in real life, this is easier said than done.

THREE QUESTIONS ON PAID, OWNED, EARNED

Ask yourself these questions to engage in a healthy debate on the choices between paid, owned and earned:

- How much reach can I buy with my current paid media budget?
- What is the typical engagement rate of previous owned media activations?
- What was my historical record of earned reach when I attempted it?

Now benchmark the cost per reach inclusive of all internal overhead cost for each of the three types of medias. There is no precise answer, but this short exercise might surprise you. See Figure 5.4.

FIGURE 5.4 The links between paid, earned and owned

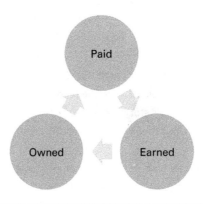

REAL-WORLD EXAMPLE
The power of paid + owned + earned = M&M Spokescandies

In early 2023, the confectionery brand M&M's launched the bold 'Spokescandies on Pause' campaign and I had the privilege of being part of the team measuring its effectiveness.

The idea followed up on a cultural controversy when minor updates to brand characters, like Green switching from boots to sneakers in 2022, ignited a massive cultural debate. Rather than avoiding the issue, M&M's leaned into the controversy, announcing the 'cancellation' of its iconic characters and replacing them with comedian Maya Rudolph. This was a brilliant move that captured the public's attention like never before.

The 2023 campaign unfolded over several weeks, culminating with the largest event in TV advertising in the United States, the Super Bowl reveal. Each M&M's character had its absurd storyline, from Red selling memorabilia on eBay to Yellow being hired by another Mars brand, Snickers, as an ingredient. The chaos culminated in the first Super Bowl ad, where Maya introduced 'Ma&Ya's Candy-Coated Clam Bites', which didn't do well with fans. After the Super Bowl halftime, another ad highlighting a press conference aired in which the beloved characters triumphantly returned.

The effectiveness data showed extraordinary results. This integrated campaign generated billions of media impressions. On social media alone, the campaign had its own life: fans created memes, shared reaction videos and celebrated the return of their favourite candy mascots. According to Morning Consult, a marketing agency, M&M's even ranked #4 as the 'most loved ad' by the general population.[5] Ultimately, this campaign demonstrated the power of combining paid, owned and earned media to create a truly viral cultural moment.

This campaign was a masterstroke in turning controversy into an opportunity. As part of the team that measured its impact, I witnessed first hand how powerful a bold, creative strategy can be when paired with intelligent measurement and analysis.

The 'Spokescandies on Pause' campaign is a standout example of integrating earned, owned and paid media effectively. The paid media placements, from the Super Bowl ad to the character's storylines across various platforms, ensured increased visibility. The owned media – M&M's social pages and website – kept fans engaged with the evolving storylines. But it was the earned media that truly made this campaign legendary, generating untapped impressions through viral social conversations, news coverage and fan-generated content. By orchestrating all three forms of media – paid, owned and earned – M&M's didn't just dominate the news cycle, it reignited America's love for its characters.

Measuring media effectiveness

I often wonder why every conversation about media effectiveness spirals into a debate about the appropriate metrics and key performance indicators. Don't get me wrong, they are incredibly important, but what's even more crucial is identifying the answers your organization needs to gain confidence in the power of media to generate positive business outcomes.

The key performance indicators that organizations seek to measure media effectiveness vary. Some brands focus on sales impact, while others prioritize the media's return on investment. Additionally, some organizations may be more interested in metrics like brand awareness or the level of buzz surrounding their brand. Identifying the relevant KPIs among the wealth of data available is crucial for gaining confidence in the power of media to drive positive business outcomes.

ALL KPIs ARE METRICS, BUT NOT ALL METRICS BECOME KPIs

Metrics are raw data points and measurements that indicate various aspects of our marketing execution. Metrics can be anything from reach, impressions, page views, bounce rate and engagement rate to email open rates and click-through rates (CTR). Metrics provide a granular view of what's happening across different channels and touchpoints. But they don't essentially indicate whether you're meeting your business objectives, they just tell you what's going on.

KPIs are a select group of metrics directly tied to business goals. They directly indicate how well your marketing efforts achieve the desired outcomes. KPIs are specific, actionable and aligned with the business strategy. For instance, if your goal is to increase sales, a critical KPI could be the sales impact of media and the percentage of new users converted. KPIs are the metrics that matter most when assessing the success of your marketing strategy in front of your board.

Next I focus on three critical metrics that every media-savvy marketer must manage: reach, CPM (cost per thousand impressions) and attention. These metrics are foundational in evaluating the impact of media, yet they are often misunderstood. I intend to discuss the fundamental principles with you, showing how their integration can provide a comprehensive understanding of effective media.

1 Reach: the balance between quantity vs quality

WHAT IS REACH?

Reach is my go-to media metric for brand growth through media (see Figure 5.5). It measures the number of people exposed to your brand communication via media. More reach is almost always better than less reach. Without enough reach, even the most compelling creative campaigns fail to have a significant business impact.

When you prioritize reach, you follow a 'reach-based strategy'. This is synonymous with new customer acquisition in marketing or penetration gains. According to Byron Sharp's *How Brands Grow*,[6] brand growth comes primarily from attracting light or non-brand buyers, who make up much of the market but only buy your brand occasionally. Reaching these customers at the expense of your existing ones is a critical way to expand a brand's footprint.

REACH AND FREQUENCY

In media planning, reach and frequency are interconnected metrics essential for evaluating advertising effectiveness. Reach refers to the total number of unique individuals exposed to an ad, while frequency measures how often these individuals see the ad. Surprisingly, they are not independent variables; increasing reach typically leads to higher frequency as some users see the ad multiple times before all targets are exposed once (see Figure 5.6).

Determining the ideal balance between reach and frequency has long been a primary focus for advertisers and media planners seeking to maximize the effectiveness of their campaigns. The ideal combination can vary significantly based on several factors, including product characteristics, customer behaviour and the specific media channels used.

The concept of 'effective frequency' has been widely studied in the marketing literature as it seeks to identify the ideal number of exposures required to elicit a desired consumer response.

A great media professional masters the trade-offs between reach and frequency of exposure in a 'reach-based strategy'.

FIGURE 5.5 Reach is a ratio of unique individual impressions divided by the target audience

$$\text{Reach} = \frac{\text{Unique Impressions}}{\text{Target Audience}} \times 100$$

FIGURE 5.6 The diminishing return curve of reach: reach reaches a plateau with the increase in frequency

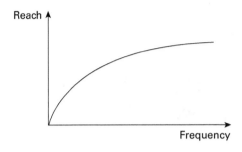

Frequency is important because numerous studies show that repeated exposure is necessary for a message to sink in, especially in a crowded media landscape. People may not act immediately, but building that mental availability that Professor Sharp emphasizes is insurance for the future. Beware of stepping into the pitfall of over-exposing your audience to your message. Once you annoy people, they pay less attention, so your ads are less likely to work.[7]

Before glorifying reach, acknowledge that it is merely a metric; it indicates how many people might see your message, but does not determine whether that exposure is effective. Your key performance indicator could instead be a specific reach goal that drives the expected brand growth. For example, for some brands, reaching 70 per cent of their target audience with a frequency of more than three times a month might be the threshold for significant impact. Don't take my word for it – find out for your brand.

THE CHALLENGES OF MEASURING REACH TODAY

Although straightforward in concept, measuring reach is difficult in today's multimedia landscape. It is relatively easy to measure reach when using a single media platform, as this quantifies the number of unique individuals exposed to your ad compared with the total target audience. However, understanding the total reach of a campaign becomes significantly more complex when it is executed across multiple platforms (see Figure 5.7).

At best, one can model a multimedia campaign's expected reach using a simplified mathematical model that uses exposure duplication today. Acknowledging that modelling reach is insufficient, the advertising industry organized itself to solve this problem. To address this, the World Federation of Advertisers (WFA) launched the HALO initiative[8] in 2019, aiming to standardize cross-channel measurement of reach and frequency and solve the fragmentation of reporting.

FIGURE 5.7   Multimedia reach overlap: in most cases, when activating different media channels, there will always be an overlap of reach. The key of a multimedia plan is to identify opportunities for incremental reach

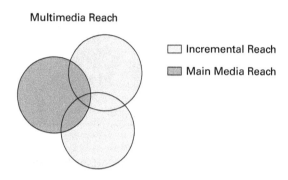

At the time of writing, in-market pilots testing the measurement solutions are yielding promising results; however, further work is required to broaden the scope to include all medias and as many geographies as possible.

QUALITY OF REACH – THE NIRVANA OF MEDIA

Beyond reach itself, any information that includes an element of quality of reach helps you plan precisely cross-channel campaigns. Because not all reach is created equal. Quality factors like past conversion benchmarks by channel, attention levels by format or hygiene metrics like viewability, fraud or brand safety rates help guide where to place future ad spending. Quality of reach is a decisive factor in balancing the ROI of each media channel.

Bad reach can dilute the efficiency of your campaigns. Take MFA (Made for Advertising) websites – created solely to generate ad revenue, not to offer meaningful content. Impressions placed on such sites may be counted as reach even without reaching real humans. Similarly, low-viewability impressions, such as display ads placed below the fold (ads positioned on the part of a webpage that users never scroll down to), are another waste. And so are TV ads shown late at night when the TV might be on but people sleep. All these impressions technically count towards reach, but they lack any potential to drive impact. To maximize the impact of your campaigns, ensure your ads are visible, in safe environments and seen by humans.

Reach drives growth, but it's not only about the number of people you reach. It's about who you're reaching, the quality of that exposure and ensuring your media strategy aligns with your overall growth objectives.

2 CPM: understanding cost efficiency

CPM is one of the most used metrics in the media buying process. It shows how much an advertiser must pay for 1,000 impressions that can potentially reach a maximum of 1,000 people (see Figure 5.8). It is a primary metric in managing media budgets.

CPM is a measure of cost efficiency, not effectiveness. A low CPM indicates you're getting a reasonable price for your ad placements, but it doesn't guarantee results to be stellar. Many media professionals fall into the trap of focusing on reducing CPMs without considering whether their ads are having the desired impact on the audience. A low CPM is a meaningless target if the ads aren't generating conversions.

To truly gauge media efficiency, CPM must be evaluated alongside engagement, conversion rates and viewability metrics. A low CPM with high conversion indicates both efficiency and effectiveness. However, a low CPM with poor conversion is a call to action.

To optimize CPMs while preserving effectiveness, you could consider the following:

- Test the formats: Some platforms, like traditional static display advertising, naturally have lower CPMs, but they might not deliver relevant audiences or impact. Experimenting with multiple formats can help you find the best balance between cost and relevance. Always consider conversions the ultimate metric of success.

- Use biddable buying. Programmatic ad platforms can optimize your CPM in real time by placing your ads where they are most cost effective, improving efficiency and performance. A good idea is to consider enhancing the bidding CPMs with a quality-of-reach metric.

- Refine targeting: A too-narrow audience can increase CPM, while a too-wide audience can lower it but hurt ROI. A good idea is to test different targeting levels to find the right balance between cost and quality.

While CPM is a valuable metric for cost control, it will never be a KPI for your business. Pair it with quality metrics to better understand how your media investment drives effective results.

FIGURE 5.8 CPM: the cost per mille (or thousand impressions) equals the total cost divided by the number of impressions

$$CPM = \left(\frac{\text{Total Cost}}{\text{Total Impressions}} \right) \times 1000$$

SHARE OF VOICE – THE PROS AND CONS

Investing in mass media or high-reach channels, or media that everyone talks about ,might be the best strategy for gaining brand fame. When any category buyer can become a potential buyer of your brand, maximizing reach should be your top media priority.

But can you afford it? The current media landscape offers a maze of multi-format options, varying in quality and measurability, to counterbalance the decline in mass reach that followed viewership patterns in TV. Navigating this digital labyrinth requires significant patience, larger media budgets and sharp analytical skills.

Advocating for mass media may seem outdated in today's era, where understanding deeply the target customer is the trendy topic. But here I am, making that case – with a twist. I'm not saying mass media is your only option; it's essential for brand scale if you can afford it. The only limitation is your budget. But what is 'mass reach' and how can you benchmark it? Is it simply achieving a higher share of voice than your market share?

The obsession with SOV as the ideal benchmark for media expenditure has always puzzled me. Sure, it's a way to benchmark media budgets, but it seems overly simplistic. There are more accurate ways to determine how much more you should spend this year than looking at your competitors.

I'll admit it: I'm not a fan of SOV. Why? Because correlation doesn't mean causation. Share of voice and share of market are often correlated but not necessarily causal. For example, in categories where private labels are growing at the expense of big brands, the relationship between SOV and SOM often reverses.

In such cases, well-established brands spend heavily on media to grow market penetration, yet private labels reap the rewards at the point of sale. Advertising stimulates category growth, not just brand growth.

In markets where brands command over 50 per cent market share, should they spend enormous budgets to maintain that dominance while competitors erode their share?

3 Attention: the new battleground for media effectiveness

Attention is often defined as the time and focus a viewer dedicates to your message. In recent years, this concept of attention has emerged as a critical metric for evaluating media effectiveness.

We live in an attention-driven media world where attention is a valuable, scarce resource. Attention has become a commodity for which brands and platforms compete fiercely. Beyond reach, media effectiveness significantly depends on how well brands can capture and hold the audience's attention. I firmly believe that attention might be the missing piece in the quality-of-reach puzzle many media professionals are trying to solve today.

And when there is focus, there is emerging complexity, too. Marketers today have a complex toolkit of measurements to understand attention effectively. There is even an industry body, The Attention Council, that promotes attention metrics and aligns stakeholders in the media and advertising ecosystem to encourage the use of new measurement tools. I was lucky to serve on the board of The Attention Council for several years, representing the advertiser's voice.

From an attention measurement fan, here are three ways to measure attention:

- Neuromarketing EEG style approaches directly measure, in specialized neuro labs, the neurological response to advertising exposure. In this case the measurement of attention has the highest quality of signal, but the lab context highly impacts the measurement and its replicability. A restricted number of companies are currently offering this service to advertisers, alongside academic laboratories.

- Visual attention tracking captures facial reactions via a front-camera device during an ad exposure. This solution's main benefit is the real-life measurement conditions coupled with scalability. Companies offering this type of service (Realeyes, Amplified Intelligence, TVision, Lumen, Affectiva and many more) use proprietary algorithms to detect eye movements and measure attention precisely in natural environments.

- Proxy attention measurements can also be derived from digital engagement metrics like clicks, time in view or skip rates. This solution has the broadest scale but lacks a clear link to human behaviours. Just because someone is not skipping an ad doesn't mean they pay attention to it. I would caution against using these unless a correlation study is run with actual viewing behaviours.

As part of the proxy attention metrics, viewability, whether an ad appeared on-screen, has been commonly used as a proxy for attention for years. But viewability alone is insufficient. Accurate attention metrics should go beyond digital engagement metrics into the territory of eye-tracking data to see where users' eyes are focused on the screen.

Attention measurement is just the beginning – the next step is incorporating it into the media planning and buying processes. The industry is leaping towards this goal, which I see within sight today.

Attention is a strong indicator of quality of reach.

The interplay between reach, CPM and attention

The easiest way to assess media effectiveness is by triangulating the information from the reach, CPM and attention metrics. Reach tells you how many people are exposed to your ad, CPM indicates the cost efficiency of that exposure and attention measures their engagement with the content.

An effective media plan requires these metrics to work together. Reach should be broad and high-quality, CPM should be optimized for cost and impact, and attention must be optimized to ensure potential message encoding.

But even when all these metrics are optimized, the main KPI of effectiveness remains media's impact on the top line, the effect on sales. But more about that topic in Chapter 7: Research.

Busting three common myths in media effectiveness

In media, myths and misconceptions abound, often leading so-called experts to a LinkedIn euphoric debate. More importantly, it drives the wrong decisions and some budget decisions for many brands.

While data has become more accessible, many brands still fail to understand and act on it. Let's debunk some of the most persistent myths about media effectiveness, their misunderstandings and why believing these can hinder a brand's growth.

Myth 1: More reach always means more impact

Reach is the buzzword that correctly enters our vocabulary as a priority of evidence-based media strategies, as Byron Sharp exposed in *How Brands Grow*:

FIGURE 5.9 Media effectiveness parameters: media effectiveness is a function of reach CPM and a measure of quality like attention

Media Effectiveness = f(Reach, CPM, Attention)

- The misunderstanding: Marketers often equate incremental reach with increased impact. They believe the more people you reach, the more successful your campaign will be, regardless of who you reach.

- The reality: Reach alone does not link to effectiveness. Yes, a large budget can achieve a lot of reach and build awareness, but the quality of reach genuinely matters. If your message isn't reaching your targeted audience and the channel is not engaging your customer, you're wasting media dollars on impressions that don't lead to conversions.

- I worked on a major campaign for a brand that insisted on hitting massive reach numbers across different media platforms. We exceeded our reach goals, but post-campaign analysis revealed a significant flaw: our programmatic buying algorithm prioritized low-engagement platforms and cheaper-to-buy display content with lower viewability potential to achieve the high reach numbers. We got reach, but not much impact. We learnt that simply focusing on reach alone is insufficient.

- The fix: Rather than chasing reach, determine your business-specific metric for quality of reach. There is no magic bullet; it depends on how savvy your media organization or agency is. Your metric could combine desired effect and user behaviours, such as attention or conversion benchmark metrics by channel.

Myth 2: More personalization always means better results

Personalization in media is the tailoring of messages and media specific to individual audience preferences and/or behaviours:

- The misunderstanding: Many marketers believe that personalization is the most significant benefit of data-driven marketing. The belief is that a customized message is more relevant to the customer and improves overall effectiveness. While personalization can improve effectiveness, there's always a tipping point.

- The reality: While personalization can improve your message's relevance, there is a point of diminishing returns. Overly personalized ads can sometimes feel invasive or irrelevant, and worse, they often narrow your target audience too much. Hyper-focused personalization usually comes at higher overhead costs and an opportunity cost that is frequently ignored.

- I've seen this first hand. In one campaign I worked on, we went all-in on hyper-targeted personalization. We created highly specific ads for multiple audience segments but soon realized our total reach was too narrow.

The media delivery mechanics for those selected audiences didn't work with 100 per cent accuracy. Each segment added to the complexity and reduced the overall impact. Worse, when put to the test, the difference in impact compared with a standard broader reach strategy was marginal.

- The fix: Always test your personalization hypothesis against a generic reach-based target. Include both working and non-working costs in the ROI equation to better understand what works best for your brand. This also applies to dynamic creative optimization, an excellent tool for executing personalization with automation. The key is to personalize just enough to feel relevant but not so much that you exclude potential customers or exhaust your existing audience and your team's workload.

- Always look for different perspectives when approaching complex topics. Another way to guide your conversation is to use the simplistic formula in Figure 5.10, crafted by McKinsey, to link the various elements that are in play in the personalization field.[9]

Myth 3: Social media is free and more effective than other media

Social media marketing is often divided into two main areas: organic and paid. Organic social media refers to content that brands post to their followers for free. These posts rely on the platform's algorithm to reach followers and possibly their extended networks. How cute! Paid social media involves advertising that brands pay to reach specific audiences through sponsored posts, ads or boosted content. If you owned a social media network, which of the two sources of income would you boost?

- The misunderstanding: There's a widely held belief that organic social media is a 'free' and therefore more efficient marketing channel. I often hear the attributes 'authentic', 'in-culture' or 'collaborative'. Unfortunately, we've known for a long time that organic reach of social media is dwindling rapidly. Platforms like Facebook, Instagram and even X throttle the reach of unpaid posts, with some studies showing organic reach as

FIGURE 5.10 Personalization formula: the value of an audience is a function of relevance and timeliness divided by a perceived loss of privacy, all multiplied by the current trust level

$$\text{Audience Value} = \left(\frac{\text{Relevance} + \text{Timeliness}}{\text{Loss of Privacy}} \right) \times \text{Trust Level}$$

SOURCE Inspired by McKinsey research above

low as 1–5 per cent of the follower base. Virality, that elusive goal everyone dreams about, is rare and massively oversold by success stories. Unless your brand stumbles upon that rare, unpredictable golden moment, organic content often lands nowhere. The time you spend to create that content is often overlooked and rarely considered as a cost.

- The reality: From a paid perspective, social media platforms are finely tuned to sell advertising. The entire infrastructure is designed to prioritize paying clients, meaning that you're playing in a crowded field with little visibility without financial investment. Brands pay to reach the right audience, targeting specific demographics, interests and behaviours. Organic social media (sometimes hidden behind influencer marketing) is like gambling on getting rich overnight: possible but highly unlikely.

- In my experience, platforms like X thrive on moments of virality, but chasing it is a risky game. If your post isn't tied to a significant trend or doesn't get a push from influential accounts, it often slips into obscurity. I've seen countless brand posts with great content that simply don't gain traction because they weren't riding the wave of a trending topic. Even when a post does go viral, replicating that success is close to impossible. Virality isn't a strategy – it's a rare, unpredictable event, much like being struck by lightning.

- The fix: So how should brands approach social media? First, consider social media a paid media channel with a complementary organic opportunity. Focus on reach, whether through ads or partnerships with creators who align with your brand values and voice. Ensure your content is tailored to the platform. And always look at social media as another media channel competing for your advertising budget.

Media has a long-term impact on sales

When did you last see a Coke or Apple ad on TV? If you're like most people today, swapping the traditional TV time for a cluttered mobile screen, you might not remember. Yet, isn't it fascinating how ads from years ago still linger in our collective consciousness? Think about *that* ad. Yes, you know the one.

For marketing professionals, Apple's '1984' or Coke's 'I'd Like to Teach the World to Sing' probably recently resurfaced on social media, shared in praise of the eternal creativity of their ad agency. But here's the kicker: it's not just industry insiders who remember them. These ads resonate with a broad audience, often becoming part of our shared cultural experience.

Whenever your brand appears on a screen, echoes through an audio ad or pops up in an immersive AR experience, it's not just a fleeting moment. It's building memory structures. The audience may not consciously recall it a week later, but what matters is the gradual build-up of brand salience. Sometimes, this memory nudges consumers in the most unexpected moments, prompting them to snap your product from the shelf. That's the subtle magic of advertising's impact.

Unfortunately, our industry has become fixated on immediate results, often overlooking the more significant benefit: the media's long-term impact.

Let's get one thing straight: if your advertising is terrible in the short term, there is rarely a long-term sales effect (see Figure 5.11). The notion of wear-in is another media myth. It's crucial to manage your media choices wisely, measuring and acting on short-term impacts. But don't stop there.

Long-term effects can be measured, though it's complex. With effort, you might uncover an effect multiplier that quantifies the expected future business impact. Some companies measure short-term impact and use multipliers to estimate long-term effectiveness. Others have sophisticated analytics to measure long-term or lifetime value. Some rely on softer brand metrics. Who's right? Perhaps all of them, in different contexts.

The role of media is to drive brand conversions today and tomorrow and build long-term brand equity.

Measuring sales is challenging long term, but quantifying long-term equity is even trickier. Media is one of the many levers in your brand's arsenal. It competes with product innovation, packaging redesign, shelf presence, price-point appeal, social buzz, sponsorships and the power of word-of-mouth to lift your brand's equity metrics. Deconstructing the driver of impact over multiple years is nearly impossible without experimentation. So, when you notice a spike in brand awareness, attributing it solely to a campaign from two years ago might be an oversimplification.

Measure or estimate the long-term impact of media on sales. It's challenging, but ignoring it is not an option – especially when the CFO comes knocking on your door.

Let's stop calling everything digital

Remember when we used to prefix everything in media with 'digital'? I hope those days are long gone in your world. The vocabulary refresh reflects a past change in the marketing landscape that is behind us.

FIGURE 5.11 The long-term effect of media is a function of the short-term effects

Media Long-Term Effect = f(Media Short-Term Effect)

In 2020, a viral meme you probably received joked that Covid-19, not CEOs or CDOs, was the true catalyst for digital transformation. Fast-forward to today and the term 'digital' has become as redundant as calling electricity 'electrical' in the early 1900s (see Figure 5.12). Today, digital technology is woven into every aspect of our lives and businesses – it's no longer a differentiator but a given.

Ten years ago, platforms like YouTube and TikTok were vying for scraps of media budgets. We were obsessed with the declining share of 'traditional' media (TV, print, OOH) versus the rise of 'digital' media. But here's the truth: this distinction is meaningless to anyone outside our marketing bubble. What matters now is each media format's potential reach and impact, regardless of its technical delivery method. After all, 99 per cent of media now travels through the same digital infrastructure.

So, what can you do?

- Embrace the diversity in media usage: there's no one-size-fits-all 'digital media'. Focus on understanding how people interact with content across various platforms and formats. Dive into the nuances of viewing habits, scrolling patterns, multi-screen behaviours and engagement metrics. Stop calling everything digital.

- Strive for newsworthy campaigns. The most memorable campaigns transcend individual channels. Aim to create compelling content that becomes newsworthy, leveraging the amplification power of all media types, including earned media and the good old TV.

- Prioritize attention over labels: Whether your content is 'digital-first' or 'TV-last' is irrelevant if it fails to capture attention. Focus on creating engaging, valuable experiences for your audience, regardless of the delivery format.

Digital technology is now as omnipresent as the air we breathe. Instead of constantly debating digital vs non-digital media channels, let's focus on the

FIGURE 5.12 Stop calling everything digital – everything is delivered digitally today

quality and impact of our marketing plans. It's less about the technology itself and more about the customer need and brand offer we want to bridge. That's the true essence of marketing in our tech-saturated world.

Stop calling everything digital.

Applied engineering for media effectiveness

Engineering Marketing Tool 5: Kaizen

KAIZEN IN ACTION: INCREMENTAL ADJUSTMENTS TO SURVIVE THE CHALLENGES OF MODERN ADVERTISING

Kaizen is a Japanese business philosophy made globally famous by Toyota,[10] the global car manufacturer that took the world by storm. It encourages continuous improvement involving employees at all company levels. The word *kaizen* is often translated as 'change for the better' (see Figure 5.13).

Today, Kaizen has evolved beyond its original manufacturing roots to become a widely applicable business improvement philosophy. In my view, it can help you become a better media practitioner. The core idea is simple: small, incremental changes applied consistently can lead to significant, long-term improvements. When considering using Kaizen for media effectiveness, I often think of a structured, data-driven learning plan that helps teams optimize spend, refine targeting and content, and increase overall sales impact and return on investment.

Think of Kaizen as a continuous feedback loop, a mental mindset that promotes iterative learning and improvement. While the concept of test-and-learn is omnipresent in marketing, Kaizen adds the discipline of breaking down challenges into smaller incremental steps and ensuring action is taken after each test.

The scope can include analysing media performance, identifying inefficiencies in the buying process and channel specifics. The key is to make minor adjustments and always ensure a robust testing protocol for success

FIGURE 5.13 Kaizen means good – change

Kai = Change   Zen = Good

is linked to the change. Today, various media metrics can be analysed in real-time and insights instantly inform the current campaign's evolution. Testing a campaign only to inform future campaigns might be sunsetting. Modern media requires instant feedback. And Kaizen, as a philosophy, fits like a glove.

Here's how to apply Kaizen's continuous improvement model for media effectiveness (see Figure 5.14):

1 Plan: Set clear objectives for your learning plan. Define specific success metrics that predict your business goals. This is when you can sort the metrics into KPIs and regular metrics. Now, focus on small changes to your media plan that you can A/B test.

2 Do: Execute your media across the chosen platforms for the test. This phase involves buying media, developing creatives and actively managing campaigns against the success metric. Importantly, every action should be data-driven and fully measurable.

3 Check: Evaluate the performance using the success metric. I highly recommend changing a single variable per test. This enables you to

FIGURE 5.14 Kaizen cycle for continuous improvement: Kaizen is more about a mindset than about a specific tool or metric

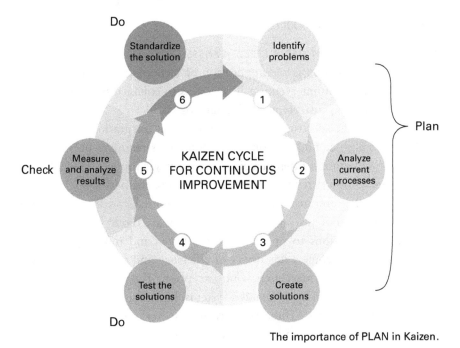

The importance of PLAN in Kaizen.

determine causation, not just simple correlations in the data. Once completed, dive into the data, measure the outcome and communicate it broadly.

4 Act: This is where you decide if the change becomes a permanent future feature. Based on your analysis, either reallocate budgets, tweak creatives or refine targeting. But please don't let the results sit on a shelf. Create a loop of continuous refinement and learning.

Some examples of practical applications of Kaizen in media effectiveness could be:

- target or audience impact optimizations
- budget allocations across different media platforms and formats
- identifying the right balance of reach and frequency within a given budget
- content refinements to adapt for platform best practices
- exposure optimizations on time of day, day of week, etc

The Kaizen philosophy offers marketers a powerful tool for continuous optimization. Focusing on minor, data-backed improvements can enhance media effectiveness, drive improved sales and potentially maximize your media ROI.

Engineering Marketing Tool 6: Automation

AUTOMATION'S ROLE IN MEDIA EFFECTIVENESS

At its core, automation is the application of technology to perform tasks with minimal human intervention. The goal is to enhance speed and precision while reducing costs, typically human costs.

In any scientific spectrum, automation is about integrating sensor data, artificial intelligence and bespoke algorithms to streamline processes. In business, automation is often perceived as a strategic programme to reduce human intervention that drives costs down and productivity up.

Understanding automation through both scientific and business lenses reveals that it is not just about replacing manual labour but also about enabling organizations to operate smarter, faster and more strategically. Automation has become a key driver of efficiency and performance across many industries, and marketing is no exception. Today, media buying is increasingly influenced by automated systems, known as the programmatic supply-chain ecosystem. These systems analyse vast amounts of data to determine when, where and to whom ads should be shown, optimizing media spend in real-time. However, as transformative as these systems are, we are far from the full potential of media effectiveness through automation.

Over the last decade, I've seen how rapidly technology is evolving in media. Programmatic advertising platforms like Google's Display & Video 360 or The Trade Desk are the main choice for transacting media, replacing traditional platform-based brand negotiations and media commitments. I've watched as once manually managed campaigns are optimized in real-time, scaling effortlessly with algorithms that make split-second decisions. But while these systems are powerful, we're not anywhere near the full potential of automation when it comes to media effectiveness.

What's particularly exciting to me is the possibility of media buying evolving into something like automated stock trading. In financial markets, algorithms process vast amounts of data to make real-time trades, minimizing human error and maximizing returns. I've often thought, why couldn't media buying work the same way? Imagine an AI-driven system that not only buys ad space but also adjusts creative content, shifts budgets and responds to audience engagement in real-time – all without human oversight. In this vision, media buying wouldn't just be automated, it would be self-learning, evolving continuously based on consumer behaviour and market conditions.

Right now, we're still dependent on human input for many media decisions. While machines are getting better at optimizing bids and placements, they're not yet able to fully control a campaign's creative strategy or higher-level business decisions. I've seen firsthand how even the most efficient programmatic platforms can stumble if the creative isn't aligned with the

FIGURE 5.15 The automation loop in media effectiveness

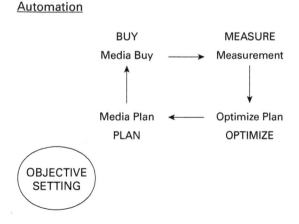

data or the wrong audience is being targeted. Automation excels at the technical level, but human judgement is still required to steer the overall direction.

To prepare for this future of automation, here are a few practical steps that I've found crucial for brands to take right now:

1   Invest in data integrations: Many brands struggle with fragmented data. Without a unified view of your audience, you're only as good as the data you feed into these automated systems. I've seen how integrating CRM, sales and offline data with digital analytics creates a feedback loop that fuels better decision-making, making future automation efforts more effective.

2   Agility in creative processes: While automation can optimize today's media placement, it cannot yet create flexible, compelling content on its own. I've worked on campaigns where rigid creative assets held back performance because they couldn't adapt to the changing insights from the data. Brands that develop agile creative processes, building modular assets that can be quickly adjusted based on performance, will win.

3   Stay informed about AI and tech developments: One of the biggest lessons I've learnt is the importance of staying ahead of the curve. Automation tools and AI capabilities are evolving fast, and the brands that experiment early with these technologies will have a serious edge. I make it a point to constantly test new features as they emerge, even if they're not fully developed. This keeps me sharp and ready for the next big technology breakthrough.

We're poised for a significant shift in how much of media buying and effectiveness are managed through systems. Automation plays a decisive role today, but the future holds even more promise. Get ready for the future of automation in media. It will be here soon.

INDUSTRY EXPERT CONTRIBUTION
Media expertise: Paolo Provinciali

The modern media landscape is awash in data. Every click, impression and conversion leaves a digital footprint, offering a seemingly endless stream of information about consumer behaviour. This data-rich environment allows marketers to dissect campaigns with unprecedented granularity, identifying what works and what doesn't with laser precision. But this wealth of information comes with a catch: the signal-to-noise ratio can be overwhelmingly low.

The ability to extract meaningful insights from this data deluge requires a new breed of marketer – one with both technical expertise and strategic rigor. This expertise is crucial not only for navigating the complexities of various media channels and platforms but also for understanding the nuances of human behaviour within each. Today's consumer flits between social media, streaming services and online marketplaces, leaving a fragmented trail of attention. A deep understanding of each platform's technical features and how they influence user behaviour is essential to capture and leverage those fleeting moments of engagement.

Yet despite the abundance of data and the tools to analyse it, many marketers remain fixated on efficiency at the expense of effectiveness. Years of optimizing media buying and placement have led to a myopic focus on tactical metrics like cost-per-click and conversion rates. While important, these metrics tell only half the story.

The bigger lever – the one that truly moves the needle – is the audience and the creative content that resonates with them. Sadly, this lever remains largely underutilized. Many campaigns are launched on the foundation of weak briefs, flawed consumer insights and uninspired creative assets. These campaigns are often 'set and forget', neglecting the dynamic nature of the media landscape and the wealth of data available for continuous optimization.

This obsession with efficiency has led to an effectiveness drought. Marketers have become so preoccupied with squeezing every last drop of performance from their media spend that they've forgotten the fundamental goal: creating impactful campaigns that resonate with their audience.

The future belongs to marketers who can strike a balance. Those who can build processes, cultivate skills and forge partnerships that optimize for both efficiency and effectiveness will be the ones who truly drive impact. They will be the architects of campaigns that not only reach the right audience at the right time but also deliver messages that inspire, engage and, ultimately, persuade.

PAOLO PROVINCIALI

Paolo Provinciali is LinkedIn's Marketing Vice President of Growth, Performance and Operations. He oversees paid & owned media, web, analytics, MarTech and business platforms. Prior to LinkedIn, Paolo was the VP of Media and Data for

Anheuser Busch InBev in the US. He ran advertising for the brewer's large portfolio of iconic brands and led the efforts to build the marketing data. Paolo also established the Global E-commerce Marketing team at ZX Ventures. Before ABI, Paolo was at Google for nearly 10 years, where he helped establish the internal media team and developed the digital and programmatic best practices to advertise Google's B2B and B2C products worldwide.

FIVE IDEAS TO TAKE WITH YOU AFTER READING THIS CHAPTER

1 Media planning starts with understanding your audience – reach is critical, but reaching the right people with the right message is even more important.

2 Effectiveness and efficiency are two sides of the media coin. Effectiveness focuses on delivering results, while efficiency ensures that you do so with the least amount of waste.

3 Not all reach is equal – focus on high-quality reach by ensuring your ads are visible, in safe environments and viewed by real, engaged people.

4 Attention is the new battleground for media success – capturing and holding your audience's attention is more valuable than simply placing an ad.

5 Holistic media measurement is key – use a mix of metrics (reach, CPM, attention) to get a complete picture of your media's performance and impact.

Media effectiveness matters: a final reflection

I believe you now have a comprehensive view of how media works, how the ecosystem players interact and what are some common strategies that can guide your media practice.

Media effectiveness relies on understanding three elements: reach, cost and a quality element like attention. Balancing effectiveness and efficiency of media is an expert task for the marketing leader in you.

Below are three questions to help you make the most of this chapter. Ask them often to make more effective decisions for your brand. As always, there are no right or wrong answers. Simply thinking about these concepts more will help you internalize them better. And for an added learning boost, consider discussing them with a colleague or a friend.

THREE QUESTIONS TO MASTER MEDIA EFFECTIVENESS

Ask these questions frequently to drive smarter media decisions for your brand:

1 How do you measure the effectiveness and efficiency of your media investments? Are these two terms confused or used interchangeably? They shouldn't be.

2 What is your ideal mix of short-term reach and long-term brand building in media? Are your current strategies focused too much on immediate results without building future equity?

3 What story do you tell internally about your media's impact? What metrics or success indicators resonate within your organization and what adjustments can you make today to improve?

ONE MORE THING…

Want to stay effective and ahead of the curve? Scan this QR code to access extra content and updates online.

Notes

1 White, D (2020) *The Smart Marketing Book: The definitive guide to effective marketing strategies*, LID Publishing, London

2 Market Research.com (2023) Global advertising market: Industry trends, share, size, growth, opportunity and forecast 2023–2028, https://www.marketresearch.com/IMARC-v3797/Global-Advertising-Trends-Share-Size-33910691/ (archived at https://perma.cc/5CSN-ALW8)

3 Stelter, B (2009) 8 hours a day spent on screens, study finds, https://www.nytimes.com/2009/03/27/business/media/27adco.html (archived at https://perma.cc/4C3T-NGCM)

4 Moyer, M W (2022) Kids as young as 8 are using social media more than ever, https://www.nytimes.com/2022/03/24/well/family/child-social-media-use.html (archived at https://perma.cc/K36H-D2DT)

5 Morning Consult Pro (2023) Most loved brands special report, https://
   go.morningconsult.com/2020_Q3_2415_Most-Loved-Brands-Special-Report_
   Download.html (archived at https://perma.cc/7HA4-QWMX)

6 Sharp, B (2010) *How Brands Grow: What marketers don't know*, OUP
   Australia, South Melbourne

7 Ghose, A, Todri, V and Singh, P (2019) Trade-offs in online advertising:
   Advertising effectiveness and annoyance dynamics across the purchase funnel,
   https://pubsonline.informs.org/doi/10.1287/isre.2019.0877 (archived at https://
   perma.cc/4GQA-NNPL)

8 WFA (2024) Halo & global cross-media measurement, https://wfanet.org/
   leadership/cross-media-measurement (archived at https://perma.cc/5HHJ-
   M3WW)

9 Boudet, J, Gregg, B, Wong, J and Schuler, G (2017) What shoppers really want from
   personalized marketing, https://www.mckinsey.com/capabilities/growth-marketing-
   and-sales/our-insights/what-shoppers-really-want-from-personalized-marketing
   (archived at https://perma.cc/PM6P-L29Z)

10 Toyota production system, https://global.toyota/en/company/vision-and-
   philosophy/production-system/ (archived at https://perma.cc/P2WB-JJLB)

06

Creative: the art and science of brand advertising

Creativity, the golden thread of our civilization

After my second child was born, I truly understood that a parent's affection must be shared equally, without favouritism among children. Each child has unique strengths, desires and feelings, but your love must remain equal. I've also learned that sticking to this principle can be challenging despite one's best efforts. The same applies in marketing levers where advertising and creativity often seem to be the 'favourite child'.

Creativity enchants us all, perhaps grabbing our attention more than it deserves. Creativity is our favourite child. This may be because creativity is an essential part of our human DNA.

Creativity is the golden thread of our civilization.

Creativity has been the golden thread of human progress, driving our evolution from cave paintings to complex digital AI models. As celebrated author Yuval Noah Harari describes in *Sapiens*,[1] our species thrived because of our unique ability to craft and believe in shared stories. This storytelling instinct is just as crucial today as it was in ancient times; marketers now harness it to build connections in an era of overwhelming choice. From Renaissance art to AI-generated content, creativity continuously adapted to the tools and technologies of the time, embedding itself into culture.

Creativity is everywhere, from visual arts to theatre, dance, music and interactive media. Today, with the rise of specialized AI models that generate art and stories, blending technology with imagination, creativity continues to be the force that shapes human lives.

In a marketing context, creativity fuels brand growth and establishes memory structures amid a flood of competing messages. Today's brands must balance the timeless appeal of creative storytelling with data-driven precision, making creativity a data-infused craft. This chapter will examine how to leverage creativity effectively, merging attention and emotional impact, simplicity and measurable results to make your brand stand out.

What makes a creative message effective? How can you enhance your effectiveness? What elements contribute to this impact? Let's explore the science behind advertising.

The art and science of advertising

The best advertising doesn't just sell products, it elevates brands to iconic status. Despite the rise of quantitative approaches, advertising still carries the aura of an art. Many students are drawn to marketing by the promise of creativity. And in a world increasingly shaped by artificial intelligence and technology, creativity may become our last true human stronghold.

Advertising is a mix of art and science.

Advertising works best when it combines creativity with scientific principles. The explosion of data sources and the rise of evidence-based decision-making have forced a scientific approach to measuring advertising.

Art is the 'idea' and science is the 'execution and measurement'.

Marketers can now accurately diagnose and refine campaigns like never before. Customer metrics and advanced analytics tools drive much of our creative effort, ensuring that each aspect of the art is optimized for the desired outcome. Yet despite this, advertising retains a mysterious, unquantifiable element. Sometimes, ads defy logic; they perform remarkably even when the initial data suggests otherwise. This magical creativity, the ability to evoke emotions, ignite curiosity or captivate an audience, transforms advertising from mere content into a true art form.

LESSON
Reality check: very few people believe in brand love.
Deal with it

A moment of honesty again, dear marketer. Despite your passion for brands, most people don't think about brands as much as you might hope they do. Throughout my career in marketing research, this realization has been the most difficult part for me in persuading my marketing colleagues.

For many years, the concept of 'brand love' was integral to our marketing education curricula. We loved to study, debate and reject it. Mid-career, I've come to terms with the fact that consumers rarely develop a deep emotional attachment to brands, one on par with their love for family, pets or favourite places.

While mythical exceptions like Harley-Davidson or Apple exist, people rarely feel a passionate connection to their detergent or toilet paper brand. Isn't that right? No one visualizes this concept better than Tom Fishburne, a.k.a. The Marketoonist.[2] To find his art related to the topic, go to his website and search for 'Inside the mind of the consumer'.

It's not that people don't think of brands. When exposed to brand messages, they might feel something and engage in an action but mostly ignore it. That's why brands build much-needed salience through immense consistency and repetition. But let's be honest: it's unlikely anyone will swap their private passions for a deep love for a car rental brand. Knowing this, why do we continue the pursuit of brand love as the pinnacle of brand success?

I like to think of brands as lighthouses, shining beacons in an ocean of choices. People appreciate them for their reliability, visibility and good reputation, not love. For this reason, the strategic decisions you make when establishing your brand are fundamental. Advertising follows and reinforces memory structures that guide consumers' decisions.

The goal? Influence their choice so much that, instinctively, they will reach and grab your product from the shelf. There are no grand declarations of love, just the quiet strength of being a salient signal of trust.

When did you last think about your brand as larger than life? Maybe it's time to review that. In a world where authenticity and trust matter more, it's time to let go of the dream of brand love and focus on building a brand consumers rely on. A good product at a great price.

Creativity is the #1 driver of growth in your marketing plan

In chemistry, a catalyst is an agent that provokes or speeds up significant reaction. When executed well, creativity can be a marketing catalyst, propelling your brand to new heights or sinking it to strange lows (see Figure 6.1). However, in a world fixated on ROIs and CPMs, the true essence of creativity is often overlooked.

Since its publication in 2017, a Nielsen research study[3] has been the go-to reference for highlighting the insight that creativity matters. Using data from

FIGURE 6.1 Sales contribution by marketing lever: the creative idea is by far the largest sales volume contributor across a wide range of communication campaigns in consumer-packaged goods

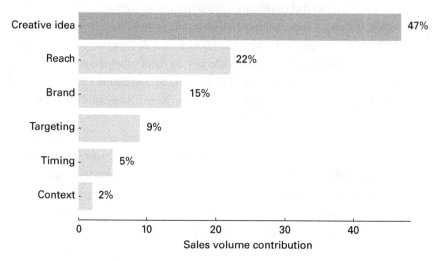

SOURCE Nielsen research[4]

consumer packaged goods brands, advertising (or creative) generates close to half of all sales contributions of all marketing communication activities. Ahead of other elements like reach, targeting or even brand, the role of creativity is so significant that it can make or break your campaigns.

Focus on creativity first!

Great advertising works across platforms and channels

Th value of the above insight (creative is #1) comes to life and is amplified in a multimedia world. A typical marketer is often overwhelmed by media choices. Should I invest in this platform or the other? Should I spend more on this non-skippable format or social media? Instead, a better use of their time would be to focus on the unbelievable power of creativity. Great creative tends to perform well across multiple platforms if its executions match with each format's specifics, influenced by viewer behaviours.

I am not arguing that media choices are not essential, far from it. However, once you establish your media channel and audience mix, success depends on one key factor: the quality of each creative message. Just imagine doubling your ROI with twice as effective creative at no extra cost. This is the potential creativity unlocks. Creativity is the driving force behind sales impact and mental availability growth.

Ineffective creative requires more media budget to perform

Throughout my years advising on creative effectiveness, I have observed the damage that ineffective advertising can cause to a brand. Poor creativity undermines both effectiveness, meaning the sales impact, and efficiency, referring to the return on advertising investment.

Similarly, great creative multiplies sales impact. In 2024, industry practitioners Adam Morgan, Jon Evans and Peter Field recognized this in their work 'The extraordinary cost of dull'.[5] This difference between non-effective and compelling creative has a significant monetary impact on advertisers' bottom lines. This research concludes that brands must over-invest in media to compensate for 'dullness' or poor effectiveness. A more straightforward path can be to craft compelling content, but that is easier said than done.

Countless case studies and research papers fill the databases of the IPA, or WARC (the World Advertising Research Center, a global authority on marketing effectiveness), showing creativity's impact on business success. Get inspired by them! Advertising is the heartbeat of effective marketing.

Advertising is an on/off switch for sales

Advertising's primary purpose is to enhance your brand's mental availability. Investing in advertising brings short-term benefits while creating long-term brand value and sales impact. However, when media investment stops, the positive effects of advertising diminish rapidly.

Various academic publications consistently highlight this insight, most often referencing the excellent work from the Ehrenberg Bass Institute.[6] The most cited research found that when businesses stop advertising for a year, sales decline by an average of 16 per cent. The longer a brand goes without advertising, the more significant the decline becomes.

Despite this widely accepted insight, the temptation of immediate profits often blinds decisions in marketing and finance departments. This leads to harmful decisions that impact long-term brand strength at the expense of short-term benefits.

Remember the duality of advertising impact: driving immediate sales and creating long-lasting memories.

But how does advertising work?

The primary function of marketing communication is to generate or sustain sales and profit margins by subtly increasing the likelihood of brand choice. This is accomplished by making the brand memorable and easy to think of and buy, fostering positive feelings and associations.

Effective advertising connects with audiences on two levels: broad-reach ads that are enjoyable and engaging, along with targeted activations that resonate as relevant and valuable (see Figure 6.2). By balancing these essential concepts, brands can maximize their campaign effectiveness.

Advertising's first goal is creating memory structures, or mental availability, for the brand. Although it sometimes educates or informs, particularly about new products, its main function is to remind the audience of the brand's existence. However, for me, advertising is effective if it accomplishes two things: it builds distinctive memory structures for the brand and drives attributable sales, which results in measurable business outcomes in the short and long term.

When simplified like an engineering process, the path of effective advertising primarily occurs between a screen and a brain. That's why managing advertising requires a deep understanding of this journey from screen to mind and finding ways to make this process smoother should be a priority for any advertiser.

FIGURE 6.2 The path from advertising impression to your customer's mind is made easy by three elements: attention, emotion and memory

When discussing effective advertising, marketers often assess the impact of storytelling and recall. However, the factors that streamline the memory encoding process are crucial: attention, emotion and memory ease. Optimize these elements and you'll enhance the likelihood of success.

All three concepts are not new to our age; they've been around since David Ogilvy started producing fantastic print work. I often recommend that any young marketer start their day by finding inspiration in his master-class book *Ogilvy on Advertising*.[7]

Effective advertising first grabs attention, sparks emotions and facilitates memory encoding through simple cognitive best practices.

THE THREE METRICS OF SUCCESS FOR ADVERTISING

Attention serves as the on/off switch for the advertising circuit: when it's off, the path to the mind ends here, but when it's on, you can move to the next stage. While attention is crucial for effectiveness, it alone does not ensure success. More attention is preferable to less attention.

Emotions serve as the oil that facilitates smoother brand encoding in memory. Most advertisers who uphold this belief prioritize emotional advertising messages that build brand equity over product-centric messages that emphasize various product benefits. Look at Super Bowl advertising campaigns: emotions are the hallmark of renowned advertising efforts.

Memory encoding occurs more rapidly when messages are simple. To better embed brands in customers' minds, successful advertisers reduce the complexity of their creative efforts to align with their audiences' busy minds and established cognitive processes. We don't want complicated, multi-layered stories, we just want to be entertained and informed straightforwardly. Simplicity always prevails.

How attention works

Human attention is a selective concentration process – a deliberate choice to focus on something while neglecting everything else. Over the past decade, this cognitive concept has gained popularity in discussions in the marketing industry. Driven by improved methods of measuring human attention, it is increasingly viewed as a valuable factor in evaluating ad effectiveness. I applaud this trend as it indicates a shift among marketers towards prioritizing people's reactions over platform metrics.

The concept of attention in marketing communication has remained consistent since the 1960s Mad Men era. Marketers continue to pursue audiences' attention in everything they do. What has changed is the approach to understanding how attention functions. We have shifted from traditional paper surveys to tracking and analysing eye movements using frontal-device cameras.

Based on this measurement revolution, attention became critical to understanding the effectiveness of advertising messages. From virtual Cannes fireside chats to Zoom conferences and countless white papers, everyone's discussing the so-called Attention Economy. In 2020, Karen Nelson-Field's seminal work, *The Attention Economy and How Media Works*,[8] attracted the attention of the marketing industry. A couple of years later, at the time of writing this book, the industry still debates a standardized definition and unified methods for measuring it.

Here's the reality: as you read this chapter, your attention is likely flickering. It's natural; we're constantly bombarded by information. Studies estimate that an average person is exposed to more than 5,000 brand messages daily. It sounds exaggerated, but even while I write this, I can spot multiple brand logos in front of me: Logitech, Dell, Apple, Sonos and Philips, all without shifting my gaze. Yet how many of these brands really capture our attention, let alone stick in our memory? Very few.

We've trained ourselves to ignore much of what we see or read. How can we expect consumers to focus on our advertising in such an environment? We know attention is limited, which is why the subject is so captivating. It's similar to the interest in climate change – we realize it's an issue, yet we have few insights into its mechanics. We know some messages break through, but we're also skilled at losing attention. Nevertheless, we continue to strive to capture it.

I'm genuinely encouraged by this renewed focus on attention. For the first time in years, the conversation isn't centred around the next technology (remember the metaverse or augmented reality opportunities), the latest platform (TikTok or Snap) or new formats (like Stories or Lenses). Instead, we're finally focusing on people's behaviours, measuring their reactions and adapting our advertising strategies to meet their needs. This people-centred approach is what marketing should always have prioritized.

Drawing on my experience in pioneering attention for creative testing, optimizing video assets for enhanced attention is a highly effective strategy. We began with the fundamental principle that more attention is always preferable to less. By accurately measuring attention second by second, advertisers can identify the current baseline of attention response and start making incremental adjustments to the creative, thereby improving each scene's attention score. Greater attention often leads to enhanced effectiveness.

Moving beyond one-off measurements when understanding attention patterns at scale enables businesses to develop more accurate predictive attention models. A predictive model of behavioural impact is a holy grail of creative effectiveness, but one that is within reach today.

ATTENTION TO BAD ADVERTISING IS DECLINING AT AN ALARMING RATE

When we increase our window of observation, most advertising signals point south. Attention to bad advertising is declining rapidly and it's clear why: people don't get moved by mediocre content anymore.

One solution is simple but challenging: marketers must develop exceptional ads to grab attention. Unfortunately, they need to fight not just with other advertisers anymore. The rise in influencer and user-generated content has raised the bar for traditional advertisers on quality. Advertisers are like salmon swimming against a powerful current of attention. We struggle against the flow, attempting to capture attention in a world where it is increasingly slipping away. The reality is harsh and there isn't much we can do to entirely reverse this trend.

We can precisely track where attention declines and present eye-catching analogies in our presentations, but we cannot change the direction in which attention flows. The troubling decrease in attention to advertising isn't solely due to poor content, it's based on a fundamental truth: time is a limited resource. We have only 24 hours in a day and people are trying to fit as much content as possible within that constraint.

In the past, when television was the main medium, there were 10 minutes of ads per hour, a manageable level of exposure. Today, we scroll through countless pages, news feeds and stories within an hour, skipping ads at dizzying speed. It's not that people intentionally pay less attention, it's that there are simply too many ads competing for a limited window of attention.

Despite this, brands still find ways to grow, campaigns continue to go viral and premium slots like the Super Bowl are sold out year after year. This indicates that while most ads are ignored, those that manage to break through do so disproportionately. The lesson is clear: to succeed in this saturated environment, marketers must create content that captures and retains attention. The standards are high and only the exceptional will thrive.

FIGHT POLITELY FOR CONSUMER ATTENTION

A series of recent business articles features alarming headlines that compare your audience's attention span to that of a goldfish.[9] I still wonder how the authors A/B tested that hypothesis. While I'm not sure if this is accurate, we, as an industry, need to capture our audience's attention with greater empathy.

If the digital advertising transformation has taught us one important lesson, it's that most people will go to great lengths to ignore, block or skip ads and our brand messages. Despite this ongoing trend, brands continue to be favoured and creativity remains a common topic of conversation around the office water cooler.

The exponential rise of ad blockers didn't kill the display advertising industry; the growth of skippable online video didn't eliminate YouTube advertising; and the increase in multitasking and second-screen viewing didn't diminish TV viewing. You might feel that all is lost. But just like in real life, the good advice I often hear is: *don't read the news, read the behavioural data.*

Is the advertising game over? I doubt it! It has become a bit more complicated, but winning is still possible. The persuasion game we play is now at an 'expert' difficulty level. Gone are the days when we could force non-skippable videos and hope for the best; it's time to put more effort into the content we create and the context in which we activate it.

Engaging visual content, appealing music and relevance will continue to capture people's attention. However, in the coming years, marketers will need to learn how to draw consumer attention with greater empathy and respect.

How emotions work

From a cognitive perspective, emotions are complex reactions that occur within the body and brain. External stimuli and the internal responses to these stimuli activate emotions. They lead to alterations in brain activity, hormone levels and physical responses such as heart rate and facial expressions. Emotions affect our behaviour and perception as strong signals influencing our mood and decision-making.

Emotions play a fascinating role in memory encoding in advertising. Advertising that evokes strong emotions, such as happiness, sadness, nostalgia or excitement, is more likely to build memory structures and be remembered and acted upon.[10] This is purely because emotions activate areas in the brain responsible for long-term memory formation, creating a stronger bond between the ad and the consumer.

Emotions are more than just feelings, they are robust connectors. Evergreen campaigns like Nike's 'Just Do It' or Apple's 'Think Differently' are perfect examples of how brands can build emotional bridges that make them memorable and relatable.

Focusing on emotions shifts attention from short-term metrics to understanding how an ad resonates on a deeper level. This builds stronger, lasting connections in brand memory. Let's explore some ways in which emotions enhance advertising effectiveness.

THE MAGIC OF POSITIVE EMOTIONS IN ADVERTISING

Let's first discuss why positive emotions are advertising's secret weapon. Even as news feeds bombard us with negative and alarming stories, advertising remains a beacon of optimism and there's real power in that position.

Consider Super Bowl ads. They're not just commercials, they're mood enhancers and mini-movies. Many people are looking ahead to the next Super Bowl ad break since advertising has become one of the few consistent sources of joy and inspiration. Strange as it may sound today, in the context of the proliferation of ad-skipping and blocking, advertising could become the premium entertainment of tomorrow.

Through my work with leading global neuroscientists, I've uncovered fascinating facts about emotions in advertising. Positive messages work better for brands. Probably because they tap into universal feelings like love, joy, pride, hope and belonging – emotions we all understand and welcome. When people feel good, they're more open to remembering your brand message.

The real magic is that effective advertising generates an emotional uplift. Your audience should feel uplifted after viewing your ad compared with before. It's like leaving them with a small gift: a smile, a warm sensation or a moment of inspiration. Combining this emotional high with your brand's distinctive assets creates powerful, lasting memory signals.

The best advice is always to ensure your brand is visible at moments of high emotional intensity. Notice how the most memorable ads, the ones people actually share online and want to watch again, almost always make you feel good. That's not a coincidence. That's the power of positive emotional advertising at work.

THE DARKER SIDE OF ADVERTISING: WHY NEGATIVE EMOTIONS ARE RISKY BUSINESS

I always thought that playing with negative emotions in advertising was like walking a tightrope. While most marketers stick to positive messages, we're sometimes tempted to tap into darker emotions. But here's why that's trickier than it seems.

The longer your audience experiences sadness, fear or anxiety, the more likely it is that these emotions will become permanently associated with your brand. Strong campaigns stumble simply because they lingered too long in the darkness. Remember those Covid ads? Every brand jumped into the sadness pool, showing empty streets and isolated people before tacking on a hopeful ending. The result? A forgettable blur of depressing content we now call 'Covid blandness'. It proved that shared suffering rarely translates to brand growth.

Negative emotions can create strong memory structures, sometimes too powerful. While your audience might remember your ad, they might also remember how it made them feel uncomfortable, sad or anxious. That's not the kind of brand association you want to build.

If you venture into negative territory, I suggest resolving the tension swiftly. Your story arc should spend minimal time in the valley of negative emotions before ascending to a positive peak. I've noticed that successful 'negative' ads focus primarily on the resolution, not the issue. Think of it as an emotional contrast: the darkness makes the light seem brighter. But never, ever leave your audience in that dark place.

How memory encoding works

Memory encoding is the brain's process of converting sensory inputs like visuals, sounds and emotions into a neural pathway that can be accessed later. Physiologically, this involves activating various parts of the brain, particularly the hippocampus and amygdala, which are central to the formation and storage of memories. The strength and emotional intensity of the stimuli play a crucial role in determining how effectively information is stored.

Over the years, I've observed a solid shift in video content consumption preferences. Viewers prefer quick snippets of entertainment over longer-form content, so the strength of the stimuli becomes critical. Ads that activate multiple senses and evoke strong emotions have a better chance of becoming memorable.

Ads that make us laugh, cry, or feel inspired are likelier to stick.

Memory encoding isn't confined to digital or video ads; storytelling can also happen effectively in out-of-home and print formats. Legendary adman David Ogilvy demonstrated the power of print advertising by crafting compelling stories that engaged readers' emotions in single-frame formats. Ogilvy's work shows that even static formats can activate the brain's memory systems when they tell a story that resonates deeply with the audience.

The lesson? Whether using a digital video, OOH or print, aim to create emotionally charged content that becomes a lasting memory. The simpler you can make it, the easier it is for the brain to process it.

MAKE IT SIMPLER

Simplicity in creative messages is more critical than ever. Your customers are bombarded with thousands of brand messages daily and don't have the time or patience to decipher complicated ads. They want quick, entertaining pieces, almost to provide instant gratification without requiring them to think too hard. This is why prioritizing a single storyline is essential. Unlike a movie with complex plots, effective advertising should convey a clear, straightforward message that viewers can instantly grasp. The simpler and more direct the story, the more likely it will engage and resonate.

The second key to simplification is asking yourself: What can be removed? Advertisers often overload their ads visually, including as much information as possible. Ads are not infomercials anymore. Eye-tracking studies consistently show that this approach confuses viewers. The brain can only process so much information simultaneously – the more cluttered the ad, the less likely viewers will remember the brand. By stripping the ad down to its essentials and removing unnecessary elements, you make it easier for the audience to digest and retain what matters most.

Lastly, don't attempt to integrate your brand too subtly into the narrative. Make it visible! Many advertisers fear too much branding will seem intrusive or distract from the story. However, using your brand prominently and frequently isn't just acceptable, it's effective. Research shows that viewers are more likely to remember ads where the brand is integrated naturally, clearly and frequently throughout the storyline. While appropriate for other forms of storytelling, subtlety is not always beneficial in advertising, where the main goal is to link to build a memory structure related to that brand. Your brand should be the anchor of the story, not an afterthought.

To ensure your campaign follows these insights, here are three questions to ask yourself:

1 Do you use a single storyline? If not, what unique story provides instant gratification to the viewer?

2 What can be removed to simplify message decoding? Review some of the visuals and text, especially if your end frame is too cluttered.

3 Is the brand prominently and frequently integrated? Do it! Ensure your brand is the story's anchor to maximize memory encoding.

The most effective ads prioritize simplicity. By focusing on a single storyline, eliminating visual and textual clutter and prominently featuring the brand, you ensure that your message is not just noticed but remembered.

WHY PEOPLE SKIP ADS – AND WHY THEY DON'T

A generalized trend every marketer is aware of these days is how consumers skip advertising. The river flows downstream, the hot air rises from the ground and viewers will avoid ads. It's the new normal in Adlandia. Please don't ignore the majority. But sometimes, people decide to watch, engage and be entertained. Why is it so?

Here are three reasons why people don't skip ads:

1 Because you've entertained them – advertising always claimed to be a form of entertainment, but this positioning might be more relevant today. We want to escape the never-ending news cycle, the worries and the anxiety of the times. We want a quick snack of fun. But we don't have hours anymore. In the past, we could dedicate a whole evening of uninterrupted viewing to a movie. Today, we've replaced that undivided attention with a split between our streaming and social media platforms. And one way to get our kick is to watch a six-second ad.

2 Because you've elicited emotions, preferably positive ones – we love a good story, and examples of good stories delivered in six seconds or less exist (anyone thinking about print or out of home here?).

3 Because they are not in front of the screen anymore – I know, it's an inconvenient truth. People don't necessarily skip advertising by clicking the skip button; they can move their eyes and attention in a different direction: to another device, another person or anywhere else than your wonderful creation.

Skipping ads is not an incurable behaviour but a growing one fuelled by our desire to dedicate our energy to multiple screen devices simultaneously. As a marketer, you spend extra hours developing your cinematic-style ad, which features product close-ups and manicured shots of the ideal consumer. You've added all the good stuff excessively: suspense at the beginning, emotional cues to trigger happiness and an excellent product testimonial at the end that glorifies the brand. Sadly, people skip advertising and do that as fast as they can.

Here are three reasons why people skip ads:

1 They don't have 30 seconds to learn about your brand story; they don't spend that much time watching their best friend's Insta Story.

2 For many, advertising is just an annoyance preventing access to the desired cat viral video. Around 80 per cent of viewers skip advertising before it finishes on YouTube.

3 They don't like to be tricked into watching a video, so don't be rude: show your brand early. Don't think they won't notice this is advertising.

Skipping advertising takes many forms: you can click the skip button after five seconds on YouTube, scroll faster in your newsfeed, swipe on Instagram or TikTok, open another tab on your browser or reload the web page in the hope that the ad will go away or even focus attention on another device entirely.

I don't have a solution for fighting this behaviour and I don't think you should fight it. Instead, you should understand it and make elegant choices about how to work with it.

How to best measure creative effectiveness

The best predictor of business outcome is the outcome.

The best predictor of a business outcome is the outcome itself. That's why measuring sales impact is synonymous with creative effectiveness. It provides marketing relevance, communicates in the boardroom language and positions advertising as a concrete value-creation process.

Measuring the sales benefits of advertising is a troublesome task. However, just because the impact is often harder to assess, it doesn't mean you should give up. Fight for it. I'll show you how I did it.

Beginning with the decision is where all great data analytics approaches truly shine. We measure creative effectiveness because we aim to make changes, learn, and adapt our creative strategies and executions moving forward. Always consider what changes you will implement in your business tomorrow rather than focusing first on the data you have available.

The best reason for measuring advertising or creative effectiveness is to guide present and future creative processes (see Table 6.1). In this context, the three most common decision points are:

• Stage one: During creative development, evaluate whether you are on an engaging creative path or need to start a new development process. The best tools for this evaluation explore memory structures and analyse standard cognitive processes related to the developed concepts. How the brain processes information is a key factor to consider here. Always be careful not to make decisions based on small sample sizes that do not represent

TABLE 6.1 Three creative decisions

	During creative developments	Just before go-live	After campaign
Decisions	Continue/Adapt/ Re-start	Tweak execution	Use again/Drop
Questions	Is this an engaging creative route, or do we need to start fresh?	Is the execution grabbing attention, emotions and is optimized to be effective?	Is the campaign driving sales and mental availability?
Method	Exploratory	Pre-testing	In-market testing

your entire audience. Some brands may opt to skip this stage and conduct a limited market test to gather real-world signals.

- Stage two occurs after final production and before the ad goes live in the market. At this stage, pre-testing is crucial and the best solutions accurately measure memory encoding ease while also serving as indicators of future sales potential. Think of attention, emotions and lack of confusion. However, it's important to note that some ads may fail in pre-testing but perform excellently in the market. This is where the artistry of advertising truly comes into play.

- Stage three is the in-market execution phase, which sometimes overlaps with pre-testing due to advancements in real-time and automated creative executions, such as DCO. Over the years, the line between pre-testing and post-testing has blurred, with a consistent focus on measuring advertising effectiveness through in-market sales impact. At Mars, we have relied on this approach for over 13 years to guide our decisions and promote a culture of creative excellence. While assessing the potential for effectiveness in earlier stages, stage three is where creative effectiveness is ultimately measured.

As stated previously, the role of advertising is to drive short- and long-term business conversions and build memory structures. We can detail what kind of measurements answer the above three questions below:

- Measure sales. Whether you call it sales, conversions, business impact or any other KPI you've chosen to align your advertising efforts with your business objectives, measuring sales is one of the most challenging yet rewarding methods to guide your creative processes.

Depending on your industry, accessing sales data and linking creativity to outcomes can vary in difficulty. My experience in consumer packaged goods indicates that unless you have access to comprehensive conversion data for your brand, as a D2C e-commerce brand does, accurately measuring creative effectiveness relies on external parties that gather this data for you. The most common sources of this data include household-level panels, loyalty card data sets and other purchase aggregators. In many instances, the availability of data is often more challenging than the analytics that follow.

- Measure memory encoding. Whether you call it memory encoding, distinctive memory structures or salience, measuring how well advertising builds your brand in consumers' minds is just as important as tracking sales.

But since reading consumers' minds is still the stuff of science fiction, the best way to understand how memory structures are formed is to measure the proxies – the three elements that guide the path from an ad to memory. The most common measurements in this area are attention, which can be represented as the percentage of attentive seconds out of the total duration of the ad or the percentage of the sample that pays attention to the ad for at least X seconds; emotions, which could be measured as the percentage of the sample that responds with a certain emotional reaction to the ad; and memory, which focuses on reducing confusion. Confusion is an intriguing measurement that closely reflects how humans process visual and auditory messages. Advertising should always strive for low confusion, which reflects simplicity and understanding.

What about brand equity? If you've read my blog or follow me on LinkedIn, you likely know I'm not a big fan of brand equity measurements. Brand equity metrics promise to encapsulate in a single number all your efforts regarding your brand's mental and physical availability. Rarely does a single campaign affect any brand equity for established brands. So why do we hold brand equity measurement in such high regard? It's probably because it's easy and inexpensive to implement. However, since it's almost free, you shouldn't prioritize it over gold standards like sales and memory.

Five hot topics in advertising excellence

Throughout my career, I've attended various industry events where I've encountered myths and stories surrounding the role of advertising. Here are five that frequently steal the spotlight. I expect you may disagree with some of my bold conclusions; that's perfectly fine. In return, I challenge you to open your mind, embrace an opposing viewpoint and then determine what is best for your brand.

1 People don't care about your brand anniversary

The widespread myth that brand anniversary campaigns drive customer engagement and preference is probably fundamentally flawed. Most customers don't care about a brand's age – they care about what it offers them now, its value compared to price, innovation features and quality.

Brand anniversary campaigns are often more about the brand's self-indulgence than customer relevance. When brands temporarily shift their creative efforts away from proven campaigns to communicate 'X years of history', they take an unnecessary risk. Consistency is a crucial factor in advertising and when brands deviate from their established visual cues and messaging, they risk confusing their audience and diluting the impact of their core communications. It's hard to be consistent with a one-off celebration of an anniversary.

To leverage your brand's history, subtly integrate it into your existing campaigns to demonstrate how tradition supports innovation. But remember, your buyers prioritize consistency and emotional connection messaging. After all, the buyers of your brand care much more about the future of your brand offers rather than the past.[11]

Don't let an anniversary campaign sidetrack your focus from the creative elements that drive growth.

2 Advertising wears out

High-quality content endures longer than you might think. Marketers frequently rush to the next campaign due to personal boredom instead of authentic consumer insight. Think again!

After 20 years in marketing communication roles, I have a revelation. We often rush to retire our successful advertising campaigns, and I admit I've been guilty of this myself. The truth is, there's surprisingly little evidence that effective ads actually lose their impact.

I remember sitting in countless meetings where we pushed for new creative simply because we were tired of seeing our own ads. You know the feeling: you've spent months crafting that perfect campaign video, watched it a hundred times during production and now you can't stand looking at it anymore. But that's not how your audience experiences the execution. Months after launching the campaign, while you may have viewed your ad hundreds of times, your average customer has likely seen it only once or twice, perhaps during a quick glance at their phone or while scrolling through social media.

My practical advice is to verify your data before extracting insights from a successful campaign. Are your metrics genuinely declining? Is consumer feedback truly negative? Or are you simply craving something new? In my experience, when an ad truly resonates with your audience, its effectiveness often exceeds our internal expectations.

Your successful creative work is more like a fine wine – it may actually improve over time, especially considering the cumulative memory structures it builds. Trust the numbers, not your personal boredom.

3 Halo effects are a superpower

One of the holy grails of marketing communication is the desire to employ halo effects to our brand's advantage. It's like possessing a marketing super-power – when executed correctly, it creates a ripple effect that influences preferences across your entire brand portfolio. But what exactly is a halo effect? A halo refers to the tendency for positive impressions of a person, company, brand or product in one area to sway one's opinions or feelings in another area. This concept extends beyond marketing into psychology and even religion.

In advertising, the halo effect refers to the expectation that attributes recognized in one area will influence consumer opinions and behaviours in another. Brands expect halo effects, which is why they spend substantial budgets on celebrity endorsements, use popular singalong music or sponsor significant sporting events despite the challenge of measuring return on investment.

One of the advantages of having precise measurements of the impact of advertising on sales is being able to demonstrate that halo effects exist and influence the point of purchase.

Here's what I've learnt about creating successful halo effects: to enhance effectiveness across the range of products, your campaign should utilize the same distinctive assets that are recognized throughout the brand, focus on the brand's unique proposition rather than promoting the extension and ensure it captures attention during moments of brand presence.

In a successful advertising campaign, your most recognized product in the brand range will often create a halo effect for the lesser-known products – meaning it drives more sales of items you don't directly advertise. The pinnacle of halo effects is the total category halo. This occurs when your advertising benefits the entire category. It is incredibly challenging to execute and plan for, but it provides a significant boost for multiple brands within the category. The more your brand dominates the category, the greater the benefits you receive.

Like every other advertising trick, there is no magic bullet. Advertising is a mix of art and science. However, there is a solid recipe for achieving halo impact: create a highly effective advertising campaign. I've never witnessed an ineffective ad generating a halo.

When I say George Clooney, which brand comes to mind first?

4 Product line extensions require dedicated creatives

There's a common myth among marketers that product line extensions require their own advertising campaigns to reach busy customers and spark growth. In most cases, prioritizing your core equity advertising is often a more effective and efficient approach, especially when evaluated from an ROI perspective.

Let's face it: most consumers who are aware of your brand recognize only your core product, the hero that built your brand's reputation. Reinforcing the core through an equity campaign, especially when using high-reach media channels, ensures you tap into the established familiarity and trust. This approach delivers the best return on investment because the core product has the scale and if executed successfully, it could enhance the effectiveness of other products under the same brand.

Developing advertising for product extensions is often an excuse marketers use to appear 'busy' during the creative development process, even when it is not needed. While it's exciting to put your signature on a new campaign, it is essential to consider whether this will create incremental value or simply add complexity. When marketers focus too much on line extensions, they risk diluting the core brand's message and spreading their resources too thin. Temporarily replacing your established core brand equity ad with an untested line extension ad presents a significant risk to your brand. Stay vigilant and manage that risk!

In some extreme cases, product extension advertising may be necessary, especially when it enhances the brand's physical availability. Tailored communication might be justified if a line extension is introduced to boost the brand's presence in a retail channel or to enter a new distribution channel. At times, it could even act as a negotiation tool with your distributor for listing. Maintaining consistency with your core brand identity cues is essential in this context. Any product extension advertisement must feel like an extension of the brand advertisement, using either the established brand campaign (if available), familiar visual elements (distinctive assets and colours), or semiotics and symbols that relate back to the core identity.

If a balanced approach is necessary, prioritize core brand equity campaigns on high-reach channels and reserve product extension advertising for closer-to-purchase points, such as retail media or in-store displays. This ensures that core messaging achieves broad reach while line extensions enhance physical availability where it matters most.

Remember, consistency in leveraging your brand's distinctive assets is crucial. Whether it's your core product or a line extension, these assets are your most potent tools in building and maintaining long-term brand strength.

5 The use of celebrities for reach and brand fame

Celebrity endorsements are a powerful marketing tool, effectively influencing consumer choices by leveraging the star power of famous individuals.

A study by Wharton professors Elizabeth Johnson and Michael Platt[12] explored the neurological responses to celebrity advertising. They revealed that celebrities can capture larger consumer attention, enhancing brand recall and purchase intent. This effect is rooted in psychological and evolutionary factors, where humans are naturally drawn to familiar and admired figures. However, the study also highlights a potential downside: the celebrity's prominence can sometimes overshadow the product, leading to a focus on the individual rather than the brand itself.

The endorser's fame guarantees that a broad audience can see your brand message, tapping into their established fan base and amplifying your brand's exposure. They often create a halo effect (see above), where the positive traits associated with the celebrity transfer to the brand. When executed effectively, this can be an influential tool – for example, linking a luxury brand with a graceful and respected figure like a movie star can elevate the brand's prestige. However, this halo effect can also have a downside – when celebrities make mistakes, those negative perceptions can also be transferred to your brand. It's a risk that marketers must consider carefully.

Linking your brand to a celebrity is not a one-off decision. In successful cases, a long-term commitment is required. If a scandal or controversy arises, your brand needs to react quickly, putting its future first. This could mean either terminating the partnership or publicly distancing the brand from the individual's actions. Agile, well-thought-out crisis management strategies protect the brand's long-term reputation.

Compared with traditional advertising costs, celebrity endorsements can be quite expensive and their ROI is often challenging to measure. Unless the collaboration is part of a long-term strategy – like George Clooney's iconic partnership with Nespresso – it can be tough to justify the expense. If you're thinking about using a celebrity for a one-time campaign, reconsider. Short-term celebrity campaigns seldom create a strong, lasting connection between the audience and the brand, making it hard to see a tangible return on investment.

What would you do if, after all the effort and budgets invested your effectiveness measurement revealed that the campaign wasn't working? Many brands face this reality, demonstrating that the mere presence of a celebrity does not guarantee success. It is essential to remember that the brand's story and message should always take priority. The celebrity should enhance the message, not overshadow it.

In conclusion, although celebrities can be valuable assets, their use requires a long-term commitment, careful brand alignment and continuous measurement. Brands should stay flexible and prepared to pivot, making sure that the celebrity consistently aligns with the brand's core values.

Applied engineering for creative effectiveness

Engineering Marketing Tool 7: Systems engineering for advertising excellence

Creating excellence in advertising isn't only about bursts of sporadic high-impacting creativity or isolated campaigns that win awards on the red carpet at Cannes. It's about building a consistent, scalable system that maximizes effectiveness and insights. It's precisely what I built at Mars for over 10 years.

Systems engineering offered me a robust methodology to establish an advertising system that drove results through continuous improvement. Here's how it can also work for you.

Systems engineering is an interdisciplinary approach that designs, manages and optimizes complex systems by understanding how various components interact and influence one another. It's about creating a cohesive structure where every part works towards a unified objective. In advertising, this means treating every aspect of your creative output – campaigns, media choices, messaging and measurement – as interconnected elements of a larger system aimed at driving brand success.

Adopting a systems engineering mindset in advertising means building a culture that sees creative work not as isolated projects but as components of an ongoing, cohesive effort. Consider your advertising as a system where each campaign contributes to a larger strategy, utilizing consistent metrics and insights to generate learning.

This system should be built around your organization's core values, brands and distinctive assets. By aligning everyone in the organization – marketing creative teams, media planners, finance and data experts – under a unified goal, you ensure that every ad execution reinforces the same story, delivering consistent results.

For example, at Mars, the advertising system aligns all creative work around core brand elements with a continuous testing, learning and optimization cycle. By measuring each campaign on the same effectiveness metric, sales impact, communicating the results broadly and ensuring follow-ups are happening immediately, we spun the wheel of effectiveness faster.

But don't trust my word for it – here's a four-step-by-step approach to building an advertising system using systems engineering principles for your brand and organization:

- Define the KPI and don't change it. Establish clear, measurable objectives for your advertising. I prefer sales lift, but you can choose KPIs aligning with your business goals.

- Design a consistent framework for measuring every campaign, from concept development to execution and post-campaign analysis. Ensure everyone follows the same guidelines, leveraging your brand's distinctive assets to create coherence across all touchpoints.

- Implement continuous testing and optimization. Incorporate testing (A/B testing, pre-testing) as an ongoing practice. Each campaign should be a learning opportunity to refine your messaging, creatives and media choices. This iterative process builds a data-driven foundation where insights are continuously gathered, analysed and applied to future campaigns.

- Build a collaborative culture. Systems engineering flourishes through collaboration. Bring together creatives, media strategists and data analysts to ensure every campaign gains from a cross-functional perspective. A cohesive team can respond quickly to market changes and optimize campaigns in real-time, boosting agility and effectiveness.

Call to action: embrace systems thinking in advertising. To elevate your advertising game, start viewing it as a system. Establish a structured process, leverage your brand's unique assets and foster a collaborative culture focused on continuous improvement. By doing so, you'll create a resilient, scalable advertising machine that not only reacts to market trends but also drives them. Systems engineering isn't just for engineers – it's a powerful tool that can transform your marketing strategy, ensuring consistent success and long-term brand growth.

INDUSTRY EXPERT CONTRIBUTION
Creative tech: Anastasia Leng

The marketing and advertising industry has a significant blind spot regarding ROI: creative. Although 84 per cent of marketing content is visual,[13] it's the least understood and analysed element.

In the 2020s, several studies have repeatedly demonstrated that creative is the largest contributor to sales uplift (i.e. Nielsen, at 47 per cent[14]) and the most important lever in brand profitability. All of these beg the question: Why aren't marketers focusing more on the creative?

The father of modern business management, Peter Drucker, once claimed that only what gets measured gets managed. Creative content has been notoriously difficult to measure systematically and objectively without an industry-wide metric that can serve as a proxy for creative excellence. If brands aren't measuring their ad creative in a scalable and objective way, how can they know what steps they can take to enhance and make it work harder for them?

The first step towards measuring creative excellence is to know your Creative Quality Score (CQS). Hundreds of studies from millions of impressions have demonstrated that there are indeed some basic creative first principles (like the need to brand your asset upfront or make your message accessible in a sound-off environment) that have repeatedly been proven to move the needle on both sales and brand growth in a statistically meaningful way.

While these learnings are platform-specific, they emphasize the need for a Creative Quality Score. This cognitive shortcut provides a quick health check into whether your creative is set up for success while giving marketers control over their ability to scale content confidently. In the last three years, KPIs like the Creative Quality Score have been systematically embedded into global content workflows of major consumer packaged goods companies like Nestlé, Bayer and Mars, resulting in impressive effectiveness and efficiency gains.[15]

An increase in the Creative Quality Score is statistically correlated with a decrease in CPM and an increase in brand recall and ROAS. Yet the average Creative Quality Score is 28 per cent, which means 70 per cent-plus of creative work is inefficient – this can mean millions in sub-optimal advertising spend. Will optimizing for CQS alone make a creative stand out with your audience? No. Creative quality is necessary but not sufficient, and while it'll help you dramatically improve your content efficiency and effectiveness, this alone won't win you any awards.

Technology is advancing our ability to measure creative excellence in a highly brand-specific way. Those who nail down creative quality are speeding further along their creative excellence journey, tracking everything from brand consistency to the diversity of their casting choices to how and how frequently they talk about their ESG (environmental, social and governance) commitments. By making this tracking near real-time and always-on, they're upgrading their existing marketing models and customizing their GenAI systems, thereby gaining a largely untapped competitive advantage that allows them to demystify creative performance, systematically incorporate those learnings into their production systems and measure the most critical part of their marketing mix. And that's a recipe for success in an AI-first world.

ANASTASIA LENG

Anastasia Leng is the founder and CEO of CreativeX, a technology company that powers creative decision-making for the world's biggest brands. Prior to CreativeX, Anastasia co-founded Hatch, one of *Time* magazine's Top 10 Startups to Watch in New York and one of the four most innovative retail companies according to the National Retail Federation. Prior to Hatch, she spent more than five years at Google, where she worked on every ad tech and analytics product, led entrepreneurship efforts in Europe, the Middle East and Africa (EMEA) and was responsible for early-stage partnerships for Google Voice, Chrome and Wallet.

FIVE IDEAS TO TAKE WITH YOU AFTER READING THIS CHAPTER

1   Advertising is a mix of art and science. Your goal is to create emotionally impactful yet measurable campaigns.

2   Focus on capturing attention, evoking emotion and memory encoding techniques in every ad.

3   Keep your messaging simple to facilitate building memory structures linked to your brand.

4   Ditch the 'brand love' myth, aiming for emotions and trust instead.

5   Measure creative effectiveness continuously and refine to optimize results at every stage of the creative development process.

The art and science of brand communication: a final reflection

All right, now you have a strong understanding of the role of creativity in building communication effectiveness.

Creative effectiveness goes beyond simply producing famous ads. The goal is to ensure that those ads resonate with your audience and deliver short- and long-term business outcomes. You can apply this understanding to improve your creative strategies.

Below are three questions to help you make the most of this chapter. Ask them often to make more effective decisions for your brand. As always, there are no right or wrong answers. Simply thinking about these concepts more will help you internalize them better. And for an added learning boost, consider discussing them with a colleague or a friend.

THREE QUESTIONS TO MASTER CREATIVITY

1   How can I know that my advertising captures attention, evokes emotion and builds a memorable mental association for our brand?

2   Are we focusing on creativity as a catalyst for growth or are we falling into the trap of pursuing 'brand love' when reliability and trust might matter more?

3   Is our message simple enough to cut through the noise yet powerful enough to drive distinctiveness across platforms and stick in the memory?

ONE MORE THING...

Want to stay effective and ahead of the curve? Scan this QR code to access extra content and updates online.

Notes

1 Harari, Y N (2015) *Sapiens*, Harper, London
2 The Marketoonist (2014) Inside the mind of the consumer, https://marketoonist.com/2014/01/mind-of-the-consumer.html (archived at https://perma.cc/X8AB-S26C)
3 The Nielsen Company (2022) When it comes to advertising effectiveness, what is key? https://www.nielsen.com/insights/2017/when-it-comes-to-advertising-effectiveness-what-is-key/ (archived at https://perma.cc/6ZVQ-MYGF)
4 The Nielsen Company (2022) When it comes to advertising effectiveness, what is key? https://www.nielsen.com/insights/2017/when-it-comes-to-advertising-effectiveness-what-is-key/ (archived at https://perma.cc/FSE2-WCSM)
5 System1 (no date) The extraordinary cost of dull, https://system1group.com/the-extraordinary-cost-of-dull (archived at https://perma.cc/EN9X-Y6ZJ)
6 Hartnett, N (2021) Ehrenberg-Bass Q&A: What happens when brands stop advertising? https://marketingscience.info/ehrenberg-bass-qa-what-happens-when-brands-stop-advertising/ (archived at https://perma.cc/68LJ-XT7B)
7 Ogilvy, D (1984) *Ogilvy on Advertising*, Random House, USA
8 Nelson-Field, K (2020) *The Attention Economy and How Media Works: Simple truths for marketers*, Springer, Singapore
9 For example, Time (2009) You now have a shorter attention span than a goldfish, https://time.com/3858309/attention-spans-goldfish/ (archived at https://perma.cc/7ZEC-FKDZ)
10 Mizerski, R W and White, J D (1986) Understanding and using emotions in advertising, *Journal of Consumer Marketing*, p. 57
11 Geoghegan, A (2020) Brand birthdays can help you realign for the future as well as celebrate the past, https://www.marketingweek.com/andrew-geoghegan-brand-birthdays-realign-future-celebrate-past/ (archived at https://perma.cc/G4F6-EJYC)

12 Knowledge at Wharton (2023) The Marketing Psychology Behind Celebrity Endorsements, https://knowledge.wharton.upenn.edu/article/the-marketing-psychology-behind-celebrity-endorsements/ (archived at https://perma.cc/E934-9DK4)

13 AdNews (2022) The crisis in creative effectiveness has new issues, https://www.adnews.com.au/news/the-crisis-in-creative-effectiveness-has-new-issues (archived at https://perma.cc/FCP6-JYGK)

14 The Nielsen Company (2022) When it comes to advertising effectiveness, what is key? https://www.nielsen.com/insights/2017/when-it-comes-to-advertising-effectiveness-what-is-key/ (archived at https://perma.cc/66U5-7DA4)

15 CPG case studies, https://www.creativex.com/resources/casestudies (archived at https://perma.cc/T57S-XWZC)

07

Research: the science of measuring marketing effectiveness

Why you can't manage what you don't measure

In marketing, measurement and research aren't just my favourite disciplines, they're superpowers. When used effectively, they transform gut decisions into strategic insights. Without measurement, you're not managing, you're guessing.

Solid customer research serves as a foundation for any effective marketing strategy. Once the strategy is implemented in the market, marketing research provides the framework for assessing all your decisions regarding tactics and execution.

What do we mean by an effective marketing research approach? It involves knowing when to ask questions and when to observe behaviours, identifying which metrics are relevant enough to serve as KPIs and transforming numbers into stories that can more effectively persuade stakeholders.

Measuring marketing effectiveness involves balancing three key factors: data, people and narrative. Although we seem overwhelmed by data, many of us are sinking in insights. Only the strongest narratives will reveal the insights that persuade people. Read this chapter to learn how to improve your research methods, explore the best practices I've relied on and uncover the science of understanding your customers.

You will find ideas on thinking holistically about marketing effectiveness across strategy, product, pricing, media, creative and business impact. Enjoy!

Five proven steps to smarter marketing research

Improving your marketing research starts with a mindset shift. From OR to AND. To adopt a more customer-centric approach, you should measure what matters equally for both your customers and the business. Figure 7.1 outlines five steps to improve your marketing research.

FIGURE 7.1 Steps to improve your research: the five steps focus on prioritizing decisions, expertise, KPIs, behaviours and empathy. Listen, understand and walk in your customers' shoes to uncover what drives their actions

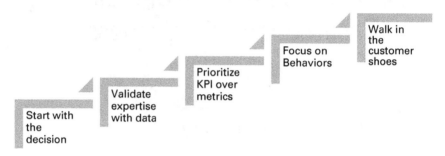

1 Always start with the business decision

Are you using research to illuminate the path forward or to confirm existing beliefs? I once read a marketing research presentation that featured an unforgettable image of a drunk person leaning against a lamp post. The caption read, 'Using the lamppost for support rather than illumination.'

It perfectly captures a common issue in marketing: we use research to support existing opinions rather than to bring to light meaningful insights. We frame questions to confirm our beliefs and celebrate when responses align with our expectations. Concept validation, for example, is often viewed as a success when it merely supports pre-existing ideas. However, accurate research does more than validate – it challenges, provokes and broadens our understanding. It's not about reinforcing what we think we know, it's about discovering what we don't.

We often start with the data we already have instead of focusing on the business decisions we can influence. When research begins with what's convenient to measure rather than what truly matters, the outcome is often shallow insights and answers to questions that no one is asking.

To make research actionable, always ask, 'What decision am I informing here?' This clarity transforms research from a passive exercise into a powerful decision-making tool. Begin with a specific business decision and concentrate on data sources that yield insights to inform the next actions. This could involve enhancing a campaign ad, determining whether to launch a product or identifying new trends.

Let's stop leaning on research like a drunk on a lamp post. Let research illuminate our future decisions.

2 Use data to strengthen your expertise, not replace it

Data insight is a superpower that helps marketers gain an accurate, deep understanding of people, their actions, thoughts and behaviour. The best researchers uncover insights that address consumer pain points and spark business opportunities. These insights are often crafted based on the expertise of the researcher, who is best positioned to explore data, ask the best questions, observe the right behaviour and draw conclusions.

Today, the role of the insights function is under scrutiny. The abundance of data and advanced analytics has created the perception that anyone can be a researcher. Many organizations are reorganizing their insights teams, moving them into IT-driven departments based on the assumption that data alone can reveal everything. However, while data is crucial, true consumer understanding goes beyond numbers. It necessitates human expertise to interpret patterns, derive meaning and validate experience-based truths with evidence.

I learnt this first hand over a decade ago when I was tasked with reshaping Mars' quantitative research approach for advertising effectiveness. Without a formal research background, I had to quickly absorb foundational knowledge, master industry jargon and understand new methods and product categories. That experience reinforced a critical truth: research is not just about data, it is about the experience that frames it. While AI, automation and behavioural analytics continue to evolve, human psychology remains remarkably consistent. Insight is still a social science, no matter how advanced the tools become.

The future of marketing insights will not be shaped by data collection but by the ability to frame data with expertise and context. The best insights emerge from a mix of experience and evidence. Technology enhances our understanding, but human intuition makes the connections. Those who master this balance will drive the most impactful marketing decisions.

Insights = experience-based truths confirmed by data.

3 Focus on KPIs that drive growth, not vanity metrics

If you want to grow your brand, focus on what truly matters: sales. Previous sales and conversions are the strongest predictors of future growth. Sales impact serves as the ultimate KPI that informs better decisions. Yet many marketers fall back on softer metrics like purchase intent, click-through rates or viewability. Maybe because they are easier to measure, but they are mostly background noise unless they directly link to a transaction.

In my experience, sales impact is the ultimate measure of marketing effectiveness. Not only does it reveal which campaigns drove action, it also fuels ROI calculations, something the C-suite cares about. Metrics like purchase intent may seem useful, but they have significant flaws. If you ask 100 people whether they will buy a product, very few will say no. Especially in a research setting, people tend to want to sound agreeable and optimistic. However, claiming they will buy something costs them nothing and rarely translates into actual purchases. Ten solid sales uplift studies are far more valuable than thousands of 'almost-sales' surveys.

Tracking sales is not always easy, especially in categories like CPG, where individual-level data can be difficult to obtain. But even with these challenges, getting closer to actual sales outcomes leads to sharper insights and better decisions. Aggregating data at the store or regional level dilutes the signal, so precision is key.

Sales is the most important KPI. Proxy metrics like purchase intent and click-through rates may appear to be shortcuts, but they can often be misleading. Always verify the correlation between any metric you monitor and the actual business outcome.

Real growth comes from understanding what drives actual purchases, not what people claim they will do. It may be harder to measure, but prioritizing sales impact leads to better outcomes.

MOST PEOPLE DON'T OBSESS OVER YOUR BRAND LIKE YOU DO

Normal people rarely think about your brand. They aren't marketers, they're real people. They don't analyse taglines, debate logos or reflect on your mission statement. They buy what meets their needs and move on.

I keep a Marketoonist[1] cartoon in my office that serves as a reminder. It depicts a human brain filled with thoughts about family, work and life – but no space for brands. The truth is, most people wouldn't notice if your brand disappeared tomorrow. A UK study by Havas[2] found that 81 per cent of brands wouldn't be missed if they vanished overnight.

People are overwhelmed by the sheer volume of brands, products and messages they encounter daily. They don't ignore brands because they dislike them but because they don't need a personal connection to every product they use. A few brands like Harley-Davidson and Apple achieve cult status, but they are the exceptions. For most, deep emotional attachment isn't part of the equation.

And that's okay. Accepting that your brand isn't central to consumers' lives is liberating. It shifts your focus to what really matters: solving real problems and delivering value. Functional loyalty – consistently meeting needs – matters more than chasing brand love for a commodity like shampoo or chewing gum.

Not every brand needs Harley-Davidson's playbook. Focus on being indispensable in your category and your brand will succeed where it matters most: in the real lives of real consumers.

4 Forget opinions, follow the data: why behaviour wins

One of the most valuable lessons in marketing is this: what customers do matters more than what they say. If you want to predict future success, focus on behaviour. Actions reveal the truth, while opinions can be misleading.

I relied heavily on survey data early in my career, assuming it provided a direct view of customer intentions. But time and again I saw a disconnect between what people said and what they did. Asking consumers if they would buy a product after seeing an ad rarely matched actual sales. Responses are impacted by different biases and even how the questions are asked.

People often respond with what sounds suitable or aspirational rather than what reflects their actual behaviour. Let's not even discuss the potential for digital surveys to be frauded by non-human respondents. While applicable in some cases, surveys should never be the primary decision-making tool.

Actions matter more than words. Past behaviour is the best predictor of future actions. If you want to understand customers, analyse what they actually do: what they buy, how they engage with ads and what drives conversions.

However, not all behaviours are equally valuable. Avoid chasing vanity metrics like click-through rates because they are easy to measure. Clicks don't always pay the bills. The focus should be on behavioural signals that lead to tangible business outcomes.

Shift to a behaviour-first mindset. Observing real consumer behaviour takes effort. It requires tracking engagement across digital, retail and social channels. But the payoff is worth it. Trust what people do, not what they say.

5 Try walking in your customers' shoes

Dear marketer, when was the last time you experienced online advertising the way your customers do? Imagine browsing with an ad blocker installed.

Millions of consumers are doing that today and it's a clear reflection of how they feel about online advertising.

Ad blockers are a prime example of 'hockey stick' growth, a slow start followed by explosive adoption. Once niche software, ad blockers are now used by one in three[3] internet users globally, with massive adoption among 18–30-year-olds in the Western world. Years of intrusive pop-ups, cluttered pages and irrelevant ads have driven people to take matters into their own hands. The message is loud and clear: consumers are fed up. This trend is emblematic of a more significant issue facing the advertising industry: the consumer pushback against advertising.

So, what does this mean for you as a marketer? It means it's time to step into your customers' shoes:

1 Install an ad blocker yourself. Experience the internet as many customers do: empty ad spaces and frustration-free browsing. This firsthand perspective can be an eye-opener and may lead you to rethink your approach to ad placements.

2 Work with your media agency. Understand which platforms and sites are more resilient to ad blockers and collaborate on tactics to protect your media budget while delivering meaningful reach.

3 Re-evaluate your strategy. Bold advertising doesn't have to be disruptive. If your ad would make you install an ad blocker, reconsider it. Respectful, well-crafted ads can win back consumer trust.

Ad blocking is an explicit behaviour of your customers. To stay relevant, don't fight it – learn from it. Walking in your customers' shoes will help you create better experiences, build trust and ensure your marketing resonates instead of repels.

Demystifying marketing effectiveness: a practical guide

Not all evidence is created equal.

In marketing effectiveness research, the strength of your conclusions depends on the quality of your data. From anecdotal observations to gold-standard systematic reviews, understanding the hierarchy of evidence ensures your decisions are backed by trustworthy insights. Here is my rough guide to the most common research methods. Consider this framework any time you measure effectiveness across the spectrum of marketing levers.

The seven levels of evidence (inspired by medical sciences)

1   Anecdotal and expert opinions: Anecdotes are personal experiences or observations, often subjective and unrepresentative. Though informed, expert opinions lack the rigor of scientific studies and should be supported by strong data evidence.

2   Animal and cell studies (pre-clinical): Animal studies and tests on isolated cells provide early insights but don't always translate to human outcomes. Human trials are needed to confirm findings. Think of proxy measures in marketing: what is valid for one brand might not be valid for yours.

3   Case reports and case series: Case reports document individual cases, while case series track multiple subjects. Helpful in identifying new conditions or side effects, they show correlation but can't prove causation.

4   Case-control studies (observational): These studies look back at two groups, one with a condition and one without, to identify potential causes. While valuable, they only show correlation, not causation. Any attempt to measure marketing impact post campaign falls into this type.

5   Cohort studies (observational): Cohort studies follow groups over time to explore the effects of exposure (e.g. smoking) versus non-exposure. They provide stronger evidence than case-control studies but can't fully prove causation.

6   Randomized controlled trials (RCTs): RCTs randomly assign subjects to treatment or control groups. Single-blind or double-blind designs reduce bias, making RCTs one of the most reliable forms of evidence.

7   Systematic reviews: Systematic reviews analyse multiple RCTs, evaluate study quality and provide a balanced, comprehensive conclusion. They are the gold standard of evidence.

Stats crash course: how to interpret data like a pro

CORRELATION ISN'T CAUSATION: HOW TO AVOID FALSE CONCLUSIONS

Many people confuse correlation with causality, but they are not the same. Correlation means that two events occur together or follow a pattern. For example, if sales increase as social media posts rise, that's correlation. However, it doesn't prove that the posts caused the sales spike.

Causality refers to the relationship where one event directly leads to another. In marketing, demonstrating causality involves providing evidence that a specific campaign, message or ad resulted in increased sales or higher engagement.

It's easy to mistake correlation for causality. A sales bump often leads marketers to credit their latest campaign. But without proper testing, other factors, such as seasonality, competitor actions or consumer trends, could be the real cause.

Marketers should rely on A/B testing to prove causality. By comparing two groups, one exposed to a campaign and one not, we can measure whether the ad had an impact or effect. Don't be misled by correlation. While it helps identify patterns, understanding causality is essential for making smarter, evidence-based marketing decisions that yield accurate results.

BIASES IN RESEARCH: THE HIDDEN DISTORTIONS IN DATA

Bias distorts research findings, leading to misleading conclusions and wasted resources. It happens when specific factors unfairly affect outcomes, making results less representative of reality. In marketing research, bias can subtly influence how we interpret consumer behaviour, often without our awareness.

From experience, I've seen how easily bias can creep into research:

- Confirmation bias is one of the most common issues. We tend to focus on data that supports our assumptions and ignore the findings that challenge them.

- Selection bias is another issue, where the sample chosen for testing does not fully represent the target audience, leading to skewed results.

- Social desirability bias is particularly widespread in surveys and focus groups. Respondents frequently provide answers they believe are acceptable rather than reflecting their genuine opinions, especially on sensitive subjects such as sustainability or health.

Reducing bias effectively requires careful study design. Techniques like random sampling, blind testing, and using neutral question phrasing enhance reliability. Importantly, challenging assumptions and welcoming unexpected findings guarantee that your insights are accurate reality.

Awareness of bias is crucial for making research genuinely actionable. Be critical in evaluating every study you run to ensure decisions are evidence-based.

PROBABILITIES: EMBRACING UNCERTAINTY IN MARKETING

Nothing in marketing is ever 100 per cent certain. Every insight is based on probabilities, not guarantees, which means there's always some degree of uncertainty in decision-making.

Probability is a standard statistical measure of how likely an event is to occur. In marketing, every insight represents a prediction, not a fact. A consumer study might indicate an 80 per cent chance that an ad will drive sales, leaving a 20 per cent chance that it won't. This uncertainty is manageable, but it must be considered when interpreting data.

When I first learnt about probabilities, p-values and confidence intervals, it reshaped how I approached marketing. A p-value indicates the likelihood that a result occurred by chance; the lower it is, the more trustworthy the finding. Similarly, when we measure ROI, amounts like $1.23 per dollar spent are median values within a range, such as $1.12 to $1.34. Even with large samples, around 20 per cent of results may fall outside expected intervals. Have you ever considered the implications of that?

Instead of seeking exact answers, think in ranges and probabilities.

When reviewing research, don't forget to ask:

- What's the sample size?
- What's the confidence interval?
- What's the p-value or confidence level?

These questions help interpret findings accurately and prevent oversimplifying complex data. By embracing uncertainty and using probabilities to guide informed actions, marketers can make smarter marketing decisions.

The three most important tools for measuring marketing attribution, A/B testing and regression

A/B testing: the gold standard for marketing and life

A/B testing is the most reliable method for measuring marketing effectiveness. By comparing two variations of an element – such as an ad, a webpage or an email – you can determine which one performs better with real users. Unlike correlation-based methods, A/B testing establishes causality, making it an essential tool for optimizing campaigns and evaluating effectiveness.

WHAT IS A/B TESTING?

At its core, A/B testing is about controlled comparison. One group sees version A, another sees version B, and their behaviours are measured to identify the winner. The key to its accuracy lies in randomizing the selection of A and B groups, which eliminates biases and external influences. A/B testing is widely used to:

- improve website conversions by testing headlines, images or call-to-action (CTA) buttons
- optimize ad creatives, placements, media channels and messaging
- refine email subject lines for higher engagement

How to run a successful A/B test:

1 Choose one element to test. Focus on a single variable, like a display ad copy.

2 Split your audience randomly. This ensures fair exposure and unbiased results.

3 Measure key behavioural metrics – conversion rates, click-through rates or engagement – to determine which performs better.

For more complex experiments, multivariate testing can compare multiple elements simultaneously but requires larger sample sizes for accuracy.

COMMON A/B TESTING MISTAKES AND HOW TO AVOID THEM

- Stopping tests too early: Allow enough time to reach statistical significance before concluding.
- Testing too many variables simultaneously: Focus on one change at a time to isolate the impact.
- Ignoring retesting: Consumer behaviour shifts, so repeat tests to validate findings regularly.

WHY A/B TESTING IS ESSENTIAL

A/B testing can serve as your strategic advantage. By continuously testing and optimizing, marketers make smarter, data-driven decisions that lead to clearer outcomes since it's either A or B, with no room for ambiguity. In a world filled with uncertainty, A/B testing brings clarity, precision and confidence to your marketing strategy.

Attribution: identifying what drives sales

Attribution helps marketers determine which touchpoints influence consumer actions, such as purchasing or signing up for a service. By understanding attribution, businesses can allocate budgets more effectively and optimize marketing efforts. However, digital attribution models often oversimplify complex customer journeys, leading to misleading conclusions.

WHAT IS ATTRIBUTION?

Attribution is the process of assigning credit to different marketing touchpoints that contribute to a conversion. Established models include:

- first-click attribution – credits the first interaction, promoting mostly awareness-driving channels
- last-click attribution – credits only the final touchpoint, often overvaluing conversion-heavy channels
- linear attribution – distributes credit equally across all touchpoints, oversimplifying influence

These models often fail to capture the complete picture. A customer may interact with multiple ads, emails and social media posts before making a purchase, yet traditional attribution methods may misrepresent the actual drivers of conversion. I am still searching for the best attribution model. Please help me if you find it.

HOW TO RUN AN EFFECTIVE ATTRIBUTION ANALYSIS

1 Choose the right model. Consider whether first-click, last-click or a more advanced method best aligns with your business goals. A combination is advisable.
2 Collect comprehensive data. Track interactions across multiple channels to ensure accuracy. The more data gaps you have, the worse the outcome will be.
3 Test data-driven attribution. Machine learning models analyse historical data to assign credit based on actual influence rather than arbitrary rules.

Attribution can be combined with A/B testing and lift studies to validate its findings.

COMMON ATTRIBUTION MISTAKES AND HOW TO AVOID THEM

- Over-relying on last-click models. Use multi-touch attribution to reflect the entire customer journey.
- Ignoring offline and cross-device interactions. Ensure attribution models account for all touchpoints, not just digital ones.
- Assuming correlation equals causation. Use A/B testing to validate whether a channel truly drives conversions.

WHY ATTRIBUTION IS ESSENTIAL

In a complex media world, attribution helps marketers understand what drives actions, leading to smarter budget allocation and higher ROI. By selecting the appropriate model and validating results with other measurement techniques, you can achieve a more accurate view of marketing effectiveness.

Regression analysis: quantifying total marketing impact

Regression analysis helps marketers measure the relationship between various factors, such as advertising expenditure and sales. It is an essential method in marketing mix modelling (MMM), enabling businesses to identify which strategies contribute most significantly to growth.

WHAT IS REGRESSION ANALYSIS?

Regression quantifies how independent variables (e.g. price, promotions, distribution, advertising, weather, inflation) impact a dependent variable (e.g. sales or equity). This helps marketers answer questions such as:

- How much does TV advertising contribute to sales growth?
- Does increasing digital ad spend lead to more conversions?
- What is the impact of seasonality or weather patterns on revenue?

You can optimize marketing budgets and improve campaign effectiveness by identifying these relationships.

HOW TO RUN A SUCCESSFUL REGRESSION ANALYSIS

1 Define your objective. Decide which variable you want to model, such as sales impact or equity.
2 Gather clean historical data. Include variables like channel ad spend, market trends and competitor activity.

3 Control for confounding factors. Ensure unrelated variables do not distort results.

More advanced models integrate AI machine learning to help address non-linear relationships and improve accuracy. The level of innovation in this field is impressive.

COMMON REGRESSION MISTAKES AND HOW TO AVOID THEM

- Confusing correlation with causation. MMM is not causal. Use A/B testing to confirm causal relationships.
- Multicollinearity in data. Remove or adjust highly correlated variables to improve accuracy.
- Overfitting models to past data. Test predictions on new data to ensure reliability.

WHY REGRESSION IS ESSENTIAL

Regression analysis offers data-driven insights into the holistic factors that drive marketing success. While it should not be relied upon in isolation, combining regression analysis with A/B testing and attribution analysis enables marketers to make more informed, tactical decisions.

The smart marketer's guide to ROI: why it's useful and when it's not

Return on investment is a metric used to assess the profitability of a marketing campaign or investment. While it acts as an efficiency metric, it continues to be the most common answer to the industry's question: How do you measure marketing effectiveness?

In reality, ROI measures the profit a company generates from its marketing expenses in relation to its costs, usually calculated as a percentage. A high ROI indicates efficient resource use, but an excessive focus on ROI can lead to negative consequences for the company's future growth.

THE THREE TYPES OF ROI

Are you confused about different ROI acronyms? So was I. ROAS, ROI and ROMI. Here is a brief explanation:

- ROAS (return on advertising spend, Figure 7.2) measures the revenue generated per dollar spent on advertising. For example, if a campaign generates $5 for every $1 spent, the ROAS is 500 per cent. ROAS is revenue-focused and does not consider broader costs such as production or distribution.

- ROMI (return on marketing investment, Figure 7.3) is often used inter-changeably with ROI in marketing. However, it can specifically focus on the effectiveness of all marketing investments, including research, brand-ing and content creation. ROMI helps understand the total impact of marketing efforts on profitability. It excludes non-marketing costs though.

- ROI (return on investment, Figure 7.4) takes a broader view than ROAS and ROMI by factoring in all campaign costs, not just marketing. ROI measures the actual profit generated by an investment. For instance, if a campaign costs $10,000 and produces $15,000 in profit, the ROI is 50 per cent. Elements of product costs are included here.

While ROI is crucial for measuring efficiency, an excessive focus on maxi-mizing it can result in business practices that impede future growth. When brands optimize exclusively for a high ROI, they often prioritize only the most profitable channels, audiences and campaigns. In a multi-brand busi-ness, this approach favours larger brands at the expense of smaller ones. These strategies mitigate risk but frequently lead to reduced spending, as marketers cut back on investments that don't provide immediate, substan-tial returns.

FIGURE 7.2 ROAS

$$ROAS = \left(\frac{\text{Advertising Revenue}}{\text{Advertising Costs}} \right) \times 100\%$$

FIGURE 7.3 ROMI

$$ROMI = \left(\frac{\text{Revenue} - \text{Marketing Costs}}{\text{Marketing Costs}} \right) \times 100\%$$

FIGURE 7.4 ROI

$$ROI = \left(\frac{\text{Revenue} - \text{Total Costs}}{\text{Total Costs}} \right) \times 100\%$$

For instance, a brand that maximizes ROI may cut back on brand-building campaigns, which usually yield benefits over the long term. In the most extreme case, that same brand might focus on targeting existing customers through retail media, ensuring a high ROI but missing out on significant growth opportunities.

Optimal ROI vs growth-oriented ROI: when to use each

There are two best practices for ROI in marketing: optimizing for efficiency (high ROI) or pushing for growth:

- Optimal ROI: Utilize this approach when the objective is to maximize profitability within a set budget. This strategy is effective in mature markets or during economic downturns when resources are limited and efficiency is crucial. Emphasizing high-ROI campaigns aids in generating profit without excessive spending.

- Growth-oriented ROI: Conversely, a growth-oriented approach to ROI involves accepting lower immediate returns to expand reach and capture a larger market share. This strategy is most effective for brands aiming to grow aggressively in competitive markets or during new product launches. In this case, marketers may invest in high-reach but lower-ROI channels such as print or social media to build brand awareness and create future demand.

Finding the right balance is critical to using ROI effectively in marketing. Brands need to identify which campaigns justify a focus on short-term profitability (high ROI) and which require a growth mindset, accepting lower ROI to capture market share. While ROI is a valuable metric, its limitations must be recognized. Always use it in combination with other metrics, and remember: ROI measures efficiency, not effectiveness.

POSITIVE ROI IS JUST THE BEGINNING – REAL BRAND GROWTH REQUIRES MORE

Advertising ROI is a favourite metric for finance and marketing teams. Savvy marketers see its value but know it is only part of the story. While ROI matters, chasing efficiency alone won't build a strong brand. ROI should be a baseline, not the end goal. Many brands hit their ROI targets and stop there, treating it as the ultimate success measure. But ROI only tells you if an ad paid for itself. It doesn't measure brand impact or future growth.

Why ROI Alone Falls Short – Cheap media can make ROI look good on paper. Take display banners. They are ignored, blocked and barely noticed, yet because they cost so little, they can sometimes break even. Compare that to high-quality online videos that convert 10 times better. If the cost is exactly 10 times higher, both have the same ROI. But which one truly grows the brand? Short-term ROI thinking leads to cost-cutting instead of brand-building. Cheap media, ad fraud and low-quality impressions can create an illusion of efficiency while doing little to drive real sales or engagement.

Economic Downturns Distort ROI – In 2020, when advertisers slashed budgets, CPMs dropped, making ROI seem higher. But consumers weren't engaging more. Market conditions can artificially inflate ROI, making it a dangerous metric to rely on alone.

For Small Brands, ROI Can Be a Trap – New brands rarely achieve strong ROI from the start. Cutting investments too soon can choke long-term growth. Instead, focus on maximizing conversions, engaging consumers and refining creative. McDonald's[4] has recently prioritized brand-building over short-term ROI, proving long-term investment matters more.

ROI is useful, but it's not the measure of success. Brands that win focus on customer engagement, creative impact and sustainable growth. Positive ROI is a start, not the finish line. Real growth comes from investing in what moves the brand forward.

How to build a marketing measurement framework that works

Building precision with the media measurement pyramid

Measuring marketing effectiveness is both an art and a science. To make informed decisions, marketers require a framework that balances ease of execution with the quality of insights provided. That's where the Media Measurement Pyramid I created comes into play (see Figure 7.5). This structured approach categorizes research methodologies into a hierarchy, guiding marketers towards increasingly behavioural, causal and precise methods as they ascend. While this framework applies specifically to media measurements, it can also be utilized for other elements of your marketing plan.

The Foundation: 'What Some People Say'. At the base of the pyramid are methods such as survey questionnaires that drive brand-lift studies. As expected, these approaches capture consumer perceptions, self-reported intentions or attitudes towards advertising. While they are the easiest to

FIGURE 7.5 My measurement philosophy: the pyramid of measurement helps you navigate methods and complexities of media effectiveness

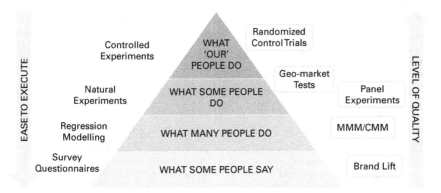

My Media Measurement Philosophy: behavioural, causal, precise

implement, they often lack precision. Why? Because they measure what people *say* they think or feel rather than what they actually *do*. These methods provide a starting point but often fail to reveal media's true impact on actual behaviour. I seldom regard surveys as a measure of effectiveness.

The Mid Layers: 'What Many People Do' and 'What Some People Do'. Climbing higher, the focus shifts from self-reported attitudes to observed actions. Regression modelling and natural experiments enter the mix, analysing historical data and natural occurrences to uncover patterns and correlations. These methods offer more profound insights into consumer behaviour, but they still have some limitations in precision, as they cannot fully isolate cause and effect.

Examples of middle-layer solutions include marketing mix modelling and cross-media measurement (CMM). These techniques analyse aggregated data to understand how media influences large groups of people. Geo-market and attribution/sales lift experiments provide additional rigour, offering causal insights by testing interventions across specific markets or audience panels. At this stage, marketers bridge the gap between broad trends and actionable behaviours.

The Summit: 'What 'Our' People Do'. The most rigorous methods sit at the top of the pyramid: randomized control trials and controlled experiments. These represent the gold standard for marketing measurement. By testing two groups – one exposed to a specific media intervention and one not – brands can isolate the true impact of their efforts. Although these methods are more complex and resource-intensive, they yield the highest-quality insights, directly linking media activities to consumer behaviour.

The Media Measurement Pyramid highlights the need to move beyond superficial metrics to gain genuine behavioural insights. As you ascend the pyramid, the methods become more difficult to implement but yield increasingly actionable and precise data. Marketers can begin at the base for a quick, broad understanding but should strive for the peak when high-stakes decisions require clarity and causation.

By adopting this framework, you can navigate the complexities of media effectiveness, ensuring that your strategies are rooted in reliable, high-quality insights. The ultimate goal? To align efforts with outcomes that drive real impact, moving from what people say to what they truly do.

FIVE STEPS TO BUILDING A MARKETING EXPERIMENTATION CULTURE

The practice of marketing experimentation was mastered in tech companies such as Google, Netflix and Booking.com. With massive access to user data and a predominant engineering mindset in their workforce, these companies shifted from instinct to data-driven decisions. Today, this strategy is transforming industries beyond technology. At its core, marketing experimentation fosters improved, evidence-based decision-making.

As mentioned before, A/B testing is the gold standard for causality and is at the core of any experimentation culture (see Figure 7.6). It isolates cause and effect, making it the most reliable method for testing. Initially used in

FIGURE 7.6 The five steps to build an experimentation culture: think about mindset, method, behaviour, scale and sharing

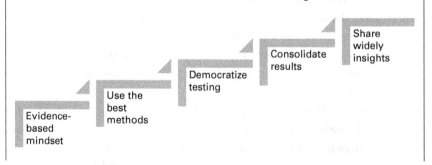

pharmaceutical trials, it has now become essential for business teams to optimize sales, product development and media investments:

1   Step 1: Embrace an evidence-based mindset where everyone trusts data over intuition. Even the best instincts can mislead, but facts reveal what truly works. While overwhelming data can cause hesitation, focusing on actionable insights reduces uncertainty. An authentic culture of experimentation starts with a mindset shift: letting evidence guide decisions.

2   Step 2: Choose the best testing methods depending on the type of research. A/B testing is the foundation of experimentation. If the pharmaceutical industry relies on it to save lives, marketers can use it to drive better outcomes. Companies with direct sales data, like e-commerce brands, can run A/B tests easily. For CPG companies relying on retailer data, natural experiments or post-hoc analyses offer an alternative.

3   Step 3: Make testing accessible to everyone in the organization. A/B testing is simple, scalable and works. It removes the guesswork and delivers clear results. Empower your teams across markets to run their own tests with a centralized framework for consistency. Partner with analytics teams or external vendors to correct execution.

4   Step 4: Centralize results to build knowledge in a learning database. In global organizations, local teams often test in isolation in their own markets, but centralized data amplifies corporate learning. A single A/B test is useful, but repeated tests across markets create certainty. In my past role, we built a shared repository of global insights, helping teams validate hypotheses across regions. Consolidating results eliminates redundancies and accelerates learning.

5   Step 5: Share insights to scale success and avoid failures. An experimentation culture should benefit every business unit, not just the ones running tests. By broadcasting successes and failures, less advanced teams can learn from proven strategies and avoid mistakes. Consolidating and sharing test results improves both marketing performance and customer experience. The more teams contribute, the stronger network effects become.

Whether you're conducting small tests or large-scale campaigns, adopting an experimentation mindset will result in smarter decisions and long-term growth.

THE ALLURE AND ILLUSION OF MARKETING AWARDS

Marketing awards have always fascinated me. No other industry seems as obsessed with self-recognition as advertising does. Yes, I'm part of it. I enjoy the excitement, the prestige and the glamour. Still, I keep asking myself why we care so much.

Every June, thousands of marketers converge in Cannes to celebrate creativity, immerse themselves in the glamour and applaud those who have 'made it'. My social media feeds overflow with posts proclaiming, 'I'm so proud to announce...' But why are we so attracted to these trophies?

I think it's because our work is rarely tangible. Builders can point to houses they've constructed. Factory workers can see their products on a shelf. But marketers live in the in-between. We help shape a brand's story, yet when a product succeeds, the credit often goes to sales teams or product developers.

Maybe awards fill that gap. They validate us, give us a moment to be seen, acknowledged and celebrated. But here's the reality: Winning doesn't always mean effective. Having judged awards myself, I've seen campaigns win for their creativity, social media buzz or industry hype, not because they drove real business growth.

I love awards. They bring the industry together, push creative boundaries and make our work feel special. But they are not the measure of success. True marketing impact is seen in long-term brand growth, not in a trophy cabinet.

Enjoy the celebrations. Just never forget what really matters: marketing effectiveness.

How Mars cracked the code on creative effectiveness

Creativity is one of the most powerful tools for brand growth. Creative excellence can make or break a campaign even in today's fragmented media world. Yet many organizations struggle to build systems that ensure creative work is measured against real business results. At Mars, for more than a decade I helped build a framework that doesn't just celebrate creativity but makes it measurable, scalable and effective:

- Start with data, not opinions. Proving the value of creativity to non-marketing leadership was challenging. At Mars, we made creativity measurable by focusing on hard data rather than subjective opinions. Instead of asking consumers what they liked, we studied how creative campaigns influenced actual consumer behaviour and sales and modelled return on investment. This approach helped us speak the language of the C-suite by directly linking creativity to business outcomes.

- Create a centralized system for consistency. To make creative effectiveness measurement a company-wide standard, we established the Comms Lab, a dedicated team in charge of marketing effectiveness across all regions and business units. By using a standard definition of creative success, a common approach to analytics and a single team to guide it all, we were able to compare campaigns globally and deliver a consistent output. This structure empowered local teams to execute while focusing our team on building long-term capabilities in marketing effectiveness.

- Invest in the best tools. Knowing what works and what doesn't is a matter of millions for the world's largest advertisers – a risk no business is willing to take. We built a data-driven measurement system, powered by the best data sources available in each market (household consumer panels capturing behavioural data only) and the most advanced analytics methods to analyse all that. One standout tool is ACE (Advertising Content Expertise), an in-house creative testing solution developed after extensive consumer behavioural research on what drives effects in advertising. ACE measures a combination of human attention and emotional impact, plus other key metrics proven to increase effectiveness. The tests run in real-world environments, ensuring accurate, actionable insights.

- Make insights easy to act on. Complex data is useless if it's not understood. We simplified creative effectiveness measurement output into a 1-to-4-star rating system, making it easy for marketers to interpret results and take action without diving into endless reports.

- Partner for long-term creative success. Creative effectiveness isn't built in isolation. We developed deep partnerships with creative and media agencies, aligning them with our effectiveness-first mindset. These relationships help balance creativity with business performance over the long run.

- The key to long-term success. The secret to our creative effectiveness culture was consistency. Building a system takes time, but staying the course is what drives sustained impact. The latest tools and trends come and go, but a consistent approach to measurement is what delivers the results.

By embedding effectiveness into our culture, we have turned creativity from an art into a measurable business driver. The journey took commitment, but the rewards – stronger brands, better decisions and lasting success – are worth it.

THE POWER OF SIMPLIFIED METRICS: TELLING A STORY THAT RESONATES

I've learnt that in marketing, numbers don't speak for themselves. The way you frame them makes all the difference. When results look confusing, disappointing or are just 'off', telling the right story around them can turn hesitation into action.

One of the highlights of my career was a simple change I made to crystallize actions in advertising research. Instead of drowning in complex ad effectiveness scores, I switched to a simple four-star rating system, like an 'intelligent traffic light'. It created a common language in the entire organization, cut through the noise of external suppliers offering similar solutions and gave teams clear next steps instead of endless debates on method. No more overanalysing or second-guessing. Just clarity.

Why this works

1 Story first, numbers last. Most marketers aren't data scientists. When faced with too much complexity, they hesitate. A 'go', 'fix' or 'stop' framework makes their decisions faster and easier. That's what you want!

2 People react to what feels intuitive. Everyone understands a star rating or traffic light system. It makes results easier to discuss, less defensive and more constructive, even when they're not what we hoped for.

3 Learning beats perfection. Not every campaign will be a home run. What matters is how quickly we learn and adapt. When results don't match expectations, the focus should be on what's next, not just questioning the data.

4 This shift changed how I approach marketing research. I always strive for simple output because intuitive metrics don't just make data more straightforward, they empower action. Less hesitation, fewer debates and a team that moves forward with confidence.

Applied engineering for marketing research

Engineering Marketing Tool 8: benchmarking

Benchmarking keeps marketing ambitions grounded in competitive reality. It helps your brand measure its performance against past results, competitors and even different industries to gain fresh perspectives and make smarter decisions.

While it's a fundamental tool in marketing research, benchmarking originates from engineering, where it guides efficiency and innovation. Used correctly, it helps align marketing efforts with broader market trends and business objectives. However, to be valuable, benchmarking must guide improvement, not just comparison.

THREE SMART WAYS TO USE BENCHMARKING IN MARKETING EFFECTIVENESS

1 Build a benchmarking database to improve future decisions. Tracking past performance, sales impact, ROI and response curves can create a roadmap for future success. For example, if historical data shows TV plus digital drives the highest sales lift, budgets can be optimized accordingly. Without repeating research, benchmarks act as guardrails, preventing wasteful spending and maximizing impact.

2 Benchmark against competitors to refine your strategy. Studying how competitors allocate media budgets can reveal opportunities and gaps. If they underinvest in emerging platforms like connected TV or retail media, that might be your chance to lead. Be mindful: benchmarking should inform, not dictate, strategy. Use it to spot trends, not to copy tactics.

3 Look outside your category for fresh inspiration. The best benchmarks don't always come from direct competitors. Luxury car brands learn from high-end fashion advertising, while CPG brands borrow from e-commerce's use of retargeting. Great ideas often come from unexpected places: benchmark beyond your industry.

4 Benchmarking is a tool, not a rule. Over-reliance fosters imitation rather than innovation. Industry norms offer useful context, but true success arises from balancing data with bold creativity. Sometimes, the best way to surpass the benchmark is to break it.

THE TAKEAWAY

Used correctly, benchmarking helps marketers make smarter investments, optimize strategies and unlock new growth opportunities. The key is to treat it as a guide, not a formula. What are you benchmarking against today?

Engineering Marketing Tool 9: Data-driven decision-making (DDDM)

Welcome to the final tool in this series. Data-driven decision making is often used as a buzzword. However, in practice, many marketers either pursue the wrong data, get lost in analysis paralysis or fail to connect insights to actual decisions. Without a straightforward process, data can become a distraction rather than a competitive advantage.

THE POWER OF DDDM

At its core, DDDM is an approach that prioritizes evidence over instinct. In marketing, gut feelings often masquerade as 'experience', leading teams down the wrong path. Data helps remove bias, providing a clear and objective view of consumer behaviour. A useful analogy is aviation. Pilots rely on instruments to navigate, not just instincts. Sensors monitor engine performance and flight conditions, ensuring precise decision-making, especially in high-stakes situations. Marketing works the same way. Creativity and intuition matter, but they need data to guide them.

START WITH DECISIONS, NOT DATA

One of the biggest mistakes in marketing research is collecting mountains of data without first defining the business decision it's meant to inform. This leads to reports packed with insights but no clear next steps. Instead, flip the process. Start with the decision, then find the data to support it. Whether it's optimizing a media budget or evaluating a campaign, the quality of data makes all the difference. Data isn't the destination, it's an enabler to get you there.

THE THREE RULES OF EFFECTIVE DDDM

1 Decision first. Before diving into data, spend plenty of time defining and aligning the business question with stakeholders. What problem are you solving? What's the goal?

2 Data quality over quantity. Not all data is useful. The classic 'garbage in, garbage out' rule applies everywhere. Make a priority to ensure your data is accurate, relevant and timely to avoid making the wrong decisions.

3 Action over analysis. Many teams analyse data endlessly but hesitate to act. A perfect report means nothing if it doesn't drive action. The best research is decisive and inspires action.

BALANCING SCIENCE WITH ART

Marketing isn't just science – human behaviour remains unpredictable. People make emotional, sometimes irrational, choices. That's why data should enhance creativity, not replace it. Some of the best marketing strategies combine rigorous data analysis with bold creative thinking. Think of it like poker: you don't control the odds, but a data-driven betting strategy significantly increases your chances of winning.

DDDM is the last mindset tool in my series because it ties everything together. It brings clarity, accountability and focus. Success comes from knowing when to trust data, when to take risks and how to act. Master this and you'll transform marketing into a powerful force for your brand.

INDUSTRY EXPERT CONTRIBUTION
Research innovation: Jon Lombardo

From synthetic diamonds to synthetic insights: the future of market research

Consider this: lab-grown diamonds are now more perfect than mined ones. Synthetic oil performs better than natural oil. Artificial rubber lasts longer than natural rubber. In each case, the engineered version has surpassed the original. The same engineering revolution is now happening in market research, where AI-powered synthetic research outperforms traditional methods in every key measure: speed, cost, flexibility and scale.

Traditional market research has always been painful. Want to survey 100 CEOs? That'll cost you hundreds of thousands of dollars. Need insights for your next campaign? Get ready to wait 3–6 months for results. Want to deeply understand your customers? Good luck getting busy people to sit through hour-long surveys. These barriers are so daunting that many marketers skip research altogether and jump straight to execution – often with costly mistakes.

Enter synthetic research, powered by generative AI. Instead of struggling to recruit real CEOs, synthetic research creates AI-powered 'impersonas' – detailed digital twins built from massive datasets of real-world information. These impersonas draw knowledge from vast amounts of market data, including earnings calls, analyst reports, news articles and social media posts. Early validation studies, including both academic research and Evidenza testing, show synthetic responses closely match human responses – typically with 70–90 per cent accuracy across different industries and contexts.

The advantages go beyond just speed and cost. Human survey respondents get bored. They rush through questions. They give quick answers to get their gift card and move on. Synthetic respondents maintain perfect focus from question 1 to question 100. They provide rich, detailed responses to every query. They'll engage in deep discussions about your brand at 3 am on a Sunday. And they'll do it all without the astronomical costs – in time and money – of traditional research.

Synthetic research will continue to transform market research by enabling:

1   the ability to keep asking follow-up questions until you get the clarity you need

2   deep understanding of brand health through multidimensional metrics – tracking mental availability, emotional connections and purchase drivers

3   access to high-quality market research for companies of any size – democratizing insights previously available only to large enterprises

But here's the key: in a world where you can get any answer you want, the real value shifts to knowing exactly what to ask. It's simple economics: as the supply of answers becomes infinite, the demand – and premium – for smart questions soars. We believe tomorrow's market leaders will be those who master the art of asking the right questions in a fast and iterative way.

Just as synthetic materials have revolutionized their industries by being better than the original, synthetic research is revolutionizing market research by making superior customer understanding accessible to all. The future isn't about replacing human insight with artificial intelligence, it's about democratizing deep customer insights for the AI age.

JON LOMBARDO

Jon Lombardo is the co-founder of Evidenza.ai, a platform leveraging AI to generate data-driven marketing plans based on marketing science principles. As former Head of Research at LinkedIn's B2B Institute, he contributed to influential studies on B2B brand growth, helping replicate established marketing laws across seven B2B categories. His team's research advanced understanding of how B2B brands grow and identified key category entry points in B2B markets. Previously, Jon directed General Electric's Social Media Center of Excellence, overseeing commercial initiatives across major social platforms.

FIVE IDEAS TO TAKE WITH YOU AFTER READING THIS CHAPTER

1   Trust behaviour over opinions. Actions predict future outcomes better than surveys: watch what people do, not what they say.

2   Start with decisions, not data. Define the business question first, then collect only the data that informs it.

3   Use the right methods for the right insights. A/B testing proves causality, MMM uncovers long-term impact and systematic research ensures reliability.

4   Culture drives research impact. The best data and methods mean nothing if your colleagues don't act on the insights.

5   Marketing effectiveness is a process, not a destination. Continuous testing, learning and adapting are the keys to long-term success.

Measuring marketing effectiveness: a final reflection

This research chapter aims to equip you with marketing science tools, enabling you to make robust, replicable and evidence-based marketing decisions.

It's not just about using data to make decisions, it's about identifying the most valuable data, clarifying the hypothesis and action standards, and applying a scientific method to testing. Always remember, it's the quality, not the quantity, of the data that truly matters.

Below are three questions to help you make the most of this chapter. Ask them often to make more effective decisions for your brand. As always, there are no right or wrong answers. Simply thinking about these concepts more will help you internalize them better. And for an added learning boost, consider discussing them with a colleague or a friend.

THREE QUESTIONS TO MASTER MARKETING RESEARCH

1   What percentage of business decisions I make are consumer behavioural data-based?

2   On a scale of 1–5, how confident am I that my hypothesis and action standard will generate business value?

3   How close am I to running an A/B test for each measurement project?

ONE MORE THING…

Want to stay effective and ahead of the curve? Scan this QR code to access extra content and updates online.

Notes

1   The Marketoonist (2014) Inside the mind of the consumer, https://marketoonist. com/2014/01/mind-of-the-consumer.html (archived at https://perma.cc/Y3SZ-7AN2)

2 Rogers, C (2019) 81% of brands could disappear and European consumers wouldn't care, https://www.marketingweek.com/brands-disappear/ (archived at https://perma.cc/VL62-XDJK)

3 Interactive Advertising Bureau (2023) Ad blocking: Who blocks ads, why and how to win them back (2023) https://www.iab.com/wp-content/uploads/2016/07/IAB-Ad-Blocking-2016-Who-Blocks-Ads-Why-and-How-to-Win-Them-Back.pdf (archived at https://perma.cc/J5QM-LZDE)

4 Marketing Week (2023) How McDonald's made marketing its centre for growth, https://www.marketingweek.com/mcdonalds-marketing-centre-growth/?utm_source=chatgpt.com (archived at https://perma.cc/T3XU-EPJ5)

08

Navigating the future of marketing in the age of AI

A possible future of marketing

Futurism, the art of preparing for the future, helps us manage uncertainty by evaluating disruptions, critical uncertainties, emerging trends and unconventional viewpoints. While I may not have a crystal ball, my decades of experience in marketing effectiveness and acquired insights from countless industry conversations and events have taught me that the question isn't *if* these emerging trends will shape our world but *when*.

Change is inevitable and everyone works on adapting to it. The future of brand marketing requires a new approach. Recent years offer some clues into what may work, but the chance of accurately predicting the future is slim since customer behaviours constantly shift.

Tailwinds like technology and automation bring opportunities, but the overwhelming flow of information makes focusing on unique ideas challenging. Future shoppers expect seamless experiences; every click, scroll or tap must feel effortless. However, with customer data everywhere and AI managing most aspects of brand communication, excellence in execution can't be a competitive advantage, it will be ground zero.

Headwinds are blowing strong, too, with growth opportunities more challenging to rely on. Customer preferences shift fast, fuelled by an enormous assortment and an explosion of purchase occasions across most categories. So far, brands have responded by jumping on purpose, inclusivity and sustainability trends. While important, these tactics are no longer optional and slowly became table stakes.

The demise of the classic brand-building model isn't a theory, it's already under way for brands that aren't agile, creative and engineered for the future.

This future is here already, irregularly distributed.

This chapter explores five pivotal trends that will transform the business world as we know it. Read them, absorb the main ideas and then think critically about their likelihood for your brand.

FIVE TRENDS IMPACTING MARKETING TODAY AND TOMORROW

1　The death of the advertising push model.

2　The altering role of brands as signals of quality.

3　The rise of automation and systems thinking.

4　100 per cent predictive marketing.

5　The empowerment of consumers over brands.

Let's explore each trend through two lenses: one where transformation is at the extreme and one that is more conservative. The reality might combine elements of both scenarios, but we won't know for sure. I can't promise you will have a complete future map, but I can offer some principles to help you better navigate whatever map you encounter.

1 The death of the advertising push model

The traditional push model of advertising, where brands broadcast messages in hopes of capturing attention and converting audiences, is on life support. Marketing is now less about speaking at consumers, it's about obtaining permission first.

Despite continuing to use advertising-supported platforms, consumers are no longer willing to be passive recipients of brand messaging; technology empowers them to curate their own experiences. Ad blockers, ad skipping, the rise of paid subscription services and content-filtering algorithms are tools that people use today to eliminate anything that doesn't add value.

For brands, this shift is existential. Future growth requires a new strategy that transitions from interruption to invitation. Success may depend on profoundly understanding consumers, enhancing relevance and meeting them where they already are. Brands can evolve from broadcasting to building connections, from demanding attention to creating value. However, that's easier said than done. No definitive future playbook is emerging. The old playbook is outdated. What comes next will determine who thrives.

Probable future path: While the decline of push advertising will continue, some brands may pivot towards the following:

- Content marketing excellence involves creating stories and entertainment that resonate deeply and occur outside regular ad breaks. Entertain or inform – don't sell.
- Inbound marketing strategies are a pull approach that draws consumers into the world of the brand through SEO, social media, owned platforms and thought leadership.
- Tent-pole advertising events will probably continue to thrive because marketers want the fame of winning a Cannes Lions or participating in the Super Bowl. However, the number and scale of these global events will likely decline.

'Crazy' future path: At the extreme, envision a world where consumers have complete control over the ads they receive. With advanced AI filters and protective legislation, brands can no longer push messages; instead, they must become whispers in the right ears at the right moments. Perhaps advertising will become extinct and everything will be decided at the point of sale; perhaps mental availability will be entirely replaced by physical availability.

Regardless of what the future holds, you can prepare today for either of the two paths or something in between:

- Build brand equity for the long term: Use emotional storytelling, craft consistent narratives and approach communication with a multimedia mindset. Frontload equity.
- Foster genuine relationships: Respond meaningfully to customer engagement, interact reactively on social platforms and build trust through listening.
- Embrace permission marketing: Shift to opt-in strategies, prioritize transparency in media buying and earn attention through respectful approaches.

2 The changing role of brands as signals of quality

Brands were once lighthouses, guiding shoppers with the benefits of quality and reliability. For decades, a recognizable logo was shorthand for 'you can trust this'. It was a quality symbol.

That authority is gradually fading. The emergence of 'dupe culture', for instance, has allowed customers to opt for cheaper, lookalike alternatives that imitate high-end fashion brands. Today, counterfeit products inundate specific marketplaces and are becoming more accepted. They blur the distinction between what is real and what is fake. Meanwhile, perhaps in response, high-quality food private labels demonstrate that premium quality doesn't always demand a premium price.

This shift has transformed customers into discount hunters. They sift through reviews, comparison videos and social proof to uncover value beyond just a brand name. The mark of quality that a brand once provided now demands evidence: performance, customer satisfaction and a low price.

Today brands must work harder to earn trust. Being recognizable isn't enough.

Probable future path: Some brands will reinvent through the following:

- Differentiation via innovation. Success might come from offering unique products and experiences that set brands apart. Continuous innovation is essential for staying ahead in a rapidly changing marketplace, but it won't be enough. Copying features is easier than ever.

- Building emotional connections. Some brands will thrive by creating deeper bonds with customers rooted in shared values and a clear purpose. Brand > Product.

- Enhancing transparency. Openly disclosing details about sourcing, production and ethical practices will become non-negotiable. Transparency is key to earning and maintaining trust in an overly sceptical world.

'Crazy' future path: Picture a future where blockchain technology allows consumers to verify every aspect of a product instantly. Brands become secondary to the verified attributes of each item. The concept of brand preference shifts significantly when transparency trumps reputation.

Regardless of what the future holds, you can prepare today for either of the two paths or something in between:

- Innovate relentlessly: Foster product creativity within teams, adopt design thinking and learn how to gain short bursts of competitive advantage via innovation.

- Strengthen brand authenticity: Be genuine in communication and always align actions with values – a negative brand story travels faster than a positive one.

- Adopt transparency technologies: Implement traceability tools, use packaging QR codes to share stories and stay updated on supply chain transparency best practices.

3 Everything AI: the automation promise

Let's agree on one point: AI is a game-changer, transforming how marketers work and engage with audiences. Agents now resolve queries in seconds, while algorithms sift through vast amounts of data to uncover insights that humans might miss. With AI, personalization can occur at scale, behavioural research is more accessible than ever and traditional content-creation processes are being challenged.

It's not just about speed. AI solutions allow marketers to predict customer needs, adapt campaigns in real time and experiment with new ideas at minimal risk and with minimal interaction. Automation handles repetitive tasks, freeing teams to focus on strategy and creativity. However, AI isn't a magic wand. It needs quality data and thoughtful oversight to deliver accurate results. Use it with a quality mindset and the opportunities it unlocks are endless.

Probable future path: AI will become ubiquitous in marketing:

- Automation of routine tasks: Freeing up humans for strategic creativity or whatever else is left.

- Hyper-personalization: Delivering bespoke experiences and content at scale will be the norm.

- Systems thinking integration: Creating cohesive ecosystems where AI tools interact seamlessly, with minimal human oversight. Think about a permanent link between strategy – product – communication – effectiveness.

'Crazy' future path: Imagine a marketplace where AI systems autonomously negotiate and transact on behalf of customers and brands. Algorithms communicate and sell brands to algorithms and humans oversee the processes like conductors of a complex symphony, focusing on strategy and ethics rather than execution. Is that even a full-time brand job?

Regardless of what the future holds, you can prepare today for either of the two paths or something in between:

1 Integrate AI across your strategy: Adopt AI tools to transform analytics and customer engagement. Explore both generative AI and traditional AI solutions. If you haven't already, start by building your foundational AI knowledge with accessible courses available on platforms like Coursera.[1]

2 Develop systems thinking: Identify the interconnections within your marketing efforts. Break down silos and promote cross-functional collaboration to improve efficiency and build future systems. Think in systems.

3 Adapt to new customer behaviours: As AI-driven tools like voice assistants and prompting reshape people behaviours, consider how interactions impact your brand. Explore AI from a user behaviour perspective, not just a way to enhance your productivity.

4. Predictive marketing: anticipating customer needs

Predictive marketing transforms how brands interact with customers by shifting the focus from reaction to anticipation. By analysing vast amounts of data, brands can now identify patterns, forecast future behaviours and provide solutions before customers even realize they need them. Wow! This trend represents a significant evolution in marketing, where insights are now even more vital than they were in the past.

Understanding the customer seems like an easier task, even though user behaviour is complex. Customer expectations from brands are also at an all-time high. Personalized experiences are shifting from retroactive to proactive.

Predictive marketing helps brands meet current consumer needs and helps shape what's next. But as this trend grows, so do ethical questions around data usage and influence, requiring actors to tread carefully and responsibly.

Probable future path: Predictive marketing will bring value in three significant areas:

- Enhanced forecasting will allow brands to identify category trends more precisely, helping pioneers stay ahead of the competition.

- Proactive engagements will enable brands to offer tailored solutions before customers realize they need them.

- Improved customer journeys will provide seamless, efficient and often personalized experiences built on predictive insights.

'Crazy' future path: Imagine predictive algorithms so advanced they manipulate consumer desires subtly and subconsciously. As predictive models integrate with significant evolutions in neuroscience best practices, marketing could be all about shaping, not just meeting, demand. This raises obvious ethical challenges about manipulation and consent.

Regardless of what the future holds, you can prepare today for either of the two paths or something in between:

- Continue to invest in advanced analytics: Build capabilities in data science and adopt new tools to strengthen predictive capabilities. It's a cost of doing future business.

- Prioritize ethical standards: Develop transparent data-use policies and always ensure compliance with evolving privacy regulations.
- Enhance customer experience: Leverage predictive insights through first-party data platforms to personalize each touchpoint if it improves customer satisfaction.

5. Brands in the hands of consumers: the shareholder model

The era of brand dominance is slowly coming to an end. Consumers now hold unprecedented power, using social platforms and digital tools to voice opinions, establish trends and impact brand reputations.

The megaphone, once solely controlled by brands, is now shared with influential individuals who can serve as either advocates or critics. This trend signifies a significant change: brand narratives are no longer just managed, they're co-owned by their audiences. New business models may also transform the structure of brand ownership.

Probable future path: Brands will adapt by:

- Embracing co-creation, inviting customers to participate in product development and even communication campaigns
- Building communities fostering spaces where customers connect, share ideas and engage with the brand
- Increasing transparency, openly sharing internal decisions and actively seeking customer input to maintain trust and credibility. Imagine voting on your favourite brand innovation pipeline

'Crazy' future path: Picture a world where brands operate as decentralized autonomous organizations (DAOs). Consumers hold voting rights, make collective decisions and own stakes in the brand. Governance shifts from corporate hierarchies to consumer-led ecosystems, creating a radical new model of brand ownership.

Regardless of what the future holds, you can prepare today for either of the two paths or something in between:

- Foster more customer participation: Engage customers in decision-making through interactive social media campaigns and idea-sharing platforms.
- Cultivate radical transparency: Share both achievements and challenges, creating honest dialogue to build trust.

- Explore decentralized technologies: Experiment with blockchain tools like token-based rewards or loyalty programmes that empower consumer participation.

As we stand at the intersection of tradition and innovation, it's clear that marketing disruption is not a distant wave but a tide already rising before us. While some ideas may appear daunting, the five trends we explored above present a wealth of opportunities for those brave enough to embrace them with curiosity.

Adaptability is my anchor in a sea of change. Although the future may be uncertain, we can chart a course towards success by embracing some of these shifts. How can you be better prepared for this future?

FIVE ACTION POINTS FOR EVERY MARKETER

1 Subscribe and engage: Read industry-leading publications and attend one webinar or conference this month.

2 Upskill yourself and your team: Enrol in a course on AI, data analytics or marketing operations and schedule team learning sessions.

3 Adopt smarter tech: Pick one tool to streamline your current processes, enhance customer experience and cut redundant technologies.

4 Lead with ethics: Update your data privacy policies and actively communicate transparency efforts to customers.

5 Test and adapt: Launch a new feature experiment this month, analyse results and adjust usage accordingly.

THREE FORCES SHAPING THE TRANSFORMATION OF MARKETING

Technology is not alone in shaping marketing's future – more profound shifts in customer, purchasing path and corporate behaviour drive it. Technology acts as an accelerator across these forces.

1. The evolving role of the consumer

Today, customers seem to hold more power, amplified by technology. They don't decide alone – algorithms influence choices, prioritizing convenience over brand equity. People expect brands to align with their values. Purpose-driven marketing is bouncing up and down, yet scepticism towards traditional advertising has increased. Influencers act as modern brand gatekeepers, gate-keeping authenticity and trust in a digital age. Brands need to blend the efficiency of technology with the authenticity of human connections.

2. The evolving role of the purchase channel

The line between advertising and sales disappears, replaced by seamless, integrated experiences. Direct-to-consumer (D2C) brands set the standard; retail media closes the path from awareness to purchase. It's time for the established brands to copy the omnichannel strategy. Traditional retail channels, meanwhile, face pressure to adapt. High-street retail is poised to evolve or die in a low-margin and instant-gratification world.

3. The evolving role of the stakeholder/business

The expectations of stakeholders have never been higher. Shareholders demand sustainable growth, faster decision-making and greater transparency. Beyond shareholders, the planet itself has become a stakeholder. Consumers increasingly demand accountability from brands, expecting them to minimize environmental impact and act responsibly. The real challenge is balancing these pressures while staying competitive and agile.

Marketing's transformation involves navigating the intersection of technology, consumer expectations and business priorities. Successful brands will use technology not just as a crutch but as a bridge to more human connections.

And then... there is AI.

Marketing in the age of AI

AI is marketing's next frontier

In November 2022, the world buzzed with excitement over a new tool: ChatGPT. I clearly remember the evening I first engaged with its prompt window. Sitting on the couch next to my wife, I attempted to express the thrill of what I had been witnessing. Together, we asked ChatGPT to summarize the latest EU legislation her department had just released. 'This AI can actually write, explain and even translate complex legal language into plain English,' I said, half in awe. She looked at me, both intrigued and a bit uneasy. 'If AI can do all that, what does it mean for us?' she wondered aloud. Her question lingered, capturing both the wonder and fear surrounding this technology. If AI could make sense of intricate pan-European legislation, imagine its potential in marketing, a field where understanding people and delivering the right message are paramount.

From campaign strategy to real-time ad optimization, from pricing to generating customer insights, AI is revolutionizing every step of the marketing journey today. Understanding AI's capabilities and limitations is essential for today's marketing leaders. The first step is distinguishing between machine learning and generative artificial intelligence. We'll dive into how AI can transform marketing decisions, allowing brands to strategize faster, optimize on the fly and even predict customer needs before they're expressed.

WHAT I LEARNT IN MY FIRST YEAR OF USING GENAI TOOLS

My 12-month journey of discovery using emerging generative AI tools in marketing has been truly eye-opening. I've explored the vast scope of possibilities and practical applications in my day-to-day marketing work and I've become increasingly optimistic about future developments. Here are three insights you might consider as well.

Generative AI is just the tip of the AI iceberg.

When we think of artificial intelligence in marketing, we often revert to generative AI solutions. These flashy, headline-grabbing applications of AI technology, made famous by ChatGPT or Gemini, took the spotlight. After using generative AI tools for one year, I concluded that AI for marketing is like an iceberg.

Above the waterline, visible to everyone, are the generative AI solutions. But these are just a fraction of what artificial intelligence offers to marketing. What's more interesting is to peer under the waterline. Most AI solutions for marketing lie beneath the surface in the form of machine learning and natural language processing applications.

Beneath the surface, AI drives analytics, dissecting massive data sets to reveal insights that would be impossible to spot manually. These insights allow marketers to understand patterns in customer behaviour, identify profitable segments and adapt strategies based on real-time data. AI also powers predictive modelling, enabling brands to anticipate what customers will want next, based on patterns in their past actions. This capability goes far beyond reactive marketing, allowing companies to engage customers with highly relevant content before they even realize they need it.

For example, ML algorithms are the workhorses powering predictive analytics, personalized media delivery and human behaviour understanding. AI deep learning models can detect facial reactions and predict emotions and attention. Today, marketers better understand happiness, sadness, confusion and surprise because of AI algorithms.

Applications like these are the backbone of AI's effectiveness in marketing. They can offer insights to drive much more business-relevant decisions than, for example, an emerging voice generation solution.

Today, visual AI beats text AI.

Let's face it: I got it wrong in the beginning. After my initial experience with ChatGPT, I was instantly afraid that text-based generative AI solutions would replace me in writing my blog and turn my dream of authoring a book into a nightmare. However, after a year of using generative AI, I realized I gained more value from image-generating AI solutions than from text-based ones.

Image-generating AI quickly and accurately transforms prompts and abstract words into surprising visuals. Initially, we made fun of the technology for its typical errors, like depicting six fingers on each human hand. But the tools improved rapidly and became easier to prompt. Today, we're astonished by the quality of the results, not their mistakes.

Visual generative AI tools have since impacted established marketing creative processes and workflows. Creative ideas are visualized faster, storyboards boast more dynamism and colour, and early creative concepts are closer to final execution than ever before. Visual generative AI is a versatile set of tools for storytelling, brand building and communicating ideas to others.

One year later, text-generating AI lacked a personal touch despite faster response times and broader real-time capabilities. Will that change by the time you read this chapter? Maybe.

This is the most basic version of GenAI you will ever use.

Lastly, it's essential to recognize that we are merely scratching the surface of AI's potential in marketing. You still have time to adapt and learn if your business model isn't fully digital. Consider this time as an opportunity to integrate AI into your marketing strategy. Improve now before GenAI advances even further.

Reflecting on my first year of using GenAI, I realize that the most rewarding business moments were all rooted in the physical world. The year-end dinner with my team, the mid-year team-building event, numerous speaking engagements and those highly successful internal workshops were standout experiences. AI had little involvement in those events, even though the topic was on everyone's lips. At no point did we believe we could replace physical connection with AI, and I still don't feel that way.

As with other technologies, a wise founder once remarked that many people overestimate the progress technology can make in 12 months, while they underestimate the significant advancements it can achieve over decades. Indeed, that founder is Bill Gates.

How AI can support your marketing processes

AI for marketing strategy

Incorporating numerous AI tools into your marketing strategy isn't ground-breaking anymore – it's like securing the floor. Whether you're shaping the business orientation, segmenting your audience, positioning your brand or delivering targeted communications, here is how I would use AI to help.

1 SELECTING THE TYPE OF BUSINESS ORIENTATION

Your first strategic decision is choosing your business orientation, whether product-focused, market-oriented, advertising-driven or sales-centric. When accurate customer and market data is complex to source or when the quantity of data you need to process is enormous, AI comes to help. AI machine learning models can track trends, competitive shifts and real-time customer feedback based on millions of brand-related signals. This offers insight that helps replace traditional market research, especially in B2B contexts. Imagine how hard it is to invite the CEOs of top companies to participate in a research study. AI can almost magically reveal what resonates in the market, reducing the need for extensive manual research for difficult-to-reach respondents.

2 SEGMENTING THE CUSTOMER BASE WITH PRECISION

Customer segmentation is where AI's analytical depth truly stands out. AI can help you clarify purchasing habits and online interaction patterns by moving past demographic or geographic segmentations into predictive behavioural segmentation. Your segmentation will also become more dynamic, as every new data point can revise it on the fly. Synthetic customers are a game-changer in this space. These AI-generated groups of personas simulate real customer behaviour, providing instant feedback on your segmentation efforts. It's like having a test market in a box.

3 POSITIONING THE BRAND IN THE MINDS OF CUSTOMERS

By tapping into the avalanche of data linked to your brand, AI-driven sentiment analysis enables you to understand how customers genuinely feel about your brand in real time. Whether through digital media monitoring, analysing online reviews or browsing Reddit discussion threads, AI tools can capture the 'emotional pulse' of the market. With these insights, you no longer have to guess about your brand's position, you are responding to market data. AI helps you continuously refine your positioning, ensuring you are seen the way you want to be seen and how customers expect you to be viewed.

To maximize the potential of AI in your strategic work, adopt these three behaviours:

- Prioritize data-driven decisions: Let insights guide your orientation, segmentation and positioning choices. Replace gut feelings with concrete data.
- Embrace experimentation with synthetic customer data. When data gaps exist, use AI solutions to complement existing human data. Use synthetic personas to test strategies in real time and refine your approach.
- Iterate on personalization: Leverage AI-driven targeting to deliver relevant, personalized experiences across all customer touchpoints, from products to communications.

AI for pricing and product

Dynamic pricing is the most frequently discussed example of AI applications. The era of static pricing across various categories has ended. AI now enables dynamic, real-time adjustments that respond instantly to market changes. The outcome? Pricing and product strategies that optimize benefits from demand.

1 REAL-TIME PRICING FOR INCREASED PROFITABILITY

By consistently analysing supply, demand and competitor prices, models can recommend the optimal price at any moment. For instance, during a holiday spike when slopes fill up, an automated system can implement additional lift fees with minimal human interaction to maximize a ski resort's revenue. When competitors offer retail discounts, models can respond instantly, suggesting a matching price or emphasizing features that justify a premium in updated communications. This adaptability is crucial in industries where price is the deciding factor for consumers' choices.

2 BALANCING PRICE PERCEPTIONS AND DEMAND ELASTICITY

AI solutions help maximize business margins and ensure that prices meet customer expectations. By analysing price sensitivity across various segments, AI can recommend minor, gradual price adjustments for high-elasticity products or more significant changes for low-elasticity ones. Monitoring brand sentiment on social media and reviews alerts companies to potential backlash if a price change seems out of line. The Snickers case study presented in Chapter 3 is an excellent example of a brand using algorithms to connect retail pricing with online sentiment.

3 FASTER PRODUCT IDEATION WITH GENAI

Generative AI tools can accelerate product development cycles by simulating customer reactions to new packaging designs. Imagine a company testing eco-friendly packaging concepts. GenAI tools can generate designs based on past preferences, evaluate them using synthetic customer data and iterate rapidly. Brands can now shorten design cycles that previously took weeks.

To maximize the potential of AI in your pricing and product work, adopt these three behaviours:

- Stay curious about innovative approaches to pricing. When making pricing decisions, think about how you can utilize AI to modify prices according to market conditions, achieving the right balance between customer satisfaction and profitability.

- Balance pricing with perception. Use AI to monitor pricing elasticity and sentiment, aligning price changes with customer expectations.

- Accelerate pack or feature testing with GenAI. Accelerate ideation and testing cycles to keep your packaging fresh and relevant. Remember that, as mentioned in Chapter 4, changing your packaging should be a last-resort strategy.

AI in media and content

Advertising is probably one of the most AI-impacted elements of the marketing mix. While the most talked-about use case of AI is the replacement of human creativity, thinking of AI as a partner in both content and media is the better lens. Here's how AI is driving a new era in advertising.

1 PROGRAMMATIC AND REAL-TIME BIDDING

AI-powered programmatic advertising systems automate ad placements and bids for ad space in real time to reach the best possible audience for each impression. On the supply side, this automation minimizes ad waste and enhances the effectiveness of the inventory. For brands, the present is one where AI adjusts bids instantly to achieve effectiveness. We are slowly moving towards a future where media is transacted through automation and minimal/zero human intervention. Before your brand heads that way, ensure your modelling signals are high-quality and predictive of business success.

2 CONTENT OPTIMIZATION AND PREDICTIVE SUCCESS

AI's biggest promise in brand communication is to enhance advertising content. Marketers can now leverage AI tools to adjust creative elements based on real-time audience feedback. AI models, trained on historical performance data, can predict which elements will likely engage: which colour, type of humour or emotion resonates best with your audience to maximize effectiveness.

3 CONTENT CREATION AT SCALE

In theory, AI tools for content creation, whether text copy, display images or video, enable marketers to produce new assets at an unprecedented rate. These tools speed up production cycles, but the system can overheat without supervision. Automated content should complement, not entirely replace, human creativity to retain brand authenticity and distinctiveness. While AI can quickly produce variations of a product description, human writers still add depth and nuance that connect emotionally with customers. Just because you can doesn't mean you should.

To maximize the potential of AI in advertising work, adopt these three behaviours:

- Be curious about programmatic precision. Test AI-driven bidding to reach the most relevant audience segments and optimize media spending. Continuously optimize your quality factors.
- Play with real-time creative adaptation. Improve impact by allowing AI to adjust ad elements based on live feedback on the fly. Ensure your content is always compliant with brand and legal requirements.

- Enhance human creativity with AI. Use AI to scale content creation across different platform requirements while preserving the unique, authentic touch only humans can provide. Always ask: do I need another ad?

AI for marketing research

AI is transforming marketing research by enabling marketers to analyse vast amounts of data with speed and accuracy that surpass established methods. But AI isn't new to marketing research, it just gets better daily. Here are three examples of how AI-driven research empowers marketers to stay ahead of customer preferences.

1 ANALYTICS FOR PREDICTIVE MARKETING

AI-powered predictive analytics allows marketers to anticipate customer behaviour, resulting in proactive strategies that enhance ROI. For example, by analysing past purchases and behavioural patterns, marketers can predict when customers will make repeat purchases or switch to a competitor. The insight enables right-on-time connections that deliver the right product to the right customer at the right moment.

2 SYNTHETIC DATA FOR RAPID TESTING

Synthetic data generated by AI enables brands to test product concepts and brand perceptions without relying on real-world data. By simulating realistic customer behaviours, AI facilitates faster and risk-free experimentation. For example, prior to launching a new product, you can use synthetic data to predict how various customer segments will respond.

3 COMPETITIVE ANALYSIS AND MARKET INSIGHTS

AI tools also provide deep insights into competitor strategies and market dynamics. With AI, marketers can monitor competitors' pricing, campaigns and customer sentiment and adjust their approach accordingly. For example, if a competitor launches a price promotion, AI can help determine the potential impact on your brand conversions and suggest strategies to retain customers.

To maximize the potential of AI in marketing research, adopt these three behaviours:

- Prioritize predictive analytics vs descriptive analytics. Anticipate customer needs, enabling proactive marketing that boosts effectiveness. Think more about the future, not the past.

- Play with synthetic data. Generate and test strategies quickly with AI-created synthetic data, reducing costs and accelerating insights. Bonus if your customers are not the types who answer research surveys.
- Gain a competitive edge. Stay ahead by monitoring market and competitor activity with AI-driven insights. Too much category data is now an ally, not a confusing enemy.

AI will not fully replace humans anytime soon

The fear that AI will completely replace human marketers is widespread but, I think, misguided. While AI is a powerful tool, it remains just that: a tool. Rather than supplanting human marketers, AI enhances their capabilities by taking over repetitive, time-consuming tasks, allowing humans to concentrate on what they do best: creativity, strategic thinking and emotional intelligence.

Think of AI as an enabler, not an eliminator. It excels at data crunching, pattern recognition and automating routine tasks. This frees up time for marketers to engage in high-value work unique to your brand. How we define high-value work in the future will be an interesting exploration. I think human intuition and creativity still reign supreme in crafting compelling messages, defining brand voice and making complex decisions.

Today, AI lacks the nuanced understanding of human behaviour that is essential for effective marketing. Emotional intelligence, empathy and an appreciation for cultural subtleties are skills that AI cannot yet replicate. I am convinced the best marketing strategies will emerge from a partnership between AI and humans. AI handles the heavy lifting with data analysis and optimization, while humans steer the creative and strategic direction.

AI is about augmentation, not replacement. It amplifies human potential, enabling marketers to be faster, smarter and more focused. Think of AI like our predecessors thought about electricity or the internet.

Your job will not be made redundant by AI – you will be replaced by a human using AI better than you.

INDUSTRY EXPERT CONTRIBUTION
Academic leader: Stefano Puntoni

Artificial intelligence is quickly transforming marketing and, more broadly, the social sciences. AI initially emerged as a technical field driven by computer science and engineering. However, as AI innovations, and particularly generative AI, are disseminated through society at massive scale and speed, AI has now become a concern for all branches of the social sciences. For marketing professionals, the rise of AI-driven technologies, such as large language models and recommendation systems, opens up new avenues for customer engagement, persuasion and personalization. However, AI's growing sophistication also raises complex challenges that go beyond technical efficiency, particularly concerning issues such as bias and inequality.

Making good decisions with data and algorithms can be difficult as the technology changes rapidly and analytics become increasingly sophisticated. Our book, *Decision-Driven Analytics*[2]: *Leveraging human intelligence to unlock the power of data*, offers a framework to help companies navigate this complex landscape and ensure that data and algorithms serve key business objectives. One of the most significant developments in AI is its ability to influence customer behaviour in unprecedented ways. Several recent academic studies show that AI systems can demonstrate super-human powers of persuasion, which has profound implications for marketing practice. LLMs, for example, are becoming integral to customer service tools, virtual assistants and even creative processes. These tools can potentially enhance productivity and deliver more personalized customer experiences, but they also carry risks, particularly when it comes to reinforcing existing biases.

A key issue here that tends to be underappreciated is that AI bias often emerges not just from the data on which models are trained, as in the old computer science mantra 'garbage in, garbage out'. Instead, bias can often emerge in unexpected contexts from interactions between algorithms and human users. For example, market forces (e.g. systematic differences between different demographic groups in prevailing bidding prices for digital advertising) can interact with algorithmic decision-making to skew ad delivery in ways that can be societally problematic (e.g. show more ads for STEM jobs to males than females). This threat highlights the importance of vigilance. It also highlights the need for firms to recruit behavioural scientists to support AI deployment. Technical fixes alone will not be sufficient to ensure safe and appropriate outcomes for consumers and society.

As AI continues to evolve, academics and practitioners must strive to better understand and mitigate the risks while leveraging AI's potential for more inclusive and effective strategies. For academics, this means approaching AI not just as a tool for improving business outcomes but as a subject of social inquiry. Our research centre, AI at Wharton,[3] is aimed at developing new insights to facilitate safe and effective AI deployment. For practitioners, this means striving to incorporate insights from behavioural science and psychology in AI development and deployment. Ultimately, it's all about the people we serve.

STEFANO PUNTONI

Stefano Puntoni is a Professor of Marketing at The Wharton School. Before joining Penn, Stefano was a marketing professor and department head at the Rotterdam School of Management, Erasmus University, in the Netherlands. He holds a PhD in marketing from London Business School and a degree in Statistics and Economics from the University of Padova, in his native Italy. His research investigates how new technology is changing consumption and society, including how humans are adopting and evolving with AI.

FIVE IDEAS TO TAKE WITH YOU AFTER READING THIS CHAPTER

1 The present brand-led marketing model is shaken and transformed by a blend of customer expectations, change of paths to purchase, and societal and business shifts.

2 The only way to get ready for an unknown future of marketing is to start experimenting today.

3 AI in marketing goes far beyond generative solutions, impacting all aspects of the marketing plan: strategy, pricing, advertising and research.

4 AI augments human capabilities rather than replacing them, allowing for more effective and creative marketing.

5 Staying flexible and curious is crucial for navigating the ever-evolving marketing landscape.

Marketing in the age of AI: a final reflection

The decline of the classic brand-building model isn't just a theory, it's already happening for brands that aren't agile, creative and designed for the future. Whether you're shaping business strategy, segmenting your audience, positioning your brand or delivering targeted communications, leverage AI to enhance your current efforts and experiment for the future. Learning about what's to come is limitless.

Below are three questions to help you make the most of this chapter. Ask them often to make more effective decisions for your brand. As always, there are no right or wrong answers. Simply thinking about these concepts more will help you internalize them better. And for an added learning boost, consider discussing them with a colleague or a friend.

THREE QUESTIONS TO MASTER AI AND MARKETING

1 Are we continuously using AI to align our marketing with customer needs and trends?

2 How can we balance AI-driven efficiency with human creativity to maintain authenticity?

3 What steps are we taking today to prepare for one of the marketing models of the future?

ONE MORE THING...

Want to stay effective and ahead of the curve? Scan this QR code to access extra content and updates online.

Notes

1 Coursera, https://www.coursera.org/ (archived at https://perma.cc/4RPJ-7ZR4)

2 De Langhe, B and Puntoni, S (2024) *Decision-Driven Analytics: Leveraging human intelligence to unlock the power of data*, Wharton Digital Press, Philadelphia, PA

3 AI at Wharton, https://ai.wharton.upenn.edu/ (archived at https://perma.cc/7QWJ-G8E3)

09

The effective marketer: mastering personal growth and building high-impact teams

The effective marketer: building skills for individuals and teams

Over the last two decades, I've been exposed to more marketing campaigns and data sets than I can count. My team and I have measured thousands of advertising campaigns and enhanced many by applying scientific principles, an intense curiosity about human behaviour and a focus on business outcomes.

I've witnessed our marketing industry evolve in surprising ways. We often talk about the technological advancements that have recently impacted all areas of marketing. While this is true, I feel the concurrent evolution of the marketing mindset is frequently ignored.

Remember when the marketing playbook depended on intuition and 'tried-and-true' tactics? For most brands, those days are far behind. Evidence-based marketing decisions have become the standard, leading to stronger outcomes. Today's marketers are certainly more analytically savvy than their predecessors. Data-driven marketing has evolved from an emerging trend to a fundamental necessity in any marketing process. Given the recent acceleration of technology's impact on marketing, driven by the rise of AI solutions, I can only anticipate that the pace of change will continue to increase. Two questions come to mind and I will explore them in this chapter.

- How can you prepare for the future of marketing effectiveness?
- How can businesses build a future-proof marketing effectiveness team?

The future of marketing effectiveness belongs to those who merge creativity with complex data. It belongs to those who abandon their biases and are brave enough to pursue innovation grounded in principles. But don't worry – being analytical doesn't mean you need a PhD in statistics, it simply means grasping numbers and making them work for your brand.

Are you ready to strip away gut instinct to 100 per cent data-powered insights?

Personal development: the five capabilities you need to win

To successfully navigate the future of marketing, professionals must upskill themselves in five areas: develop an analytical mindset, improve communications skills, embrace a life-long learning ambition, superb networking skills and an ambition to build a personal brand (see Figure 9.1).

FIGURE 9.1 The five capabilities future marketing effectiveness leaders need to develop

Analytical Mindset

Communication Skills   **Personal Development**

Networking Skills

Personal Brand Building

Life-long Learning Ambition

1 Discover your analytical mindset: play, understand and aim to enjoy data

Analytical skills in marketing include the ability to accurately collect, interpret and utilize data to make informed decisions, optimize strategies and anticipate future customer behaviour. These skills enable marketers to assess different facets of their marketing plans, focusing on performance, optimization and, ultimately, effectiveness.

Today's marketing industry sets a high premium on an analytical mindset that requires more than just skills or data. If you still rely on 'what feels right', you're not competing at the same level as the top marketers.

An analytical mindset is about translating numbers into actionable insights that guide brands towards growth. Begin by identifying trends. One of the biggest lessons I've learnt during my years in marketing effectiveness at Mars is the significance of staying ahead of the curve. Anticipating key trends before they become mainstream enabled me to appear proactive and detect shifts before others could.

Three ideas:

- Tools like SparkToro[1] and Semrush[2] helped me stay ahead with my personal brand-building exercise for the Marketing Engineer blog. SparkToro has been invaluable for understanding where my blog's audiences spend time online and which LinkedIn influencers impact their opinions. It's like having a behind-the-scenes look at where conversations are happening. Semrush, meanwhile, has become my go-to tool for trend analysis and keyword monitoring. It's incredible how much insight you can gain by seeing which search terms are gaining momentum. These tools enabled me to adjust my LinkedIn posting strategy quickly, aligning messaging with trending topics before others do so.

- But tools alone aren't sufficient; active engagement with peers is essential, too. I prioritized joining various LinkedIn groups, industry events and communities like WFA[3] or ANA.[4] These forums serve as invaluable resources for connections and insights. The conversations that occur there often reveal the direction of the market. It's not just about under-standing what others are saying, it's about engaging, asking questions and sharing your experiences. As a result, I've joined a network of marketers who exchange insights, tips and even warnings about upcoming changes

- I use a system based on Feedly,[5] Pocket[6] and Evernote[7] automation to manage the flood of information reaching me. I've set up feeds from the top business publications and trusted industry blogs, so regularly I receive a digest of the latest developments without having to remind myself to visit multiple sites. The time I spend curating and reading through my feeds has paid off repeatedly, giving me the foresight to pivot when needed.

In my opinion, developing an analytical mindset involves technology, active engagement and effective content management. It requires knowing where to search, who to listen to and how to utilize tools to convert insights into actions. By integrating these approaches, I've been able to keep a competi-tive advantage and consistently stay ahead in an ever-evolving industry.

Here is a great tool I use to learn.

THE FEYNMAN TECHNIQUE

The Feynman Technique is a learning method developed by the Nobel laureate in Physics, Richard Feynman. It was designed to simplify complex topics by teaching them as if explaining them to a beginner. Here's how it works:

1 Pick a topic to study and map it: Choose the topic you want to understand. Dive into the basics, gaining a foundational grasp of the subject by drawing a visual map of your current understanding.

2 Explain it in simple terms: Imagine explaining the concept to a 12-year-old or someone without domain knowledge. This forces you to break down ideas into their simplest components, revealing weak points in your understanding. Using simple language is vital.

3 Identify gaps in your understanding: As you attempt to explain, you'll likely uncover areas where your knowledge is unclear or incomplete. Take note of these gaps.

4 Review and refine: Return to the source material or research to clarify these gaps. Repeat the cycle, refining your explanation until it's clear and complete.

This technique is incredibly useful for marketers. You can deepen your knowledge and gain recognized domain expertise by breaking down complex marketing concepts like DCO, distinctiveness or price elasticity into digestible explanations. Try it with your partner, parents or kids and let me know how it works.

2 *Enhance your communication skills: storytelling, prompting, design*

I vividly remember when I started in marketing research. I believed that collecting customer data and creating detailed reports were the keys to demonstrating my value to the business. However, I soon realized that numbers alone don't tell a story. The most important skill I developed was interpersonal communication: effectively translating complex data into clear, engaging narratives that resonate with different audiences.

Simply providing a chart of campaign performance is not enough, you need to make that data relevant and turn the insights into actionable recommendations for the team, the client or the leadership – those who are in listening mode. This requires strong interpersonal and presentation skills – in short, effective communication skills.

To improve my communication skills, I joined Toastmasters,[8] an organization providing a safe space to practise public speaking and presentation skills. At first, attending my club every week felt daunting, but each session taught me how to structure my ideas better, speak up confidently and engage any audience. Suddenly, explaining campaign metrics and strategies became less about jargon and more about emotions, weaving stories people could relate to and feel excited about.

Another lesson was the significance of active listening. When I collaborated on creative campaigns with cross-functional teams, I recognized that understanding other people's perspectives is just as vital as sharing my own. Taking the time to listen to my colleagues, whether they were sales teams struggling to meet targets or creative agencies seeking insights and inspiration, enabled me to communicate more effectively. It's a simple skill, but it can transform a conversation and promote alignment. For this skill to develop, there's no better path than embracing VTS.

INTRODUCING VTS

VTS, or visual thinking strategies, was one of the highlights of my learning path. I was so lucky to participate in the IRG 2024 program in Oxford/St Paul de Vence, where I was introduced to VTS under the guidance of my instructor, Dabney Hailey.

Together with over 100 global marketing leaders, we discovered the joy of looking at art for extended periods of time. And we loved it!

What is VTS? VTS is a powerful educational approach encouraging profound observation and discussion of visual stimuli. This method builds critical thinking, empathy and communication skills, making it applicable across various business domains, especially marketing.

Dabney Hailey, a museum curator, MIT lecturer and founder of the Hailey Group,[9] has dedicated her career to bridging the gap between art and modern learning techniques. VTS emphasizes engaging with visual materials to enhance understanding and collaboration in groups.

During a memorable training session, 50-plus marketing leaders spent over 45 minutes looking at a single painting. Rather than being a waste of time, this exercise proved to be a profound discovery experience. It allowed us to practise observation, listening, empathy and interpretation – skills essential for a business leader.

By taking the time to reflect on art, we learned to appreciate nuances that can easily be overlooked in fast-paced environments. Our facilitator taught us how to engage with everyone who contributed without judging or projecting our views on their comments.

Here are three actionable ways to incorporate VTS in your daily marketing life:

1 Start meetings with visual analysis: You can begin meetings by visualizing your current project. It can be a PowerPoint slide or even an Excel report. Then, ask open-ended questions like, 'What do you see?' or 'What emotions

does this evoke?' This encourages diverse perspectives and stimulates creative discussions. After all, every document we produce, even a lousy Excel report, should grab attention and generate emotion from a diverse group of people. If it doesn't, it's not working.

2 Analyse feedback visually: When reviewing consumer research, use visual data representation. Instead of just reading comments or statistics, create visual maps or infographics that illustrate trends and emotions. This will help your team gain deeper insights into customer needs. Sometimes, the beauty is hidden between the rows of numbers.

3 Create content with visual storytelling: When working on your next marketing campaign, utilize VTS principles by examining successful past campaigns visually. Do a gallery walk (design thinking technique), make a visual collage of what you like and use your eyes more than your memory. Discuss what is effective and how similar strategies can be applied to new content.

As marketers, we always seek to capture people's attention in a world full of distractions. Yet we can become so focused on our brands that we overlook the details around us. By applying VTS techniques, we can train ourselves to observe more thoughtfully and engage more meaningfully.

Marketers are uniquely positioned to understand human behaviour. We can become better marketers and business leaders by honing our human attention skills through VTS.

3 Nurture a lifelong learning ambition: never settle, growth is a marathon, not a sprint

Marketing is one of the fastest-evolving industries today, fuelled by constant technological innovations, shifting customer behaviours, improved research methods and an explosion of business models.

What worked yesterday may not work tomorrow and marketers face the challenge of remaining relevant and effective in an ever-changing landscape. In this dynamic environment, lifelong learning becomes a necessity.

One way I developed adaptability was by placing myself in new situations. I took on cross-departmental projects, working with IT, product development and customer service teams. It wasn't always easy. I was used to the marketing world, where creativity and brand building reigned supreme. Suddenly, I had to learn about Agile planning and Clean Rooms terminology, topics in which

I had no experience. However, these projects were game changers for my career. They compelled me to adjust my marketing perspective and discover ways to align with the goals of other teams and, ultimately, the organization.

I've constantly sought out mentors who have navigated similar challenges. One of my mentors, who had experienced multiple shifts in the industry, shared valuable insights about staying flexible and seeing changes as opportunities rather than obstacles. Those conversations helped me frame setbacks not as failures but as lessons.

Marketers must commit to continuously expanding their technical skill sets, updating their knowledge and monitoring industry trends to remain competitive and effective.

The days of earning a degree and relying solely on that knowledge throughout your career are long gone. Marketing today is a marathon and the most successful professionals view learning as an ongoing journey. The fast pace of change requires us to adapt quickly, whether it's mastering new tools like generative artificial intelligence, understanding the implications of data privacy regulations or adjusting strategies to align with emerging consumer trends. Marketers who remain curious, proactive and committed to self-improvement are the ones who not only survive but thrive in this industry.

ONLINE LEARNING PLATFORMS: ACCESS KNOWLEDGE ANYTIME, ANYWHERE

We live in the golden age of learning. We are privileged by the abundance of high-quality online education tailored for marketers. Here are three of my favourite learning platforms:

- Coursera: Partnering with leading universities like Stanford and Yale, Coursera[10] offers certificates and degrees many employers recognize. With thousands of courses, it's ideal for those wanting to advance their career or explore new fields. Courses I tried included *Digital Marketing Specialization* by the University of Illinois and *Marketing Analytics* by the University of Virginia, covering topics like data analytics, digital strategy and customer behaviour. *Best for*: Accredited certificates.

- MasterClass:[11] Learn directly from industry icons like Bob Iger and Richard Branson inside this video platform, which is known for its high production content quality. While not focused exclusively on business, courses by experts like Steph Curry and Michael Pollan offered me valuable insights that enhanced my leadership skills. *Best for*: Learning from experts.

- LinkedIn Learning:[12] Perfect for professionals seeking to build practical, career-relevant skills, LinkedIn Learning offers 17,000-plus bite-size courses on business skills, tech and marketing specializations. Certificates can be added directly to your LinkedIn profile, enhancing your visibility and credibility for future employers. *Best for:* Deep skill-building.

Other platforms, such as Udemy and Skillshare, offer shorter, focused courses on various topics, such as SEO, email marketing, programmatic advertising and more.

4 *Elevate networking skills: gain comfort around senior management, stage charisma and connection*

Networking skills, such as confidence around senior management and charisma on stage, are essential for your career growth. Attending industry events keeps you updated on trends and enables you to connect with peers, but speaking at those events is the transformative experience you should try.

For me, there are three must-attend events for serious data marketers: Cannes Lions, Advertising Week and the I-COM Summit Experience. Here's a quick introduction, plus one personal insight on how to make the most of these events:

- Cannes Lions:[13] Often called the 'Oscars of advertising', Cannes Lions is an annual festival celebrating creativity and innovation. Here, top marketers from brands, agencies, platforms and industry leaders gather to discuss creativity and debate the future of marketing. Attending the Cannes Lions just to see the campaigns win awards is only half of the pie. Equip yourself with comfortable shoes and stroll along the Croisette to discover innovation and inspiration and make new marketing friends.

- Advertising Week:[14] With sessions held across continents, Advertising Week covers everything from brand marketing to emerging tech trends. Top brands and agencies offer practical insights and case studies on their successful marketing strategies. It's an ideal event for learning real-world applications of buzzword approaches. Pick your continent and learn.

- I-COM Summit Experience:[15] This invitation-only event offers smart marketing executives the opportunity to create lasting connections and explore the industry's edge capabilities. A carefully curated list of speakers, amazing venues, fantastic food and content that seems always ahead of its time.

Personal tip for making the most of events: Don't just attend events passively – engage actively. Be the first to ask questions and make yourself visible to your network. If you can, be on stage.

USE YOUR PHOTOGRAPHY SKILLS TO BUILD CONNECTIONS

Consider taking photos of speakers and sending them right after their talk. This personal touch can help initiate a conversation and 99 per cent of individuals will highly value your effort. Afterwards, sharing insights from the event on social media can boost your visibility and demonstrate your engagement in the industry conversation.

Attending events is one of my favourite ways of learning, but nothing compares to a personal heat experience that makes you grow. Here is an example of how I challenged myself and became a better communicator.

LEARNING THE DUTCH LANGUAGE, A PERSONAL STORY OF ADAPTABILITY

Here's a story about how I learnt Dutch in just two months. Early in my career, I moved from Romania to the Netherlands to take on the role of brand manager for British American Tobacco in Western Europe. Several months later, I had to present a significant new product launch to a Dutch-speaking audience of sales representatives. I assumed they would be comfortable with English, so I confidently started my presentation. However, halfway through, I noticed they weren't fully engaged – most were on their devices and my message wasn't getting through. I concluded to lukewarm applause, realizing I needed to adapt to the local language to connect more effectively.

Determined, I set a goal to deliver my next big presentation in Dutch. I enrolled in an intensive language programme, where I was fully immersed in Dutch for a week in a small village, speaking only Dutch with instructors and locals. Two months later, I returned to the same stage to present to the same audience, this time entirely in Dutch. Through demonstrating vulnerability, learning skills and adapting to local customs, the outcome was completely different. Although I relied somewhat on memorization, my Dutch message resonated, breaking through any barriers. I received a standing ovation from the field force and contributed to the future success of this campaign.

This experience taught me two valuable lessons: never underestimate the impact of speaking someone's language, and when changing your environment, first adjust yourself to its unique dynamics before asking it to change. Doing so can make all the difference.

5 Personal brand building: design and craft your brand, be content creator

Personal brand building is the process of creating a distinct, memorable identity for yourself that reflects your skills, values, expertise and personality. It involves strategically sharing your knowledge, achievements and unique perspectives to establish a reputation that resonates with your target audience, whether that's within a professional field, industry or broader community.

A strong personal brand positions you as a thought leader or expert in your field, builds trust and helps you attract opportunities that align with your goals and values. Building an externally recognizable personal brand is essential for marketers today. It's not just about reach and noticeability, it's a way to demonstrate expertise in arguably the most critical skill in marketing: brand building.

If marketers can successfully create and grow their brand, they're proving their ability to apply those same skills to clients, employers or products:

1 Career growth and networking: Building a personal brand establishes a professional identity that transcends a specific employer, making your name and image memorable to potential employers, clients and collaborators. This visibility leads to expanded career options and potential independence. A marketer with a powerful personal brand is more likely to attract attention from headhunters and industry leaders looking for talent.

2 Increased visibility and recognition: A distinct personal brand helps marketers stand out in a crowded industry, positioning them as thought leaders. This visibility opens doors for opportunities that might not otherwise come their way, such as invitations to speak at conferences, guest lecture spots or participation in industry working groups. People naturally want to hear from you and engage with your ideas when you're tagged as an expert.

3 Becoming a recognizable brand beyond the employer: A well-developed personal brand allows marketers to become known independently of their current job or company. This independence builds resilience and increases their value in the marketplace. When a marketer's reputation precedes them, they bring additional credibility to any organization they join and can often command better opportunities and higher levels of trust from leadership and clients.

What can be your first step? Start a blog.

YOU SHOULD START A BLOG

With the world in lockdown in 2020, everyone seemed to be picking up new skills at home. Some people took up carpentry, others tried painting by numbers and many started fitness routines. I chose to start a blog. Launching the Engineering Marketing blog, which you can find at sorinp.com (archived at https://perma.cc/EGE4-9BR8), turned out to be one of the best decisions I've made in the last decade.

Starting a blog isn't easy. At first, you'll feel the sting of imposter syndrome. You'll wonder if anyone will read your writing or if your ideas are valuable. But trust me, stick with it. The more you write, the better you become. In the beginning, I set a goal to write 50 posts in 50 weeks. Naturally, I didn't reach that goal – life happened and I had a newborn on the way – but I still published 32 posts in that first year. Not bad. The following years were less productive, but I established the habit of writing.

The best part of my blog is that it serves as a permanent record, a testament to my thoughts and creations from 2020 and beyond. That blog led to bigger things: it fuelled my commitment to reading one book a week and sharing my insights consistently on LinkedIn, launched my 'Audio-Vision Project' on Instagram and opened up new creative opportunities and friendships.

If you're an expert marketer or aspire to be one, there's no better way to build your personal brand than by creating content. Just look at the amazing people who have built strong personal brands through consistent content creation. Everything you need to build your brand is available in you: just start and be yourself.

Team development: the DNA of a high-impact marketing effectiveness team

The ABC of marketing effectiveness skills

To build an effective marketing team, you need to balance skills across three core areas: analytics, insights and business acumen (see Figure 9.2). These elements work together to form a data-driven, customer-oriented and financially savvy team capable of executing impactful marketing strategies.

It's rare to find the three skills in a single person. Don't chase the impossible. Build a team of complementary experts that will cover the three areas for your business. Here is what you should be looking for:

- Analytics: Robust analytics are essential for modern marketing. Understanding AI, machine learning techniques, regression analysis and experimentation enables your team to interpret data, forecast trends and

FIGURE 9.2 The three magic elements every marketing effectiveness team needs: analytical expertise, deep customer knowledge and a strong business acumen work in sync to create the profile of a marketing effectiveness expert

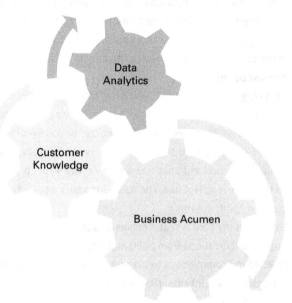

optimize decisions based on measurable metrics. By collaborating with data analysts, they can automate processes, uncover insights and enhance customer understanding methods. For instance, regression methods and A/B testing assist the team in understanding the impact and refining strategies for maximum effectiveness. Knowing the basics of these methods is just the beginning. Analytical acumen enables you to ask the right questions, interrogate data and transform it into actionable insights.

- Business acumen: Having strong business skills is essential for aligning marketing strategies with the organization's broader goals. Team members with finance expertise and product knowledge can speak more fluently when presenting future investment scenarios and make strategic decisions that foster profitability and growth. Financial acumen empowers the team to manage budgets effectively and prioritize efforts that yield the highest returns. Moreover, product expertise allows the team to have a deep understanding of the offerings they are marketing, resulting in more authentic and compelling messaging. Learning how a business makes money and how it loses money should be a priority for every marketer.

- Customer insights: Understanding customers is crucial for effective marketers. Some expertise in psychology, behavioural sciences and demographics enables marketers to predict audience responses, craft resonant messages and create content aligned with consumer motivations. Curiosity is a great enabler for learning the basics in those fields. By integrating behavioural and demographic data, the team can refine its measurement approach to meet real consumer needs and deliver relevant, impactful marketing campaigns.

Combining these three skill sets creates a well-rounded, effective marketing team ready to tackle complex challenges and deliver effectiveness.

Say hello to the marketing scientist

A narrator fluent in business and an engineer skilled in data.

Imagine a marketing scientist. They likely embody a strong empathy for consumers, a marketing heart, an analytical approach to decisions, an engineering mind and the tools to make the right brand choices. The marketing scientist masters the art of applying marketing science to grow brands. Science empowers businesses to make smarter decisions, innovate effectively and achieve sustainable success.

Today's successful marketers are engineers of consumer understanding, adept in analytical reasoning and proficient in making data-driven decisions.

The good news is that you can become a marketing scientist without an academic background. Adapting requires three relatively easy shifts:

- a mindset shift – from creative to analytical
- a decision shift – from gut-reactive to proven methods
- a focus shift – from inner to goal-oriented

A checklist for the marketing effectiveness team of the future

Building a marketing effectiveness team is about more than just data and insights it generates. It's about people, culture and influence. After more than 13 years leading a marketing effectiveness team at Mars, I crafted a list of 10 principles that I believe matter the most. Curious to know what you think.

☐ Recruit with relentless focus: Never get tired of investing time in hiring. Every recruitment decision has long-term consequences. A great hire will amplify your team's impact, while a bad hire will drain time and energy.

Be patient, be picky and always hire for both skill and mindset. I always look for curiosity, adaptability and strategic thinking before testing technical expertise.

☐ Forge strong relationships with senior leadership: Marketing effectiveness lives at the intersection of marketing and finance, often influencing the CEO's decisions. You won't get far without deep relationships with your CMO, CFO and CEO. Understand their priorities, speak their language and position effectiveness as a business enabler, not just a reporting function. Make them your allies.

☐ Build a culture of shared learning: Encourage continuous learning. Create internal playbooks, best-practice libraries and knowledge-sharing sessions so insights don't get lost when people move on. A learning culture ensures your team stays ahead. Because without structured learning, every insight dies in a PowerPoint deck.

☐ Make marketing effectiveness visible: Marketing effectiveness teams that remain in the background lose influence. Make your work visible, relevant and indispensable. Use case studies, success stories and internal PR to showcase impact. Position your team as the go-to source for marketing decision-making, not just a back-office function of the media director.

☐ Create consistency for long-term impact: Organizations lose effectiveness when they constantly switch tools and methodologies. Stick with proven approaches and let compounding results take effect. Breakthroughs come from sustained application, not constant reinvention. Never get tired of a good method.

☐ Get the team out of the office: Strong teams aren't built in meeting rooms. Take people out of their usual environment, bring in a facilitator and focus on relationship building over strategy creation. Shared experiences create the trust and camaraderie that high-performing teams rely on when things get tough.

☐ Expand beyond marketing to increase influence: Marketing effectiveness doesn't exist in isolation. Build partnerships with finance, procurement and commercial/sales teams to expand the impact. The more integrated your team is across departments, the more influence it will have on big-ticket business decisions.

☐ Balance speed with rigour: Marketing effectiveness teams need to move fast without sacrificing credibility. Avoid endless data validation loops, but also ensure insights are solid enough to drive action. It's a fine balance between agility and depth. Fast insights that are wrong are useless. Perfect insights that come too late are also useless.

☐ Leverage external networks to stay ahead: The best teams stay plugged into the outside world. Engage in marketing science forums, attend conferences and build external networks. Learning from outside the organization ensures the team leads, not follows trends.

☐ Measure the team's impact like a business unit: You measure marketing effectiveness, but do you measure your own team impact? Define KPIs for your team's influence, adoption rate of recommendations and business impact. Track progress and prove value through measurable results.

INDUSTRY EXPERT CONTRIBUTION
Data translation expert: Thomas McKinlay

Marketers have terrible options when they're looking for ways to improve their results. It's either 'experts' sharing their opinions based on their personal experience (with no evidence that it will work for others) or sketchy case studies and 'stats' published by those trying to sell something.

The best marketers know that these options are unreliable and don't drive results. So they turn to the only option they believe they have left: they spend massive resources testing and learning from their own data – even though others have probably tested the exact same thing thousands of times over. In essence, they're stuck with reinventing the wheel.

This is absurd. There is a better way, a way that allows us to reliably learn from what others have already discovered: scientific research.

Scientific research is peer-reviewed by other scientists, closely screened by journal editors and publicly shares all methodologies, experiments and limitations used – for anyone to scrutinize. It's vastly better than any other data we have. And there's a lot of it. Brilliant scientists in top business schools all over the world are constantly exploring ways to make marketing more effective. Every year, they publish over 10,000 marketing-related research papers.

Sadly, most of these studies sit unused and undiscovered by marketers for years. No one has the time to sift through all of them, find what is practically useful and then spend three-plus hours going through a dense research paper to understand how to put it to use. I created Science Says to change that. My team of marketing PhDs and I analyse the latest scientific studies published in marketing and turn them into short, actionable recommendations. Tens of thousands of marketers read and apply Science Says insights every week to improve their marketing results.

Scientific research is not perfect. But it's orders of magnitude better than anything else we have. Let's put it to use to become better marketers.

THOMAS MCKINLAY

Thomas McKinlay is the founder of Science Says, where he works with his team of marketing PhDs to translate the latest scientific findings in marketing into practical insights. Previously, he was a marketer at Google and in the startup ecosystem.

FIVE IDEAS TO TAKE WITH YOU AFTER READING THIS CHAPTER

1   Embrace an analytical mindset: Future-proofing your marketing team starts with developing a love for data. Analytical thinking isn't just about crunching numbers – it's about using data to predict trends, refine strategies and drive decision-making for maximum effectiveness.

2   Master the art of storytelling: Data is only as powerful as the story it tells. Learn to translate complex insights into compelling narratives that resonate with diverse audiences, from creative teams to senior executives.

3   Invest in lifelong learning: The marketing landscape evolves constantly, making ongoing education essential. Explore new tools, experiment with innovative approaches and regularly update your knowledge to stay ahead of industry trends.

4   Balance analytics and creativity: Success in marketing lies at the intersection of hard data and creative thinking. Use insights to inspire innovative campaigns that resonate emotionally while being grounded in measurable outcomes.

5   Build a collaborative team with diverse skills: A truly effective marketing department thrives on complementary expertise. Blend analytics, consumer insights and business acumen to create a team capable of tackling complex challenges and delivering impactful results.

The effective marketeer: a final reflection

Congratulations on finishing another chapter and uncovering the key traits of an effective marketing leader. The future of marketing effectiveness lies with those who fuse creativity with qualitative, complex data sets. Are you one of them?

Below are three questions to help you make the most of this chapter. Ask them often to make more effective decisions for your brand. As always, there are no right or wrong answers. Simply thinking about these concepts more will help you internalize them better. And for an added learning boost, consider discussing them with a colleague or a friend.

THREE QUESTIONS TO MASTER PERSONAL AND
TEAM DEVELOPMENT

1   Are we fostering a culture of curiosity and data-driven decisions? Marketing effectiveness begins with a mindset shift: from relying on instinct to trusting evidence. Ask yourself: Do our teams have the tools, resources and freedom to question assumptions, experiment with new strategies and learn from both successes and failures?

2   Do our capabilities reflect a balance of analytics, insights and business acumen? A successful effectiveness department is built on three pillars: data analytics, consumer understanding and strategic thinking. Is your team structured to bring these elements together seamlessly? If not, how can you complement existing strengths with new hires, training or partnerships?

3   Are we measuring and communicating impact effectively? Insights are only as valuable as their ability to drive decisions. What metrics and success indicators do you use to communicate your team's value internally? Are they resonating with leadership and do they align with the organization's broader goals?

ONE MORE THING…

Want to stay effective and ahead of the curve? Scan this QR code to access extra content and updates online.

Notes

1   SparkToro (n.d.) Audience research tool for understanding online behaviour and influence, https://sparktoro.com/ (archived at https://perma.cc/39QE-TKLA)

2   Semrush (n.d.) SEO, content, and digital marketing analytics platform, https://www.semrush.com/ (archived at https://perma.cc/FV2K-PG3S)

3   World Federation of Advertisers (WFA) (n.d.) Global organization representing marketers and brand owners, https://www.wfanet.org/ (archived at https://perma.cc/CM7X-RP7F)

4   Association of National Advertisers (ANA) (n.d.) The US-based association for marketing and advertising professionals, https://www.ana.net/ (archived at https://perma.cc/Q37T-R8GT)

5   Feedly (n.d.) News aggregator for tracking blogs and publications, https://feedly.com/ (archived at https://perma.cc/YE8W-ZPJ6)

6   Pocket (n.d.) App that saves and organizes articles, videos and web content for reading, https://getpocket.com/ (archived at https://perma.cc/3A6B-D3B9)

7   Evernote (n.d.) Note-taking and organization app for productivity, https://evernote.com/ (archived at https://perma.cc/DA88-84Y4)

8   Toastmasters International (n.d.) Public speaking and leadership development organization, https://www.toastmasters.org/ (archived at https://perma.cc/RB2K-STRH)

9   Hailey Group (n.d.) Consulting firm specializing in visual thinking strategies, https://www.haileygroup.com/ (archived at https://perma.cc/WHL3-DCKK)

10 Coursera (n.d.) Online learning platform offering courses from top universities, https://www.coursera.org/ (archived at https://perma.cc/6356-UG5C)

11 MasterClass (n.d.) Video-based courses taught by industry leaders and experts, https://www.masterclass.com/ (archived at https://perma.cc/LM9R-GUSQ)

12 LinkedIn Learning (n.d.) Professional development courses on business, tech and creativity, https://www.linkedin.com/learning (archived at https://perma.cc/59EN-JCVP)

13 Cannes Lions (n.d.) Global festival celebrating creativity in advertising and marketing, https://www.canneslions.com/ (archived at https://perma.cc/JX2V-DHE6)

14 Advertising Week (n.d.) Conference series covering advertising, media and marketing trends, https://advertisingweek.com/ (archived at https://perma.cc/U5M2-5VMQ)

15 I-COM Summit Experience (n.d.) Data-driven marketing and measurement conference, https://www.i-com.org/summit-experience (archived at https://perma.cc/KV2M-NRUH)

10

The 10 books that shaped the marketing engineer in me

Sharp, B (2010) *How Brands Grow: What marketers don't know*, Oxford University Press.
This book challenges established marketing beliefs and offers evidence-based insights derived from scientific principles and robust research to help marketers understand how brands grow.

Kahneman, D (2011) *Thinking, Fast and Slow*, Farrar, Straus and Giroux.
This book explores the two systems of thinking, System 1 (fast, automatic thinking) and System 2 (slow, deliberate thinking), and how they influence human decisions. Nobel Prize laureate Daniel Kahneman provides valuable insights into human behaviour and biases, offering marketers a deeper understanding of how consumers think and act.

Binet, L and Field, P (2013) *The Long and the Short of It: Balancing short and long-term marketing strategies*, IPA.
This book offers insights into effective advertising best practices and how to manage marketing investments between equity building and short-term sales-based campaigns.

Rumelt, R (2011) *Good Strategy, Bad Strategy*, Crown Business.
This is my go-to book on strategy. It provides a clear framework for developing effective strategies. It highlights the key differences between true strategic thinking and superficial planning. It offers insights into how focusing on core challenges and making tough choices can lead to powerful results.

Lafley, A G and Martin, R L (2013) *Playing to Win: How strategy really works*, Harvard Business Review Press.
This book outlines a straightforward approach to strategy that emphasizes making clear, deliberate choices. It breaks down the essentials of strategic

thinking, defining where to compete and how to win. The authors provide actionable guidance on identifying unique strengths and creating a sustainable competitive advantage. They offer a practical playbook for achieving lasting business success, as they did at Procter & Gamble.

Burggraeve, C (2020) *Marketing Is Finance Is Business: How CMO, CFO and CEO co-create iconic brands with sustainable pricing power in the galactic age*, independently published.

This book provides a compelling framework for collaboration between marketing, finance and leadership teams. It highlights how the goals of the CMO, CFO and CEO can be aligned by focusing on sustainable pricing power.

Nelson-Field, K (2024) *The Attention Economy: A category blueprint*, Oxford University Press.

In this compelling sequel to her first publication, *The Attention Economy: How media works*, the author takes an in-depth look into the dynamic world of marketing and advertising. She unveils the pivotal role that human attention measurement plays in the present and future landscapes.

Binet, L (2018) *How Not to Plan: 66 ways to screw it up*, WARC.

In the sink-or-swim world of media planners, strategists and their clients, now more than ever there is a need for a practical handbook to guide us through all the main parts of the process. Sharp, thoughtful and a must-read for aspiring strategists.

Ogilvy, D (1983) *Ogilvy on Advertising*, Vintage.

Often considered the definitive guide to advertising, this book details the essentials of crafting successful advertising campaigns. Ogilvy's extensive experience shines through in his practical advice on copywriting, which remains valid even more than 40 years after its first publication.

Romaniuk, J (2018) *Building Distinctive Brand Assets*, Oxford University Press.

Successfully complementing Byron Sharp's *How Brands Grow*, this book offers a deep dive into creating and managing distinctive brand assets – elements like logos, colours and brand characters that help brands stand out and become mentally available to consumers. It's practical, evidence-based brand building 101.

INDEX

Looking for another book?

Explore our award-winning
books from global business
experts in Marketing and Sales

Scan the code to browse

www.koganpage.com/marketing

From 4 December 2025 the EU Responsible Person (GPSR) is:
eucomply oÜ, Pärnu mnt. 139b – 14, 11317 Tallinn, Estonia
www.eucompliancepartner.com

www.ingramcontent.com/pod-product-compliance
Lightning Source LLC
Chambersburg PA
CBHW070940050326
40689CB00014B/3277